Bao Lac
Ha Giang
Hokow
Cao Binh
RTE 3
RTE 2
That Khe
5
Lang Son
1
Tuyen Quang
Yen Bay
Phuc Yen
Kep
RTE 4
Mon Cay
Son La
Son Tay
Moc Chau
8
Hon Gay
Hanoi
Haiphong
Hoa Binh
Nam Dinh
Ninh Binh
Gulf of
Bai Thuong
4
Thanh Hoa
NORTH-
Muong Sen
Cua Rao
RTE 1
RTE 7
Phu Dien Chau
VIETNAM
Tonkin
3
Ha Tan
Vinh
7
Ha Tinh
UTH
TNAM
Dai Hao
DIEU
RTE. 1
ang
Tuyen Hoa
Dong Hoi
Vinh Linh
2
CEASE-FIRE LINE
JULY 22, 1954
Quang Tri
6
Hue
Ashau
Phu Bai
Da Nang

From the Shadow of Death

From the Shadow of Death

Stories of POWs • J M. Heslop & Dell R. Van Orden

Published by Deseret Book Company, Salt Lake City, Utah 1973

Library of Congress Catalog Card No. 73-88328

ISBN No. 0-87747-509-1

Copyright 1973
by
Deseret Book Company

Lithographed by

DESERET PRESS

in the United States of America

PREFACE

The American prisoners of war have come home. After years of captivity—the longest of any prisoners of any war in United States history—they have come home with a fascinating and moving story. Involved in this great episode are the experiences of a number of Latter-day Saint prisoners.

The eight POWs interviewed for this book should, by all elements of human reasoning and understanding, be dead. But for reasons known only to God, they are alive, some still severely injured, but alive and greatly aware and appreciative of their blessings.

The story of these LDS men is one that must be told. It is replete with warm and wonderful faith-promoting stories—stories of miracles, of courage, of prayers being answered, of trials that have tested the faith of both the prisoners and their families.

The men interviewed represent a cross section of the prisoners. They come from Utah, Idaho, Texas, and California. The material was obtained through exclusive personal interviews with the men and their families.

The story of these men is the story of the travesties of war. They were subjected to all types of punishment, torture, and deprivations—and yet not one ever denied the gospel of Jesus Christ and his faith in his Heavenly Father.

The story is inspiring. One cannot read it without a sense of gratitude for his blessings, without a feeling of thanks for the country in which we live. One cannot read it without a greater appreciation for the principles of the gospel and for The Church of Jesus Christ of Latter-day Saints.

We feel that the story of the LDS prisoners of war can be a faith-building experience for everybody—a story that all will want to read.

J M. Heslop

Dell R. Van Orden

ACKNOWLEDGMENTS

Grateful appreciation is expressed to the management of the *Deseret News* for providing us the opportunity to write this book, through our experiences in meeting and covering the activities of the prisoners of war as they have returned home. News stories of many of the men and women included in this book were previously printed in the *Church News*.

Appreciation is extended to the POWs and their families for their warm and understanding hospitality as we gathered the facts necessary to write this book.

Photographs not taken by the authors were provided by the men and their families, as well as by the United States Air Force, Navy, and Department of Defense. Photo credit is also given to Don Searle, Gerald Silver, Doug Campbell, and O. Wallace Kasteler.

Our thanks to Geraldine Avant, Mary Larsen, and Kathy E. Lund for manuscript typing, and to the members of the *Church News* staff for advice and support.

Appreciation is gratefully given to W. James Mortimer, manager of Deseret Book Company, and to Linda Calderon and Eleanor Knowles, who read and prepared the manuscript for printing.

Finally, we express gratitude to an understanding public for its love of and support to the prisoners of war and the missing in action, many of whom made the supreme sacrifice for their country.

TABLE OF CONTENTS

Major Robert D. Jeffrey

Air Force, Dallas, Texas

Shot down December 20, 1965, near Lang Son, North Viet Nam
Released February 12, 1973

"I'm Not Going to Die Here"

"I'm not going to die in this airplane," Major Robert D. Jeffrey said very firmly to himself. But there was real reason to be concerned. His two-man F-4C had disintegrated into three large pieces and a thousand scraps as it was hit by North Vietnamese anti-aircraft fire.

"There was fire in the cockpit; flames were coming up over the back of the seat and around the sides. I closed my eyes to keep them from being burned and tried to reach the ejection handle, which was just above my head."

The force of gravity was so great as the broken plane tumbled through the air that Jeffrey could only strain as he reached for the ejector. It was like a dream—a nightmare. The muscles of his neck stiffened, but he could not raise his hands. He tried again, frantically, to pull down the face shield and blow the canopy. The heat was intense.

"I couldn't get my hands above my waist. I opened my eyes again for just an instant to look around the cockpit, and I had a very strong—I don't know what you call it—maybe an impression. I just said to myself, 'I'm not going to die here.' It was so vivid, so dramatic. I had this special will to get out of the airplane."

1

In the next moment, his mind working with new clearness, his hands, as if by inspiration, moved quickly to an alternate ejection handle located between his legs. With both hands he grasped the handle, and with new determination—"I will not die"—he pulled it.

In an instant the canopy jettisoned. Jeffrey was still bent over the seat. In a split second the ejection followed, catapulting him into the air. Jeffrey knew nothing; he had blacked out. Because of his bad position, two of his vertebrae were crushed by the tremendous force. The flames were licking at his neck and wrists.

This was Jeffrey's first mission, December 20, 1965. He had arrived in Southeast Asia only a few days earlier. He was one in a flight of four F-4Cs covering a bombing strike on a bridge north of Hanoi. Their assignment was to prevent any MIGs from attacking before they reached the target.

"We flew up the coast until we approached the Chinese border, and then we turned inland. The plan was to descend to a cloud cover below us at about 4,000 feet. As we descended through the cloud, I was one of two on the left, and two other planes were on the right. We leveled off just below the cloud and flew over an airfield near Lang Son, only a few miles from China. The Vietnamese opened up heavy anti-aircraft guns immediately.

"It was a gun, not a missile, that hit my plane in the tail section. As soon as I was hit, I pushed the throttles into afterburner to make the gunners' tracking problem more difficult by accelerating. I didn't think I was hit seriously at first because the plane just shook, but then it started buffeting. The warning lights in the cockpit flashed on and the plane pitched and started tumbling."

The silver plane with a blue star—U.S. Air Force

—was on fire. It broke into three pieces as it tumbled to the ground. The other pilots in the mission did not see Jeffrey eject from the broken aircraft. It went down in flames.

Jeffrey came to in the air in time to hear his parachute open. "I must have decelerated quite a bit from the time I left the aircraft because when the 'chute opened, I didn't feel any opening jerk from sudden decrease in speed.

"I looked down. My eyes were fuzzy, but it appeared as though I was about two hundred feet above the ground. I realized that I had gotten out of the plane at the very last second."

Jeffrey ejected over a populated area. "I could see people on the ground. Some shots were fired at me as I drifted down, but I wasn't hit. After a very short trip I landed in a plowed field near a dry riverbed. I was only about twenty yards from a Vietnamese with a gun. I was captured immediately."

Several Vietnamese gathered around him. During their momentary indecision, Jeffrey was able to assess his injuries. He had a terrible pain in his back from the cracked vertebrae. He was spitting blood and could feel that he had bitten through his tongue. Apparently it had been out when he ejected. He also had cracked his teeth and cut his lip, which was beginning to swell. As he wiped the blood from his mouth with his sleeve, he realized that his wrists were burned. Then he found that his neck below his helmet and his face were also blistered. He had difficulty focusing his eyes. The force of the ejection had caused the blood vessels to burst. Shrapnel had grazed his ankle.

His attention was brought back to his captors, who had now been joined by several others. It appeared that they had made a decision, and with guns in their hands and an excited chatter in their voices, they began to tie his hands behind him.

"I worried that they would kill me," he said. "But I think they had orders from their government to capture us. There may have even been a bounty on prisoners captured alive. I happened to be the sixtieth American POW and was somewhat of a novelty," he said.

After tying his hands behind his back, his captors tried to remove his flying gear. Zippers and the complicated "G-suit" seemed to be more than they had patience for. They took a knife and began cutting his clothing. By tugging and pulling they activated the underarm life preserver, which inflated and swelled. The bright orange color and the instant action of the life preserver startled the Vietnamese, and they jumped back, bringing their guns and knives to a position of defense. As they realized what had happened, there was laughing among them and they relaxed. Jeffrey would liked to have smiled, but his sore tongue and lips and the nature of the event prevented him from enjoying the humor.

The well-armed captors unexpectedly brought Jeffrey to his feet and led him down a road. Fear seized him as he limped along. Perhaps they were going to shoot him.

"We went down a road with an embankment on one side and a drop-off on the other. Before long, we came to a circular area that had been dug out of the embankment. It looked like a truck turnaround. They stopped me in this protected place and searched me.

"A civilian carrying a medical bag came up and had a look at me. He applied salve and bandaged the burns on my wrist, neck, and face. After that treatment they put me in a military ambulance and had me lie on the stretcher. I fell asleep almost immediately, reflecting that Divine help was the

4   *From the Shadow of Death*

only thing that got me out of the aircraft. I knew there was a reason I didn't die. I was not quite sure what it was, but there was a reason."

Chapter 2

In the Valley of Death

The bouncing of the stretcher and the groans of the Vietnamese who were carrying it awoke Major Jeffrey. It was dark, and he had been removed from the ambulance and was being carried along a trail in a deep gorge. The soreness and bruises were becoming more noticeable. The stretcher was placed on the floor of a room, fashioned by using the walls of the gorge as two walls of a crude shack. It was part of a military camp.

Using hand signs, the Vietnamese language, and a few prods, the soldiers got Jeffrey off the stretcher and seated on a chair at a crude table. In a few moments, three Vietnamese came into the room. Two of them took seats across the table and the third brought a chair to the side of Jeffrey. The one at his side was an interpreter.

The process of questioning began without any introduction. Jeffrey listened carefully to the interrogators, who seemed to be wording their questions very carefully, but he could understand nothing.

"What is your name?" the interpreter asked. It seemed like a short question for so much conversation between the two Vietnamese.

"Robert D. Jeffrey, captain [he was promoted to major while in prison], United States Air Force

FV3117985, born 23 July 1939," he answered firmly with a nod of his head.

There were smiles on the faces of the interrogators as they looked at each other, and with the help of the translator they wrote the information at the top of a piece of paper. Then there was more conversation between the interrogators. When they came to agreement and a question was put, the translator spoke.

"What type of aircraft were you flying?" he asked, and then looked confidently at his prisoner for an answer.

Jeffrey hesitated only a moment and with a firm press of his swollen lip and some difficulty caused by his cut tongue, he answered, "Robert D. Jeffrey, captain, United States Air Force, FV3117985, born 23 July 1939."

There was a startled look on the translator's face. The eyes of the interrogator turned quickly from Jeffrey to the translator. It was the translator who hesitated now. The anxious eyes of the two men across the table and a short demand brought the same answer from Jeffrey. Their faces turned long; a flash of anger was apparent.

Jeffrey could almost understand them asking to try again. The translator asked the question. Slowly, and with a fixed tone, Jeffrey gave the same answer.

For about twenty minutes the process continued, the Vietnamese becoming more and more irritated and Jeffrey more and more determined. His back was aching and his mouth was bleeding again.

Two more interrogators came in and went through the same routine. Jeffrey showed less interest in the questions, but he answered with the same determination—name, rank, serial number, and date of birth.

He felt more pain every time he shifted on the chair. He hoped the interrogation was over when the second pair of Vietnamese left the table in anger.

It was not over. A rather elderly man, dressed in a military uniform, came into the room and sat across the table from Jeffrey. It was as though he were the dean of interrogators and he had confidence.

The questions started the same. The answers from Jeffrey were also the same. Then the tone of questioning changed. There was no anger in the eyes of the elderly interrogator, but a display of concern and compassion.

"Are you married?" he asked in broken English. There was a look of real interest on his face.

"Robert D. Jeffrey, captain, United States Air Force, FV3117985, born 23 July 1939," was the answer.

The old man showed no disappointment. "Do you have children?" he asked next.

"Robert D. Jeffrey, captain, United States Air Force, FV3117985, born 23 July 1939," Jeffrey said, uneasy, but still determined.

"Think about it for a minute. Tell me about your home in the United States," the Vietnamese interrogator requested, looking as though he would receive an answer.

He did; the answer was the same.

"Look, captain, you are very young, you have a lot to live for. Answer the questions and you will have no trouble. Tell me, what was your mission?" the old man said, now a little more stern.

Jeffrey bristled a bit and again gave his name, rank, serial number, and date of birth.

"Don't be a foolish hero; it could cost you your life. Think of your wife and children. Where did you fly from? We know, but we want you to tell us. Now where?" was the question. The patience was disappearing, but the old man hid it well.

"Robert D. Jeffrey, captain, United States Air—"

He was interrupted. "Foolish man, you have had your chance. You can answer my questions or be shot."

The answer was in Jeffrey's set eyes and the firm curl of his mouth, still marked with blood.

Acting on a signal, soldiers came, marching with a quick step, and in a rough manner, they half walked, half dragged Jeffrey back down the trail. The pain in his back was like a knife jabbing. There was a Vietnamese on each arm.

Jeffrey was forced to kneel at the edge of the ravine. His eyes were focusing better now and he could see through the darkness to the valley below. Had he escaped death in the plane, had he survived the ejection only to die at the edge of this dark valley?

The interrogator walked up to his side. "You have two minutes to talk. If you don't talk in that time, you won't talk at all. You will be shot."

There was no sound from Jeffrey. Some quiet inspiration assured him of his standards, of his commitment to his country.

"You have one and one-half minutes left," the Vietnamese said.

Jeffrey could not see what was behind him, but he heard men shuffling about and guns being cocked. He couldn't understand the commands.

"One minute."

Jeffrey was thinking of his wife and son, Bill. There was a prayer in his heart.

"One-half minute," rang out in the quiet night.

Jeffrey stiffened. He was tempted to count the thirty seconds in his mind.

"It's your last chance. Your time is up," the interrogator sternly said. Then turning on his heels— Jeffrey could hear his shoes in the gravel—he gave a command.

The rifle rang out. Jeffrey heard the shots. "They

must have shot over my head or into the ground, because I was not hit. They stood me up and took me back to the shack, and that was the end of that. Three times I had escaped death," he recalled.

They put him on a truck and took him to Hanoi, about one hundred miles to the south and east of Lang Son. The truck drove down the valley paralleling North Viet Nam's major rail link to China.

He was stiff all over when he arrived at Hanoi. "They put me in the Hoa Loa prison, called by prisoners the Hanoi Hilton. I was put in a section known as New Guy Village, where they put the new shoot-downs, and was secluded in a small cell about seven feet square.

"There was a concrete bunk on each side of the cell with a narrow aisle down the center. They gave me a copy of the camp regulations, which said that Americans who were captured were criminals and were not entitled to the benefits of prisoners of war.

"We were ordered not to communicate with any other prisoners. If we were asked questions or told to do anything by the prison officers or guards, we were to answer the question or obey the command without hesitation. We had to obey all camp regulations. We were stripped of all our basic rights," Jeffrey said.

The concrete beds were not comfortable, but they were good for his back. He still wore his flying suit. For the three days he was allowed to keep it, it gave him the warmth needed for the cold December nights.

He was not left long without another interrogator. "Have you read the regulations?" the camp officer asked.

Jeffrey indicated that he had.

"You understand that if you violate any of the regulations you will be severely punished," the officer said, referring to the notice on the bottom of the printed sheet.

Jeffrey nodded that he understood.

"What kind of aircraft were you flying?" the prison interrogator asked. He was very businesslike.

Jeffrey gave name, rank, and serial number as he had so many times before.

"What was your mission?" The question got the same response.

For more than an hour the questioning went on. The Vietnamese were determined to get the answers. Jeffrey was stubborn enough not to give them.

"If you don't answer, you will not receive any medical attention." Still Jeffrey remained silent.

"If you continue to refuse to answer, you will be punished," the officer threatened.

Still no answer.

They threatened him with starvation, denial of clothing, and the comfort of a blanket. Jeffrey gave them no answer.

For three days interrogation continued, officer after officer, threat after threat. Between questioning periods, Jeffrey lay on the concrete bed. He was so exhausted that sleep was easy. The guards would awaken him periodically and take him for interrogation.

"One night they came in and took my flying suit and gave me a very thin prison garb. They began feeding me tea and soup, but my mouth was so sore I wasn't able to eat much. About the third day a medic came in and put some salve on my burns. I never did receive medical care for my broken back, or for my eyes, tongue, teeth, or the shrapnel grazes on my leg. They didn't treat my burns after the third day. They were trying to use this denial of medical attention to get me to talk.

"The night they gave me the thin clothes, they

took me to another room where they interrogated me again. I still refused to talk. They said they were going to punish me. Two guards got me down on the floor and tied my arms together with ropes. They used thin manila rope and tied me around the middle of my upper arm and ran the rope around my back, forcing my shoulder blades together and cutting off circulation.

"Then they asked me the questions again. I still refused, so they turned the light out and left me alone still tied up. About fifteen or twenty minutes later they came back and asked the questions again. I still refused, so one guard got on my back and started bouncing me. This punishment was excruciating, but I still refused to talk, and they left me alone again. They returned several times to tighten the ropes and question me. It wasn't long until I lost the feeling in my arms. After about three hours they wrapped more rope around my legs, cutting off the circulation, and then put long leg irons on me so I couldn't move. The irons were large U-shaped bolts that fit around the ankles with an iron rod that slipped through, making it impossible to stand up.

"The guards stood on the iron and grated it up and down on my shins to intensify the pain. I finally reached the point where I couldn't stand the pain any more and started answering some of their questions. Surprisingly, the questions were of no real military value. They could have read the answers in the magazines or newspapers. They also asked me about my family."

This was the fourth day of concentrated interrogation. It was the North Vietnamese way of teaching Jeffrey that he was a prisoner and subject to their will.

Jeffrey was left then to reflect on the treatment of the past four days. It was some time before he could move. He had escaped death; they had stopped short of that, but he felt he had tasted the tortures of hell.

It was the day before Christmas—Christmas Eve. He thought about one-year-old Billy and longed to be at home with him. He thought about his wife, Joy. She would make sure Billy had a good Christmas. He thought about the Savior and His gift to mankind.

"My faith in God was a constant source of strength. There never really was a time when I thought I was going to die. Nor was there a time when I thought I would never return home."

Jeffrey, who was twenty-six years old when he was shot down, had been baptized into the Church when he was thirteen years old. He is now a prospective elder.

That Christmas Eve, 1965, he prayed for strength and for release from pain.

Chapter 3

An American Voice

Following four days of ordeal, Jeffrey was placed in a section of the prison called Heartbreak Hotel, in a small block containing eight cells. He was dumped into his cell by the guards, who half carried him there. He was almost too sore to move. He was depressed; it was a breach of his personal standards to give in to the North Vietnamese demands. He felt as though he had been stripped of absolutely everything.

When there is nothing left, a man must turn to someone. Jeffrey turned to God. He prayed for help. "I called on him for strength and courage on many occasions. He never failed me. I asked not only for strength and courage, but also for the smallest things. It never ceased to amaze me the way my prayers were answered," he related.

Here, in solitary confinement, he received an answer to his prayer.

"Psst, hey, buddy," came a sound through a vent over the door. It was an American voice, the thing Jeffrey needed so much. He moved quickly but cautiously, getting up on the bed and looking out of the vent in the door.

"To be caught talking to another prisoner would mean punishment. They called the treatment that I had just endured punishment, and I didn't want any more of that."

Through the vent in the door Jeffrey saw the entrance to the cell block. He was in the first cell. Across from him was the shower. He didn't know how many other POWs were in the cell block.

Looking to see that all was clear, that there weren't any Vietnamese in sight, he softly asked, "Who is it?"

The voice was that of Colonel Robison Risner, then the highest-ranking POW in North Viet Nam, who had been captured on September 16, 1965. He was in the cell next to Jeffrey.

"What is your name?" Colonel Risner asked.

The question sounded familiar; he had been asked that so many times since his capture, but this time there was no hesitation to answer. "Robert Jeffrey," he replied.

"How are you?" was the next question.

Jeffrey described in short terms the injuries he had suffered. Risner gave him some reassurance and they talked for a while. It was a God-send.

"You be our lookout," Risner directed. "I want to talk to the other prisoners."

In the days that followed, Risner taught Jeffrey the tap code used in the prison to communicate. "We practiced for a while, tapping on the wall, back and forth. I was pretty slow at first, but my speed picked up and I could soon handle the basic code. We developed this code to a point where we had a shorthand and we could communicate pretty rapidly."

He continued to use the code when he was taken to another camp in Hanoi called the Zoo. He stayed there for about five months.

"I was fortunate at the Zoo, because I was not in solitary confinement. Because of my injuries, I was put in a room with two other men. One of them was Art Black, a paramedic. [Sergeant Arthur N. Black, Bethlehem, Pennsylvania, was captured September 20, 1965.] The other was Jon Reynolds [Major Jon A. Reynolds, born in Philadelphia, Pennsylvania, was captured November 28, 1965], who had been flying a 105. Jon had both his arms broken, a broken jaw, and a dislocated knee.

"Art had been taking care of Jon, so they moved me in the same room so he could take care of me too. Actually, he didn't treat any of my injuries. The Vietnamese didn't give him any medicine or anything to treat us with, but he was trained, and he helped us a lot. He did things for me that I couldn't do for myself.

"By February 1966, when Jon and I were recovering and able to take care of ourselves, they moved Art out into another room and Jon and I were together until May.

"The Vietnamese called us in one at a time and asked us to write our biographies. We refused to write, and they began to harangue us and threaten us with punishment.

"The next thing we knew, they had split us up and put us in separate rooms and on a starvation diet. We were given a crust of bread and one-half cup of water twice a day for about eight days. Finally, they gave up. They tried starvation punishment on a lot of prisoners and found it didn't work. When the men started eating again, their bodies would reject the food, and they would vomit. They would become weak and ill and lose weight.

"They next put me in solitary confinement in a room with the window blocked off so no light or air could come in. As in all other rooms, there were bugs and mosquitos. I was not allowed out of the room— I was not allowed to bathe or shave. The guards opened the door and pushed food in twice a day. This treatment lasted three weeks.

"I still refused to write my biography. They then moved me to another camp where the facilities were very good for separating prisoners. There was an outer wall and a compound inside the wall, which was divided into nine smaller compounds, with a hut in the center of each of these compounds. The hut was divided into four rooms. One man would be in each room—not allowed to see any other man or talk to anyone.

"Violation of the rules meant punishment. One common form of punishment used here was to sit the prisoner on a stool in the middle of the room. He had to sit there night and day—day and night. The guards would come by and harass and scream and threaten him with their rifles, looking for an excuse to beat him. If he lost his temper, they would hit him.

"They twisted our arms and put handcuffs on us, cutting off circulation. They would put ropes around our necks and pull us, blindfolded, through the compound, or they would make us run, swinging on the rope and smashing into trees or buildings.

"If the war was not going well for the North Vietnamese, they would increase the harassments and mistreat the prisoners.

"One American voice I did not want to hear was that of any of the American peace delegations. We knew that these people were not representing our government, and we suspected whom they did represent. They were not there in an official capacity, and we knew that what they were doing was not in our interests or in the interests of our country.

"There were delegations from the Soviet Union or East Germany. Fortunately, I was never asked to meet any of the delegations. Those who were forced to meet the visitors were tortured if they did not do exactly as they were told. They had to be polite.

"If the delegates had looked closely, they could have seen the signs of torture, though it is amazing the amount of pain and suffering that can be inflicted on a person in a short period without leaving noticable marks on his body."

Prisoners were moved often. After ten months in the Zoo, Jeffrey was moved back to the Hanoi Hilton to Little Vegas, and then to Son Tay, about forty miles west of Hanoi, in May 1968. This was the camp where the United States rescue attempt was made late in 1970. Even though the prisoners had all been moved earlier, this raid greatly shook up the Vietnamese and they moved all prisoners from the outside camps into the main prison in Hanoi.

"I moved out of Son Tay about four months before the raid—about mid-1970. I think this move was an attempt to improve our treatment because of the tremendous pressure that had been brought to bear on the DRV (Democratic Republic of Viet Nam) by the voice of the American people—the letter-writing campaign and the wives' trip to Paris.

"My wife was in the first group to go to Paris. They hadn't expected to see the DRV delegation. Their main purpose was to make the public aware of the situation.

"We called one prison Camp Hope. We heard about the cease-fire in November, and we had hopes that we would be going home from there. Instead, we were moved to another camp. We named it Camp Faith because that was what we were subsisting on— our faith.

"In May 1972, when the bombing started again, the Vietnamese moved half of us (208) to a camp to the north, near the Chinese border. Both Larry Chesley and I were among those who were moved. We had been roommates in Hanoi and were in the same building at the China border.

"I don't know why we were moved, unless they thought we were in danger because of the bombing. Previously, in 1967, they had taken some of us from the camps and placed us at various positions around Hanoi. One time we were at the power plant. It was well publicized that POWs were at key positions in Hanoi. This was to deter the bombing of these places."

The feeling of many of the POWs is that the bombing raids late in the war were a great help in bringing the war to an end.

"While we were at the Chinese border camp, the Vietnamese would play tapes for us, telling us about the October 1972 negotiations, and about the agreements for the cease-fire. They made it look like we, the United States, stalled the signing and that our government was to blame for the delay.

"We all prayed for peace," he added.

Chapter 4

Wife or Widow?

Mrs. Robert D. Jeffrey (Joy) went to Paris September 15, 1969, for a meeting with the North Vietnamese to find out if she was "a wife or a widow."

She was one of four Dallas, Texas, women married to U.S. airmen who had been shot down over North Viet Nam. None of them knew whether their husbands were dead or alive. Mrs. Jeffrey knew only that her husband had been shot down December 20, 1966.

"I wasn't given any hope at all. I was told to accept his death. I prayed for miracles, hoping that he had survived the explosion that broke his plane apart, even though his fellow pilots, who had observed the explosion, believed he was dead. They felt he had no chance of getting out of the explosion. I had no proof, I only hoped and prayed, and I can sympathize with the families who still do not know what happened to their husbands and fathers," Mrs. Jeffrey said.

Each of the four women—Mrs. Jeffrey, Mrs. Bonnie Singleton, wife of Captain Jerry Singleton, captured November 6, 1965; Mrs. Sandy McElhanon, wife of Major Michael McElhanon; and Mrs. Paula Hartness, wife of Captain Gregg Hartness—believed her husband was alive.

When the POW list was first released, only Singleton and Jeffrey were on it. The list contained 587 American prisoners, including 24 civilians.

Three days after the women arrived, they gained an audience with members of the North Vietnamese delegation to the Paris peace talks.

"We were surprised, like everybody else, when they agreed to see us," Mrs. Jeffrey said. "We had planned to give them a hard time, and as it turned out, they were forced to see us."

In the meeting, which lasted two hours, the wives heard their husbands described as war criminals. They were shown photographs of destroyed buildings and wounded civilians and told it was the result of U.S. bombing raids. They were propagandized and asked to denounce the United States and its participation in the war.

Promises were made by the North Vietnamese that the letters brought by the four women would be delivered to their husbands if they were alive. Xuan Dahn, a North Vietnamese official, promised to contact Hanoi and write each of them concerning the fate of her husband, but said that no information was available at that time.

"I found out that Bob was alive when I received the first letter from him in May 1970, nearly five years after he was captured. His name had been on a list in 1967, but even the government didn't believe he was alive; no one had seen him.

"My heart goes out to the wives and families of those who are missing in action. I wish these people could at least find out what happened." she said. Nearly 1,300 American servicemen are still missing.

Mrs. Jeffrey received other letters during her husband's imprisonment, most of them through peace groups.

"I found it very difficult at first to deal with the peace groups, but then I told myself I really didn't care who took my letter to my husband, as long as he got it. I was grateful to get some letters, but there was a bitter taste in my mouth every time I accepted one. Every time I received a letter, there were enclosures, which were very much like the propaganda we listened to in Paris. I found out later that it was the same kind Bob was getting in prison every day.

"Between letters from Bob, I would get letters from the peace group with all their propaganda. It was a torture treatment they used on the families of prisoners. They were using us, and trying to use the situation to torture us.

"I would get a letter with the peace group name on the envelopes, and there would be nothing but garbage in it. I would not upset myself by reading it. At least I had the ability to throw it in the trash. I felt sorry for Bob; he was forced to listen to that stuff every day, but I did have an understanding of what he was getting. It is very hard to explain it to people who do not know what you are talking about. It was frightening.

"The Communist line is based on hate. Their hard line was their bitterness and hatred to the men, and they tried to instill hate in us. This is what they feel will keep Communism going. It took me months to get over the bad feeling after I read some of the literature.

"In Paris, they were so bitter and hateful about the POWs. As I sat there listening, I was glad I didn't have the bitterness toward them that they obviously had toward my husband. It upset me greatly to know that the POWs were living under those conditions of hate.

"I prayed all the time for Bob. I had a feeling that he was alive. I feel that it was a miracle that Bob did survive, and it may have been God's will. I feel there was a reason that he did survive. On the other

From the Shadow of Death

hand, if he had been killed, I wouldn't have felt that that was God's will," she said.

Mrs. Jeffrey wears a gold bracelet with her husband's name on it. "I am going to wear it until all the other men are accounted for. Everybody we knew in Dallas wore Bob's bracelet. They all felt as if they knew him.

"The original reason for selling the bracelets was to make the POWs and MIAs real people. Those who wore the bracelets came to feel as if they knew the man and could relate to him. They could feel a little of what his family was going through. It was very difficult for people to relate to seventeen hundred POWs," Mrs. Jeffrey explained. They have a large jar of bracelets in their home, bracelets that friends returned to him when he arrived home.

"I found out he was going to be released when everybody else found out. There was no advance notice. It all seems like a blur. I was nervous when things started happening. I wanted to get him out of there.

"Bill was less than a year old when his father left. Now he is nearly eight years old. He went with me to meet my husband. Bob saluted him and waved from a distance. It was hard waiting, but I had already waited for nearly seven years.

"I was saddened to see him on television get off the plane at Clark Air Force Base. It was very depressing to think that I wasn't there."

Major Jeffrey called three times from the Philippines.

"We sat up and talked until one o'clock in the morning Philippine time. Bob had only four hours of sleep. He had waited up until everyone else was asleep and then he called and we talked for more than two hours.

"It was quite a happy time because I realized that we were laughing and joking from the first moment that he called. It was just as if he had left yesterday, despite the fact that we had both been through a great deal. I think the first thing I asked him was how he was. He had a lot of questions to answer and to ask. We just caught each other up on things," she said.

"As far as knowing each other, there has been no readjustment problem like I feared there would be. I tried to be realistic, and I think I was prepared for what was to happen," she said.

They have a lot of decisions to make about their home, about Bill, about church. (Mrs. Jeffrey is not LDS.)

"Dad has got to get acquainted with Brandy," Bill said. Brandy is the family dog.

There are two full baskets of mail to be answered. They want to answer every letter, a monumental task, because they feel very deeply the support and appreciation of the people who write to them.

Mrs. Jeffrey received two letters from her husband in April 1973, letters that had been written while he was still in prison. They had been mailed from Hanoi in March, a month after Jeffrey was released.

"It is interesting that they are the only letters I ever received other than letters from the peace group, which I resented so much. According to the Geneva Convention agreements, mail was to come through the regular channels and not through peace groups.

"These two letters had North Vietnamese stamps on them. One stamp had a very unattractive prisoner of war featured on it. He was sitting in a cell and it showed in front of the cell a United States Air Force plane going down—being shot down. The second stamp showed a North Vietnamese missile shooting down an American plane which was in flames.

From the Shadow of Death

"The stamps were very interesting, but I think they had their nerve sending them to me, and so late at that," Mrs. Jeffrey maintained. "But who needs letters when he is home?"

Major Robert D.
Jeffrey receives
welcome from his wife,
Joy, upon arrival in
Dallas from North
Viet Nam

Sign in front of the
Jeffrey home in Dallas,
Texas, sums up Joy
Jeffrey's feeling of having
her husband back home

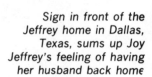

From the Shadow of Death

Major and Mrs. Robert
D. Jeffrey enjoy being
together at their
Dallas, Texas, home,
following his release
from POW camp in
Hanoi

Major Robert D.
Jeffrey saved jar
full of bracelets
returned by POW
supporters

Major Robert D. Jeffrey is welcomed back to freedom and his home in Dallas, Texas, by his wife, Joy, and son Bill

From the Shadow of Death

Major Robert D. Jeffrey enjoys thrills of giant slide with his son Bill at Six Flags Over Texas amusement park near Dallas-Fort Worth, Texas

Major Robert D. Jeffrey enjoys bike ride with his son Bill

Captain Larry J. Chesley,

Air Force, Burley, Idaho

Shot down April 16, 1966, north of Demilitarized Zone
Released February 12, 1973

Chapter 5

"No Rescue for Me"

It was Saturday afternoon. First Lieutenant Larry J. Chesley of the United States Air Force had been up most of the night before on a combat mission over North Viet Nam. When he got up about noon and went to breakfast, little did he realize that he had only four hours left of freedom—four hours left before he would become a prisoner of war.

The date was April 16, 1966.

The war was intensifying. Back in the States the headlines that day recorded: "Marines Smother Viet Cong Attack." United Press International reported that "U.S. Marines routed Communist attackers in a hand-to-hand battle 375 miles north of Saigon Saturday despite one of the most massive Red mortar barrages of the Vietnamese war."

After breakfast, Lieutenant Chesley, 27, from Burley, Idaho, standing 5 feet 8 inches tall and weighing 155 pounds, walked down to the flight line for briefing on that day's mission.

"I've picked an easy target for today," Lieutenant Hal Sheads, the scheduling officer, told Chesley. "There are no guns there." The target was a cave in some rocks just north of the Demilitarized Zone. That seemed easy enough.

"We walked out to the aircraft," Chesley said. "It was an F-4C, a phantom fighter-bomber. At this time, the 105 was the workhorse over there, but in 1968 the F-4 became the workhorse since almost all the 105s had been shot down."

"That day I was to fly with Major Sam Johnson. He was the pilot and I was the GIB (guy in back), which was then a pilot. Major Johnson had previously flown with the Air Force Acrobatic team. He was a soloist and sometimes slot man for the Thunderbirds.

"We climed into the plane at 4:30 p.m. and set out for our destination. I told Major Johnson that the guns on the plane didn't work. I had flown in it the night before."

Chesley, a veteran of six years in the Air Force, had flown seventy-six missions since arriving in Southeast Asia in December 1965. Fifty-four of these missions were over North Viet Nam and counted toward his one hundred missions required before he would be able to go home. His other flights were over Laos. He had written home earlier and said he had completed more than half of his obligation. Just forty-six more missions—forty-five after today.

He thought of home. He thought of the new house his parents had moved into in the Star Ward on the outskirts of Burley. He thought of a lot of things. He thought of the five hundred dollars he had placed in his Book of Mormon a few days earlier and wondered if it would still be there when he returned. The two hundred dollars in cash was for tithing. The other three hundred was in the form of a check.

It took thirty-five minutes for Major Johnson and Lieutenant Chesley to fly from their home base at Ubon, Thailand, to their assigned target some twenty miles inside North Viet Nam.

It was now 5:05 p.m.

Contrary to reports, there were guns at the site. The F-4 was hit by enemy fire. "We didn't even

From the Shadow of Death

know what hit us," Chesley said, "but the plane became uncontrollable, and we later learned it was on fire."

"Get out!" yelled Major Johnson.

Chesley first pulled the ejection handle located on the seat between his legs. "I pulled the handle, but it wouldn't fire [eject]." Another ejection device was located behind him, and as he turned to grab it with his left hand, a tremendous pressure, seventeen times the force of gravity, was thrust against his twisted body, fracturing a vertebra.

"It worked and I was ejected into the air. As I was descending to the ground, I saw the Vietnamese coming from all points of the clock to capture me, and I could see there would be no rescue for me.

"Oh, my God," Chesley recalls uttering, "give JoDene [his wife] strength to endure this hardship."

As he hit the ground, he landed in an open pasture and was knocked unconscious momentarily. "I was captured almost immediately. The Vietnamese tore and cut my clothes from my body until I was stripped to my garments and my white wool socks. They cut my clothes off with machetes because they didn't know how to work the zipper on my flight suit. I took some of the clothes off myself, but they didn't want me to touch anything because they were afraid I would pull a booby trap or something.

"After they got my clothes off I just looked toward heaven, and said, 'Oh, dear God, I may have to walk a long way and I can't do it without my boots.' About one minute later my prayer was answered and they brought back the boots without explanation. That was the only piece of clothing they brought back."

It was now almost dark. "The Vietnamese made me run across the field. The pain in my back was excruciating. They knew that search-and-rescue planes would be sent out to attempt to locate us and they wanted us out of the area as fast as possible.

"A little later, shock set in and my legs were paralyzed for about twenty minutes. I was really scared I was going to be crippled.

"Later that night I was put on a truck. They tied my arms behind my back and then tied my wrists to the top of the bed of the truck, so that I was hanging by my arms.

"I said, 'Oh, Lord, I can't go on this way. This is just hurting too much.' We'd only gone about five miles when the knot came untied and I fell back to the bed of the truck, gaining some relief from the pain."

Sometime during the night the truck came to a halt. Chesley wondered what was happening. He heard the Vietnamese guards chattering, but he couldn't understand what was going on. He soon realized, however, that the truck had broken down and they would have to walk.

"We walked the last four or five miles into a town. Every time a plane would come over, a guard would beat me. I was especially beaten on the right arm, which became black and blue and swollen."

Later that day, about noon, Chesley was given a shot for the pain in his back, the only medical treatment he received for his broken back during his entire imprisonment. "I was in an awfully lot of pain. A doctor came in and cut the back out of my garments so my back was exposed. He gave me a shot to ease the pain."

Later that same night, Chesley was taken to a small room where he was questioned, the first of many interrogations to which he would be subjected. With his hands securely tied behind his back, he looked around. Two kerosene lamps, about three inches high, which were used to light the room, flickered in the night, giving an eerie effect. A gun

From the Shadow of Death

lay on the table. Four Vietnamese were seated at the table.

"They asked me several questions: What base was I from? What kind of plane was I flying? What ordnances were we carrying?

"And each time they asked me a question, I would reply, 'Larry Chesley, first lieutenant, 3147498, born 27 September 1938.' "

He thought of the Code of Conduct that had been drilled into him so many times in various phases of his training.

"They questioned me five or six times, and each time I would reply only with my name, rank, serial number, and date of birth. When they found they weren't getting anywhere with me, they took me outside and threw me onto an anthill. I lay there quite awhile—I don't know just how long." Time didn't seem important anymore.

The pain in his back was almost unbearable. He wondered what was going to happen to him. He thought of his family—his wife and his two small children. His daughter, Debbie was four and his son, Donald, was only two. How he longed to see them, to be with them, to hold them close.

After lying on the anthill for some time, left alone with his thoughts, Chesley was taken back into the building where he had been interrogated.

The next day the abuse continued. He was thrown in a trench. As many Vietnamese watched, his captors dragged him up and down the trench. He still carries scars from that mistreatment.

The next night he was put in the "ropes," which he explains is "a method of torture where they tie your arms behind your back so tightly that circulation in your arms is cut off." To increase the pressure, he was forced to lie on the ground. "It was extremely painful to my fractured vertebra," he emphasized, "so much so, in fact, that I passed out."

Chesley stayed in the town for two days and then was placed on a truck again, which inched its way through the black night toward Hanoi.

"I was never so glad to see the sun come up. I had ridden in the back of that truck for so many hours; my back hurt, and I just had to endure it. At daybreak all movement on the roads stopped, so we would not be seen from the air by U.S. planes flying overhead."

Enroute to Hanoi, Chesley became the object of derision and curiosity. "Many people, women particularly, would come up to me and feel my garments to see what the material was.

"It took twenty-one days to travel from where I was captured to Hanoi. The roads were bad, and they took us to out-of-the-way places. After twenty-one days of rolling around in those trucks and sleeping on dirt floors, by the time I reached Hanoi I was filthy. I had been tortured, I was cold, and my back ached—but I made it."

Chapter 6

"Grandma Taught Me Courage"

A rice mat for a bed. Four walls, dingy and peeling, cell windows blanked out, and a bucket in the corner for defecation. These were all that Larry Chesley had to look at during those first frightening, lonely days in prison.

He stared at the gray, stained ceiling. It served almost as a motion picture screen where he could take his mind from the thoughts and agonies of imprisonment. He didn't know when he would be placed in the ropes again, but at least for a moment he could escape in his thoughts. He lived his life now with thoughts of the past and hopes for the future. The present needed courage.

"My Grandma Chesley taught me courage," he remembered, as his mental picture returned him 9,000 miles to the small central Idaho town of Arco. "She taught me to face danger, not to be afraid of it. She taught by example."

It was the summer he had ridden the race horses. Larry was small. That was an advantage for a jockey.

He could feel the pride, even a bit of arrogance, as he rode those winning horses to the cheers of an excited crowd.

There was one horse that was hard to ride. Proud and haughty, it had bolted and run away with Larry. There was no stopping it. It was all he could do to stay on; jerking the reins did no good. It was a flight of terror until the horse ran himself out and stopped at a fence, panting.

Larry was greatly relieved when he slid off. Jerking the reins, he scolded the horse, "I'm never going to ride you again, you spooky critter." The horse tossed its head about, unashamed, as he led it back to the stable.

Larry's legs were weak from the frightening experience. He didn't want to ride that horse ever again, and he told his grandmother so.

"You're not scared of that horse, are you?" Grandma Chesley asked.

"Yes I am," replied Larry.

"Never going to ride him again, huh?"

"Don't care if I never see him again!"

"Now, lad, if you're ever going to be a man and face life, you can't be frightened of little things like a spirited horse. You stick with it; don't you give up," she commanded.

"It could be dangerous," Larry retorted.

"Don't be afraid of danger; ride the horse," his grandmother insisted.

Larry was scared, but he rode again.

Even in the darkest days in prison when there was so much despair, Larry remembered this lesson of courage and would not allow himself to quit. "If you even admit that you can quit, that is the first step," he said.

Larry thought of his father many times during the days that followed his shoot-down. Before he went to Viet Nam, the last thing his father had said as he threw his arms around him was, "Be a good boy, Larry. It will take courage, but be a good boy." His father had given him that counsel many times.

"I told him I would, and I was," Larry said.

Probably the most difficult time in prison for

Larry was from December 1966 through April 1967.

"I had a bad case of beri-beri. It took all the courage I had just to want to live. I was in pain almost all the time, and I would get only twenty or thirty minutes of sleep during a twenty-four-hour period, when exhaustion overcame the pain. My roommate was having just as bad a time as I was because he could not help me. He could only watch me suffer. I hurt so bad I could hardly think. Yet, I did think. I always kept saying, 'Man, I don't want to die. I don't want to die. I would rather have the pain than die,' and I just kept going and going on that thought.

"The thing that really kept me going was my love for my wife and my children. I thought about them nearly all the time I was in prison. But during this period of time, the pain was so bad that it was all I could think about. For days I would go without thinking about my wife and children, and that was terrible.

"One day I was hurting so badly that my roommate called for a doctor. The guard unlocked the door, came in, and started beating me. My roommate jumped off his bed and threw the guard out of the room—just physically picked him up and threw him out of the room, up against the wall. They had told us in survival school never to hit a guard.

"Well, the guard got all excited and pulled off a shoe and was going to beat my roommate with it, but my roommate shouted at him, 'I'll take that shoe away from you and beat the hell out of you with it if you don't get out of here and get a doctor.'

"Of course, the guard didn't understand English, but he got the message. Finally he left and returned with four or five others. I thought, 'This is going to be it,' but they didn't do anything to my roommate. The next time he got caught for breaking a rule, he went out for an interrogation. He told the interrogator that I needed a doctor badly, and if something wasn't done soon, something bad might happen.

"A few nights later, they took me to the hospital, which was a big farce. A woman doctor looked at me, checked my reflexes, and sent me back. About a month later they started treating me for hepatitis, which I didn't have, but that is what they said I had. They started giving me shots. I got shots for thirty days, plus extra food, which at that time meant that I was getting fatback and a tiny sliver of meat. They were taking it from all the other prisoners and giving it to me. I also got bread while the rest were getting rice."

Eventually he started a comeback, but the illness had lowered his body resistance so much that the slightest thing knocked him down again. If he took part in the calisthenics that were an important part of the prisoners' well-being, he would become sick again.

"I'd just have to start from zero again, and finally, in 1971, I just quit exercising because anytime I'd get in any kind of physical shape, I'd just get knocked down by some setback in my body. So I just walked and used that as my exercise."

Courage with faith and prayers was the sustaining strength of the prisoners. Each day of confinement was a struggle. The men strengthened each other, built each other's courage. Sometimes it was just a look or a word exchanged in the courtyard where they did their laundry. Just having a companion was important. It was frightening to be alone.

Larry found courage by turning to his Father in heaven.

"Those first days, and weeks, and years I prayed a lot—all through '66, '67, and '68. About '69 I started to think that perhaps God had forgotten where I lived. I started slacking off for a while. I

From the Shadow of Death

communicated with him some in '70 and '71, but then I decided that I'd been neglecting something important and I started doing a lot of praying again. That is when I got the news that I'd been divorced.

"I turned again to prayer for courage and that strengthened me, but I was no different from the others. Every POW was an example of courage; they are the bravest men I have ever known."

Chapter 7

School Without Books

Larry Chesley sat alone in his cell. It was really not much more than a closet. There was no softness to his bed, and he found himself trying to analyze the mixture of smells that accounted for the odor that lingered in the prison. He sniffed the humid air, looked in the dim corners, brought his newly acquired prison uniform to his nose, and filtered the air through it. He could discover the smell of damp bricks, mildew, sewage, human beings, and somewhere in there, the smell of Hanoi.

This was one of the first of many, many mental exercises that Larry put himself through as his prison days wore on. It was not easy to concentrate at first. The pain in his back was severe, and most of his mental exercise was devoted to trying to find a comfortable position. Time and time again he analyzed his physical condition, seeing in an imaginary X-ray vision his fractured vertebra and trying to figure how to best position his back so it would heal properly and so the pain would diminish.

It is hard to think clearly when the message of pain comes through so strongly. But thoughts of his family were strong, and he rehearsed in his mind the last detail. Well, not the last detail, he thought to himself. There is the little detail of being with them.

44

He mentally built a house. "But I had no talent for building houses, so I didn't do that anymore," he said. He "bought" a bicycle—coaster brakes, chrome trim, the whole works—only to discover that it was too big for Debbie. Larry kept track of every day. He thought about Primary for Debbie and Donald on Tuesday. He "took" them to school the first day and imagined Christmas, their big family day.

Larry came to realize that his mind could not be kept in the prison cell. It was free to wander, and more often than not it wandered back. He thought of his youth. Mentally, he walked up and down the streets of Burley, Idaho, remembering the shops and stores and who lived in every house in his neighborhood. He recalled the event of his baptism and later receiving his patriarchal blessing from Brother Knight. He had many occasions to rehearse in his mind the details of his blessing. There was a promise of returning home. He weighed his life, wondering if he had lived up to the promised blessings.

He found himself going over the Boy Scout laws and reviewing every merit badge that had earned him his Eagle. He started recalling his classes at Weber College in Ogden, Utah, and officers training. He brought into focus every fact he could. He discovered he was in school—both as a student and as a teacher.

In analyzing his situation he came to realize that he needed physical exercise, but there wasn't much room for that as he paced two or three steps at a time in his cell. He needed mental exercise, but it would be a school without books. And he needed spiritual strength, so he talked to his Heavenly Father every day.

There came to his mind a poem, "or was it a story?" he tries to recall. "I don't know what is the source of the rhyme, but I plan to find out." Reaching into his mind, he found the words: "Stone walls do not a prison make, nor iron bars a cage."

"That is the way I felt; we all felt that way. They could lock us in a room by ourselves, but we would never be alone.

"It says in Second Corinthians 3:17, 'Now the Lord is that Spirit: and where the Spirit of the Lord is, there is liberty.' Now, you see, they cannot hold us down."

There was pain, there was misery, there was sickness for Larry, but his mind sorted and classified the truths and principles that made endurance possible.

A thousand times he wished for a pencil and paper. "I would like to write a book," he said. "If only the North Vietnemese would give us some books and paper, or a game to play or some crafts to work with. But they won't, so I will make up my own games." The games were mental games that he could play by himself. "I wish I had just an old magazine," he said to himself after winning a game he had played alone.

It was a welcome event the day Larry and another man were placed in a cell together. There was no increase in the size of the room. One man had to be on the bed while the other took a few steps for exercise. The beds were no softer, the blanket was still the same, the light was dim, and the prison odor, though dulled by its constant presence, was still there.

The thing that had changed was that the population had doubled. The brain bank was now twice as big as it had been before. A whole new world of experiences was available to the two prisoners of war.

"One of the first things I did after I received a roommate was to learn some of the poems that he remembered. The first one I learned was 'Invictus,' by William Earnest Henley.

"Dark is the night that covers me," he started. (Larry learned the poem slightly wrong in prison. It

was written, "Out of the night that covers me.")
He continued:

Black is the pit from pole to pole,
I thank whatever gods may be
For my unconquerable soul.

In the fell clutch of circumstance
    I have not winced nor cried aloud.
Under the bludgeonings of chance
    My head is bloody, but unbowed

Beyond this vale of human tears
[Correct words: "Beyond this place of wrath
    and tears."]
    Looms but the terror [horror] of the shade.
And yet the minutes [menace] of the years
    Time has found me unafraid.
[Correct: "Finds and shall find me unafraid."]

It matters not how strait the gate
    How charged with punishment the scroll,
I am the captain [master] of my fate;
    I am the captain [master] of my soul.

"That is the prison version I learned. We realized that not everything would be accurate, but we figured that if it was only eighty percent right it was better than nothing. This poem gave me a lot of strength along with the twenty-third Psalm. I would say it to myself virtually every day."

Prison school for the next few years was with one teacher and one student. "It was hard to tell which was teacher and which was student because we taught each other. We recalled our personal experiences, confided our deepest thoughts, expressed our fondest hopes."

From time to time there were rotations of prisoners and a new roommate would bring with him a new set of experiences and new things to learn. "Part of the time Jay Jensen, from Sandy, Utah, and I were together. This was wonderful because we both had Mormon backgrounds. Jay knew a great deal about the Church. We were very close and had many gospel discussions and rich spiritual experiences. Sunday was always a special day. We always knew what day it was. On Sunday, we always had church services. Even back as early as 1966, when I was shot down and lived alone in a small room with others nearby, we would pass a signal on Sunday throughout the building. At that given signal we would kneel down and pray together. Then we would repeat a scripture. The twenty-third Psalm was most popular because everybody knew it:

The Lord is my Shepherd; I shall not want.

He maketh me to lie down in green pastures;
he leadeth me beside the still waters.

He restoreth my soul; he leadeth me in the paths
of righteousness for his name's sake.

Yea, though I walk through the valley of the
shadow of death, I will fear no evil: for thou
art with me; thy rod and thy staff they
comfort me.

Thou preparest a table before me in the presence
of mine enemies; thou anointest my head with
oil; my cup runneth over.

Surely goodness and mercy shall follow me all
the days of my life; and I will dwell in the
house of the Lord for ever.

"Sometimes we would say the Lord's Prayer," Larry said. These scriptures soon became well known to all the men. "After the prayer and the scripture we would face east and pledge allegiance to our flag and country. Just in our individual rooms,

From the Shadow of Death

we would do this. And then we would worship in our own individual ways.

"The scriptures say somewhere that if two are met in God's name, there he will be also. I felt—we all felt—that when one of us would kneel down and have our own church services in his name, then God's Spirit would be there also.

"In our building ninety-nine percent of the prisoners would participate in church services. We kept faith in God, our country, our president, in the American people, and in each other. This is what gave us strength to continue.

"After December 1970 we were moved to larger groups. There were forty-eight of us, and we were able to have our own services. Everyone would take a turn and conduct the service in any manner he wished. We even had a small choir. The person conducting would assign someone to give the prayer or to pledge allegience to the flag or to speak, or he could do everything himself.

"We didn't need a chaplain. Almost everybody took a turn conducting the services, and everybody listened.

"We had a cross that was put up for church services. Some of the men wanted it as a reminder. My mother had sent a red towel in one of the packages that I received. We tore up some handkerchiefs and with a thread taken from a blanket, a white cross was sewn with an improvised needle on the red towel. We also had an American flag made from rags, and it was hung up along with the cross during our church services. A North Vietnamese guard discovered the cross and took it away. I complained, and for some unknown reason they brought it back, which was very unusual. The towel cross was turned over to the U.S. Air Force to be placed in its museum.

"These church services were some of the most moving, touching experiences I ever had," Larry recalled. "One experience that especially impressed me was a talk given by Julius Jayroe from South Carolina. We called him Jay. Jay had never been on his feet in front of a church audience before.

"When he got up to give his talk, he looked nervous. Dressed in his black prison uniform, he first looked at the floor and then at us, as he told of receiving his orders to go to Viet Nam. He was in England and it was hectic getting his family moved back to the United States and settled down.

"His talk went something like this: 'We were in South Carolina visiting my family for the last night. The children had been put to bed early. About fifteen or twenty minutes after I had put them to bed I heard my son David calling me to come to him. I supposed it was for a glass of water or a stomach ache or something.

" 'I was just a little upset, being disturbed from our conversation and my family, but I went up the stairs and in an almost demanding tone asked, "What do you want?"

" 'David looked at me and said, "I love you, Dad."

" 'That really set me back and I grabbed him in my arms. That little eight-year-old boy had waited until his younger brother, Steve, was asleep because he didn't want Steve to hear him tell me he loved me. He thought it wasn't manly to say I love you. Oh, how I would like to take him in my arms today.'

"This talk hit every one of us. It meant a lot to us," Larry said.. "In prison, we had our own song. It's one of my favorite songs, and I found out later it is Billy Graham's theme song. The first verse goes, 'Oh Lord, My God, When I awesome wonder and consider all the world Thy hands hath made, I see the stars, I hear the rolling thunder, Thy power throughout the Universe displayed.' We called our bombing attacks against North Viet Nam rolling thunder, so it seemed significent to me.

From the Shadow of Death

"One of our prisoners wrote a second verse to that song:

In foreign lands, You're even there to guide me,
Your Holy Spirit in my heart yet dwells.
When nights are cold, I feel your light inside me,
Imparting warmth through these cold hostile cells.

"That is just one of the songs that we would sing to keep our faith up," Larry explained.

"On Christmas and Easter, after 1970, we were allowed to have the Bible for an hour to copy off the Christmas story and the account of the resurrection. Then the Bible would be taken away again. These were special occasions.

"Since I have been released, many people have asked me, 'Did the POWs find God in prison?' The answer is that I don't know. I believe there is a statement which says, 'There are no atheists in a foxhole.' Maybe that statement could be extended to, 'There are no atheists in a parachute coming down over enemy territory.' I think that during the hard times most of the men found the need for strength greater than their own. Many men, I think, became prayerful, humble, and thoughtful. But I could see a difference as our treatment improved slightly; there was a slacking off. The men who brought God to prison with them will take him out with them. Those who found God in prison may leave him there. There are exceptions, of course, for there were men who discovered new strength they never had known before."

The idea that "the glory of God is intelligence" (D&C 93:36) never left Larry's mind. The same spirit seemed to exist among the other prisoners. The desire for education seemed more than just an escape from boredom.

When living conditions in the prison changed,

and forty-eight men were confined in a large room, the opportunity came for group education. Although no study materials, paper, or pencils were available, and books were denied the prisoners, they thrilled at the idea of having school. In January 1971, the education officer took a piece of brick that had been chipped from the wall, and with it he wrote on the concrete floor, much as children draw their hopscotch games on the sidewalk. He listed the subjects that would be offered in the education program. The men expressed their interests and their talents, and the list grew quite long. The dusty brick moving across the coarse concrete spelled out the categories—psychology, sociology, history, mathematics, religion, music, geometry, astronomy—the list grew.

The list completed, the men, one by one, stepped forward, and thoughtfully taking the brick, which had grown smaller, made marks by the subjects they were most interested in studying. The classes were organized, meeting in the morning for a session and then continuing in the afternoon.

"The most popular subject was history, and the second was religion." said Larry. "When they asked for officers to be in charge of different sessions, I volunteered for religion, and I taught Sunday School for more than a year. I taught them everything I knew, mostly drawing from what I had learned in seminary. First of all, I taught them about the Bible. I remembered that there were thirty-nine books in the Old Testament and twenty-seven in the New Testament. Then I started with Adam and Eve and the Garden of Eden. We talked about Cain and Abel and then the law and history, the poetry, and the major and minor prophets."

Every day Larry would search his mind, dig back in his memory as if he were taking a final exam. As he would lie down to sleep on the concrete slab bed, his mind would research the material he had gathered in his life.

"When we finished with the Old Testament, we started the New Testament. I didn't know as much about it as I did about the Old Testament, but with the help of the other men, I could put a class together.

"The Baptists were great scripture memorizers. They knew the passage and I knew the interpretation. I did not try to push my religion on them; I would explain principles when anyone was interested. Most of them were, and I would talk to them in private, not in a group," Larry said.

In addition to the Sunday School class, a devotional was held. "The Vietnamese did give us wine for sacrament on Easter and Christmas, and we broke bread. The sacrament was in the charge of two Baptist prisoners, who blessed it."

The Sunday School class had been successful, and a new subject was needed. Larry suggested a program called family home evening. He remembered back to before 1966 when he was with his family. They had studied together and had enjoyed outings and other family activities, using the manual provided by The Church of Jesus Christ of Latter-day Saints. Now he had no manual, but the subject drew the immediate interest of the captured men, who had been for so many years away from their families. The news of peace negotiations had filtered into the prison, mostly from the recent "shoot-downs," and the thoughts of returning to their families sparked even more interest in a family-related subject.

"The men responded well to the idea of family home evening," Larry said. "Many of them decided to follow the program and practice the principles when they got back to their families."

Many of the men studied in earnest, not knowing

that their families had already been broken by divorce while they were in prison. Wives who had not had any communication from their captured husbands for four years or more had thought them dead and had turned to divorce and remarriage.

It was while Larry was teaching the concepts of family home evening in the Sunday School class that news came that the prison would be opened and they would soon be returning home.

The "school without books" was soon to come to an end. No one regretted this fact, but none of the prisoners will forget the brain-searching exercises that helped to fill their long days with interest and purpose.

Chapter 8

"I Never Laughed So Hard"

A roar of laughter echoed from the hard walls of the Hanoi Hilton. The Vietnamese guards watched in amazement—almost in disbelief—the capers and antics of the POWs as they entertained each other with skits and shows and jokes.

There was a lighter side to prison life. As the conditions improved and the men were allowed to associate with one another, they entertained themselves. The ingenuity of the American serviceman is a thing to behold.

In prison many things were funny because they were funny, but many things were funny because they were pathetically sad. For example, to find a whole chicken foot or the webbed foot of a duck in the bottom of a soup bowl would bring a laugh in a motion picture, but it wasn't so easy for the POW who had to eat the soup to laugh.

During those long years in prison the POWs had good days and bad days. "Relative to a good day in America, there never was a good day in prison," Larry Chesley explained. "But relative to a good day in prison, we had good days and bad days.

"One of the things that the Vietnamese never understood about Americans is how we could laugh at our plight. They just could not understand when we would have programs and laugh at each other. It was beyond their comprehension. And yet, I cannot remember ever laughing as hard as I did in prison. I think this is one of the things that kept us going, one of the things that kept our morale so high."

During the dark and restricted days of prison life, before 1970, when the men were not allowed to speak or even look at each other, humor still existed. The POWs communicated by tapping the walls, and they made hidden peepholes to get a glimpse of the outside world.

"One of the things I used to watch out of my little peephole that brought me a chuckle and provided a lot of entertainment was the fellow in our camp who had an imaginary motorcycle. He used to wash the motorcycle in the courtyard. He would polish it and ride it everywhere he went—to bathe, to pick up his food—everywhere—making the noise of the engine with his lips. He was just having some fun. The Vietnamese thought he was crazy, and some of us did too, at first. Then word got around that the camp commander, the highest official in the Vietnamese camp, called this man into an interrogation and told him that he could no longer be allowed to ride his motorcycle in the camp. 'There isn't room to maneuver it in here,' the serious-faced Vietnamese commander said. 'Besides, we don't let the other prisoners ride their motorcycles and so you are not allowed to either.' "

In the prison camps where there was electricity, a light burned in the cell all night and was turned off in the daytime. The shadows a prisoner could create on the wall were often the only entertainment he could find.

There were loudspeakers throughout the prisons. They weren't designed for entertainment, but for propaganda and prison control. Without notice, the "Voice of Viet Nam" would come over the speaker with reports of the glorious victories of the Vietnamese military and the shame of America.

"One time they read a letter from a GI who was killed on the battlefield. The letter said, 'We don't have to ask Neil Armstrong what the craters of the moon looked like; we can see them in the bomb craters of Viet Nam.' When we heard that, we knew that Armstrong had landed on the moon and we all jumped for joy."

Holidays were not overlooked, even in the most restricted periods. Every American holiday was noted either by secret signal or, after the men were allowed to associate in groups, by a POW party.

"We kept track of every day and would try to observe holidays in special ways. Usually they told us when Easter was, but we knew how to figure that out anyway. One man kept track of the phases of the moon all the time he was there.

"When Jay Jensen, Bob Jeffrey, and I were together, we would celebrate the Twenty-fourth of July in a quiet way. Even when we were apart and we would pass each other, we would say, 'Happy Twenty-fourth. See you next year in Salt Lake City,' or something like that," Larry recalled.

Christmas was always a special and touching time for the prisoners. "We tried to make Christmas as enjoyable as possible under the circumstances. We would make our own little Christmas trees out of anything we could find, and we would give each other Christmas presents, always imaginary. For Christmas 1972, my Christmas gift was a book on photography. You see, in a photography class we had used the pictures sent to me by my mother as examples of 'how not to take pictures.' She had cut the heads off some of the subjects. My fellow prisoners wanted to be sure that I would get this book home to my mother as soon as possible so she could take some good pictures," Larry explained.

The text was a mental book written by the men and presented verbally to Larry, who accepted it with gratitude.

"Another present that was given to a friend of mine was an almanac. It was one of those world almanacs that have all the facts that anybody could want. But this almanac was just slightly different from the usual almanac. All the pages were blank, so he could fill in the right answers, because he knew them all." All the gifts were given in fun, and the men learned to laugh at each other as well as with each other.

"One time two of the guys in our group decided they would get a car to match the personality of each person in our room. They had a 1929 Packard for one man. They 'gave' him a black shirt and a white tie and called him a hood. They 'gave' me a checkered cab, but they never did say why. I thought it was probably because I had the attitude, get out of my way or I'll run over you," Larry said.

This ability to laugh was one of the things that kept the prisoners going. It helped keep morale high and gave them something else to occupy their minds.

The POWs would scrounge anything to make a costume for a skit, and skits were popular in the evenings when the men occupied the large rooms. "I took the part of a little Salvation Army woman collecting nickels on the corner," Larry related. "I put on a couple of black pajama shirts backwards, and it looked pretty much like a dress. We had some of the best skits you can imagine. They might not have been very funny to others, but they were funny to us."

The men would make fun of each other, and everyone had his turn. They would do take-offs on television commercials, and they would "beat any you've seen on TV, I guarantee."

For hours the men would recall and tell movies. It was not only an exercise in memory, but also an excellent entertainment. It was not uncommon to hear one POW say to another, "Have you heard the latest movies?"

They also used books they remembered as the basis for evening-long adventures, and sometimes they would combine the two.

"We made some pretty good movies, had a lot of fun entertaining each other. Saturdays and Sundays were movie nights. There was no acting; it was just telling the scenes and putting in the dialogue," Larry explained.

"At the end of a year of movie-telling, there was a judgment day. We had our own form of Academy Awards. I was fortunate to win two awards—one for the saddest scene and the other for the funniest scene.

"The saddest scene was from *An Affair to Remember*, when Deborah Kerr was running across the street in New York and she was looking up at the top of the Empire State Building and got hit by a taxi. Cary Grant was up on top of the building waiting for her to come, but she never made it. The funniest scene was from *Boys Night Out*.

"We had a lot of fun entertaining each other. During the two years when we were living together, we put on two musicals, *South Pacific* and *The Sound of Music*.

"The Vietnamese did not like us to sing because they thought it meant disorder, but we put on the musicals anyway. One man would narrate the scenes and then some of the guys would come out and sing in high-pitched voices for the girls' parts and other men would sing the male parts. I was not in these productions because I was not a singer, but I did enjoy them very much," Larry said.

The ability to find humor in something that is

not funny, the spirit to laugh when conditions are sad, and the ability to entertain and enjoy each other with their own efforts was a saving factor for the depressed and weary POWs.

Chapter 9

"I Knew I Would Come Home".

"I never doubted for a minute that I would come home," Larry said as he thought of his patriarchal blessing.

He was a serious-minded boy of sixteen, a junior in high school, when he went to Brother Alfred N. Knight, the Burley Stake patriarch, to receive his blessing. His seminary class had increased his interest in the gospel.

With encouragement and the spirit of seeking, Larry visited Brother Knight. There was a short talk, and then Larry sat, his head bowed, and the warm hands of Brother Knight rested on his head.

"I bless you, Larry, with a promise of a happy life," the blessing began. It was a phrase that Larry would hear several times as the blessing proceeded, and a phrase he would remember and think of often. It was a phrase he would ponder many times in a lonely prison cell.

The blessing continued, counseling the young man to be prayerful and telling him that he was "entitled to the guidance of the Holy Spirit."

The weathered hands of Brother Knight grew heavier, and the promises, based on faithfulness, continued.

"You are entitled to a knowledge of the gospel, if you study it diligently. . . . You shall be an instrument in the hands of the Lord in doing much good, both in setting a worthy example and teaching the gospel to others," the blessing said.

Young Larry did not realize at the time that he would spend many hours teaching men in prison the very things he was preparing for in those Aaronic Priesthood and seminary classes.

The blessing assured him that no matter "what may come or what may go," he would be blessed through his faith. He was cautioned to marry in the temple.

Larry struggled to remember everything that was being said. He sensed that it had deep meaning.

"To this end I bless you that you may have a happy life. Remember, however, that the world is full of strife and trouble and turmoil, and you may be called into service that you do not like at times, but if you keep your mind and body free from what the Lord has forbidden, you shall return again to your loved ones in case you have to serve in the armed forces."

These words struck home, for only the day before, the newspaper headlines were "President Asks Congress to Extend Draft Four Years." Larry and the other boys his age were mindful that military service might well be part of their lives, a thought that didn't especially alarm Larry. He might like being in the Navy or the Air Force.

His thoughts returned to the spoken words of the patriarch: "Let this be a guiding light in your life, for you shall always know the gospel is true."

Larry was thoughtful as he returned home that Friday in 1955. A few days later, a written copy of the blessing was read and reread and then carefully placed for safe keeping.

Shortly after Larry graduated from high school he enlisted in the Air Force. This was the first time he had been away from home for any length of time.

From the Shadow of Death

His home had become a source of strength, especially now that his father was active in the Church and serving as bishop of the Burley Sixth Ward.

Larry had been baptized when he was eleven years old. The next year he became a Scout and was ordained a deacon. He enjoyed Scouting and went on to become an Eagle Scout.

"I also worked up in the priesthood, and about that time Dad started becoming active in the church, mostly through the influence of a ward member."

Larry was proud of his father. On June 8, 1952, nearly nine months after he was ordained a deacon in the Aaronic Priesthood, his father was ordained an elder.

A month later to the day, Mr. and Mrs. Chesley went to the temple, and five days later, July 13, Brother Chesley became bishop and served until 1960.

"About the time Dad was made bishop or a year or so later, I became less interested in the Church and started doing things I should not be doing. Then I joined the service at age seventeen. Six months later I got married, just before I went to Japan with the service," Larry explained.

"Well, Alice and I were not married in the temple as my patriarchal blessing had told me to do. A year later while I was serving in Japan I got word that my wife was divorcing me."

It was a blow, and Larry weighed the regrets and pondered them in his mind.

It was this same time that he became acquainted with Don Hathaway, a convert to the Church from Texas. They were serving together, but Don was older. His testimony of the gospel was strong and his heart was generous.

Don reached out for Larry at a time when he needed help. "If I needed help, Don was there. If I needed to talk, Don listened; if I needed a ride,

Don had a car. If I needed rescuing, Don was there to rescue me," Larry said.

And rescue it was, for Larry was in need of help.

"I remember when I joined the service, my mother said, 'Larry, it may not always be prudent to kneel down and pray, but the most important thing is to have a prayer in your heart; whether you kneel or whether you are walking or awake, always have that prayer in your heart.' She also said, 'Larry, when you go into the service, promise me that you will look up the Church wherever you go. At least promise me that you will look it up.'

"I did as I promised. I didn't always keep going, but she knew that if I ever looked the Church members up, that they would keep looking me up, and it finally worked out because eventually there was a change in my life. I started living what I thought was a good life."

Larry was ordained an elder while he was in Japan. "One night in July we were having a district conference for all the branches and groups in Japan. All six of us from our group went to the Saturday night priesthood meeting. We were anxious to hear President Paul C. Andrus, one of the greatest speakers I have ever heard in my life.

"That night he said, 'I don't have anything to say to you tonight. I'm turning the meeting over to you, the congregation and anyone who has anything to say, just get up and tell me why you are here tonight.'

"One man got up immediately. Those who wanted to talk moved up to the front bench in turn," Larry recalled.

A second and third man got up, and then Larry, responding to deep feelings, took his place on the front bench. When he got up to speak, he started to cry unashamed.

" 'Well, I guess I am here for a selfish purpose,' "

he said. " 'I thought that maybe I would be ordained an elder tonight.'

"I then bore my testimony and told the people there how sorry I was for things I had done wrong. It was a very emotional experience for me, but I did have a testimony and felt compelled to bear it," Larry said.

Then President Andrus got up and said, "Brother Chesley, I'm sorry that I overlooked your ordination. I was supposed to ordain you an elder tonight, and I forgot to do it." Larry was found worthy and was ordained that night.

"I have since thought about that night a million times. I had no idea I was to be ordained. I didn't know why I said it."

Following completion of this first tour of duty in the Air Force, Larry enrolled at Weber State College, where he completed his bachelor's degree requirements with honors in three years and also received an Air Force commission. And he met JoDene, whom he married and to whom he was later sealed in the temple. "It was a beautiful marriage," Larry recalled.

Then Larry's wife and two small children received word from the Air Force that he had been shot down and was missing. For four years there was nothing—no word at all.

Larry received word in July 1972 that for the second time in his life he had been divorced. He didn't know any details. He tried to understand. He struggled to put things right in his mind.

"Neither my parents nor my wife knew that I was alive for four years, and I'd given JoDene instructions that if anything should happen to me— talking about death—that she was too young not to remarry and that she needed a husband and my children needed a father, and that I wanted her to marry a good man," Larry explained.

At his homecoming he said, "I would like to publicly tell you, as I am sure all of you know, that my wife has divorced me. And I want to publicly tell you that I have no malice or hard feelings in my heart whatsoever for her. If I don't have, who of you can? You do not know what she went through; you do not know what we talked about before I went to Viet Nam. So please do not judge her."

When Larry's parents found out that he was coming home, his father went to see Brother Knight, who was very ill in the hospital. One of Brother Knight's sons said that his father was not feeling well. "He is not coherent, but if you'd like to go in, please do," he said.

"When Dad went in, Sister Knight told her husband that a special friend was there to see him.

"Brother Knight said, 'Hello, young lady' to my father.

" 'This is Bishop Chesley, Brother Knight. I have come to tell you my son is coming home,' " Larry said, filled with emotion.

"Brother Knight looked at him and said, 'How long ago was it, Bishop Chesley, that I told Larry that he would come home? Twenty years?' "

"Dad said, 'Yes, Brother Knight—about twenty years ago.'

"When Dad left the room, Brother Knight was talking and conversing with his family in a rational manner.

"I'd like to bear my testimony to you that I know this is the true church. I want to tell you some of the things I learned being a prisoner, but let it suffice for now to tell you that I believe that we have a prophet at the head of this church and I believe that we have had a prophet at the head of this church since Joseph Smith. These prophets have been guiding this church just as surely as Noah directed the people of his day," Larry testified.

"I had given my testimony many times to the men in prison and many of them promised me that they would check into the Church. I loved some of those men so much. I wanted them to have that opportunity. My testimony has been my strength.

"I never doubted for a minute that I would come home. I hever doubted that I would return."
said with tear-filled eyes.

Chapter 10

"A Constant Ache in My Heart"

"I really didn't believe he was home until he was in my arms," said Mrs. Verl Chesley, who had waited for seven years for her son Larry to return from Hanoi. It had been a hard seven years for Mrs. Chesley. There had been an ache in her heart ever since she had received word from her husband that Larry had been shot down.

Military personnel from Mountain Home Air Force Base brought them the sad news but assured them that rescue efforts were being carried out. "I prayed so hard just to know that he was alive," Mrs. Chesley said. Each moment was an anxious moment; each day carried with it hope, darkened by a shadow of fear.

It was depressing when a second visit by military officers brought word that rescue efforts had been concluded. There were quiet tears, days of fasting, a community united in prayer, and continual calls of reassurance from friends and neighbors.

Mrs. Chesley read and reread Larry's last letter. It was written on his father's birthday, March 29, and contained a folded five dollar bill. "Today is your birthday. You have always been tops, Dad. I love you, Dad, and Mom too. I can never repay you for all you have done.

"I am nearly half through with my missions,"

the letter went on, with a promise to be home by late summer and an assurance that everything would be all right.

Carefully Mrs. Chesley folded the letter and placed it with the money in the envelope. It was to become a source of strength in the years to come. "Our prayers continued, but I had a terrible time to say 'thy will be done,' because I wanted Larry to be home with his family," she said. Mrs. Chesley thought that word would come in a month or two at most. Every day was an anxious day. The steps to the mailbox were always quick and eager. Every phone call was answered with hope, every knock on the door brought mixed thoughts to a burdened mind.

As each month dragged on there were three letters written by a loving mother, written in hope and mailed with uncertainty. The first part of each month one went to the Red Cross. On the sixteenth day of the month, the date Larry was shot down, a second letter was sent, and later a third. Many were addressed to the Camp of Detention, Hanoi, North Viet Nam.

After several months she was advised to write only once a month. Not knowing that no letters would be delivered for the next four and one-half years, she continued to send messages of love and family pictures.

"A mother, no matter how often or how long her children are away, always wonders if they are hungry or cold. I wondered every day, and not being able to help was a terrible feeling," she said.

Larry's last words to her kept ringing in her mind: "Don't worry Mother, I will be all right; whether I come home or not, I will be all right," he said as he hugged her and kissed his wife and children goodbye in 1965.

The first real hope came in the fall of 1969 when

a prisoner who "came out" thought he had seen his name on a list. Then news came—a call from Larry's wife, who was living in Ogden, Utah: "Larry is alive, I have a letter," she said. The call came March 29, 1970. It was a wonderful birthday gift for Mr. Chesley.

"A year later we received our first letter. I continued to write with more hope, and we sent some of the things we thought he needed most. Only a few packages got through. I sent a Bible, but he never got it."

It was the realization of a long dream when Mr. and Mrs. Chesley were invited to Travis Air Force Base in California to meet their son. Years of waiting melted away as he came from the plane to his mother's arms. "Our prayers have been answered," she cried as mother, father, and son mingled their tears in a happy reunion.

Captain Larry Chesley gives his parents,
Mr. and Mrs. Verl Chesley of Burley,
Idaho, homecoming hug

Larry Chesley learned
courage from riding
race horses at his
grandmother's ranch
in Arco, Idaho

Captain Larry Chesley
spoke as often as ten
times per week after
his release; here he
addresses school in
Ogden, Utah, attended
by children, Debbie
and Don

Captain Larry Chesley,
sitting between his
children, Debbie and
Don, becomes
emotional at
sacrament meeting at
Star Ward, Burley,
Idaho

At San Francisco party, actor John Wayne poses with
Captain Larry Chesley and Annette Huntsman, whom
Captain Chesley married in the Salt Lake Temple
June 19, 1973

Scale model of camp at Son Tay, where Captain Larry
Chesley was confined in large building in corner of
walled area

Major Jay R. Jensen

Air Force, Sandy, Utah

Shot down February 18, 1967, near Vinh, North Viet Nam
Released February 18, 1973

Chapter 11

His Scout Training Paid Off

Major Jay R. Jensen of Sandy, Utah, did not realize the full value of his Boy Scout experience as he responded to the command, "About face," and saluted his Eagle board of review.

Later, in a Hanoi prison, as he tapped a signal on the solid brick wall, he knew that the training he had received as a Boy Scout was helping him in his plight as a prisoner of war.

"The training I received as a Scout was used many times in the prison camps of North Viet Nam," he said. "From knowing how to tie knots to signaling, which was used extensively by the prisoners during their confinement, I appreciated all parts of my Scouting experience. We used many signals and codes, flash codes, light codes and a variety of communication codes, some directly from the Boy Scout handbook.

"First aid was especially helpful; also fire building, cooking and camping, and knowing what it is like to sleep on the hard ground. The prison beds were very hard indeed. I was very thankful for my Scout training," he said.

Major Jensen was shot down when a SAM missile found its way to his plane on February 18, 1967, just a month and a half after he had arrived in Viet Nam. He was flying a mission over North Viet Nam during adverse weather conditions when he was hit. He was an electronic warfare officer aboard an F-105.

There were no broad headlines in the local paper that day, only a one-column headline that said, "B52 Raids Increase Red Losses." Jay flew a fighter bomber, much smaller than the eight-engine Stratofortresses that could carry up to thirty tons of bombs.

The next day the headline of the *Deseret News* told the story of the biggest American combat force thus far in the war moving to squeeze the Communists from South Viet Nam: "Viet Reds on Run in Fierce Fighting," the headline read.

The story went on:

"Leapfrogging by helicopter, crack government troops kept fleeing Communist guerillas under constant attack. American B52 bombers, hitting with unprecedented frequency, rained tons of bombs on Communist positions in four massive raids along the Cambodian border and South Vietnam's central and southern regions.

"It was the 14th raid in three days over North Vietnam. U.S. fighter bombers pilots were limited by poor weather to only forty-one missions, but one flight of U.S. Air Force jets broke through the overcast to hit a key rail complex eighty-five miles northeast of Hanoi."

"My plane was hit by a missile that exploded directly under me. I wasn't injured, and I tried to see if the plane would still fly," he said. He tried desperately to get the plane to respond to the controls. There was no response—the craft raced on uncontrollably.

There was no choice; Jensen reached between his legs and pulled the ejection ring. In a quick moment he was free from the crippled plane and was floating down from the gray overcast sky. The plane

From the Shadow of Death

tumbled on to crash. Jensen looked about and breathed deeply from the oxygen bottle that was part of his flight suit. He could see a village below.

Then he suddenly came to the realization that he was in extreme danger. He hadn't expected to land in friendly territory, but now he was alarmed. "As I descended, the people on the ground started shooting at me. One bullet struck my helmet, but I was not injured," he said. He was extra nervous during the last few hundred feet of descent. "I landed in some trees and was surrounded immediately by angry people who began tearing my equipment from me."

It was utter confusion for the downed pilot. He was pulled and pushed and battered as his flight suit and equipment were stripped from him. He looked about for help or relief, but there was none. He feared the hostile crowd. There was hate in the eyes of the people.

"The thing I remember most, from that uncomfortable situation, was an old woman who picked up slimy mud from a rice paddy and threw it at me. She would have made a good pitcher on any team."

Automatically he wiped the mud away, spit it from his mouth, and felt the deep pangs of regret at being shot down. It was his thirteenth mission from Korat Air Force Base in Thailand, where he was stationed.

It was only a matter of time until he stood before Communist interrogators at the Hanoi Hilton prison. He gave them only his name, rank, serial number, and date of birth. Because he would not answer their questions, he was tortured.

Tourniquets were placed around both arms and pulled tightly. Jay felt the pain, but he would not give in. He was left, tightly tied, for hours until his arms turned black and he feared he might lose them.

"During this time of trial and torture I came to realize that I had one important ally. I had the Lord on my side, and I talked with him frequently. In the midst of that depravation and inhuman treatment I had many occasions to pray to my Heavenly Father. He answered my prayers, sometimes in an almost miraculous way. It was one of the most wonderful feelings of my life.

"I had other allies, too. Two big weapons against the treatment I was receiving were my faith and my testimony. They gave me much strength," he said.

Jay was placed in solitary confinement following his interrogation and torture. The cell was small and smelly. He grew accustomed to the odor, but he never adjusted to the cramped confinement of a prison cell.

The first weeks in captivity were unbelievably devastating for Jay. No one at home knew what had happened to him. Soon his letters would stop, and his family would be faced with the uncertainty of his fate. The headline in the *Deseret News* a week after he was shot down read "Hanoi Spikes U.S. Hope for Viet Talks." The story went on to say that because of a tough North Vietnamese rejection of American peace feelers, the Viet Nam War now seemed more likely to be settled on the battlefield than at the conference table.

Jay had no idea that he would be in prison for six years.

"I was in solitary confinement for about three months after the torturing sessions. During that time there were many ways I tried to keep my mind active. Many of these concerned the Church.

"I was born in 1931 and grew up active in the Church. I had been a Sunday School teacher and superintendent of the Sunday School. I had been an elders quorum president and a Scoutmaster, but for

From the Shadow of Death

a year or so just before my assignment in Thailand I had not been active.

"After arriving in Korat, I did go to church at every opportunity. We had a small branch, a very active branch with a few civilians attending, but it was mostly composed of military men."

About a week before Jay was shot down he had traveled to Bangkok with other men from the base to attend a servicemen's conference. "We had a wonderful time together. The meetings were spiritual; the activities were fun," he said.

In his cell, he recalled these pleasant religious experiences and many others.

"I tried to remember all of the scriptures I could, and all the stories from the Bible and the Book of Mormon. I thought about the songs from the hymnbook. I used to sing them to myself and was surprised how many of the words I could recall as the tune went through my mind. We weren't allowed to make noise.

"One of my favorite hymns was 'Master, the Tempest Is Raging,' and another was 'Ere You Left Your Room This Morning.' The words of these songs went through my mind many times. Every time I would feel sorry for myself in my plight, I would think about the song 'When upon Life's Billows' and remember the words 'Count your many blessings, name them one by one.' Even in solitary confinement I could find some to count.

"The most important song that I was able to remember—it was my theme song—was 'It May Not Be on the Mountain Height.' I found strength in the words 'I'll go where you want me to go, dear Lord," he said.

Sitting on the hard bed in the dim light of his cell, Jay could lift himself from the boredom of the prison. The mental pictures that accompanied the tunes, softly hummed, were his bit of freedom.

"There was a lot of time for thinking and contemplating. I did a lot of thinking. I did a lot of praying, and I did a lot of repenting. I thought about my future. I came to a greater realization of what was really important. I realized that my family, the Church, the gospel, and my country were the important things to me."

Jay was married to Ruth Meyers of Virginia in 1955, the year following his graduation from Brigham Young University in accounting, banking, and finance.

"Ruth was very much interested in the gospel, and with the help of the stake missionaries and the Lord, she was converted to the Church. Later, in about 1961, we were married in the Salt Lake Temple," he said. They had three children, Carrie, Sherrie, and Jay Roger, Jr.

Jay thought about his family a great deal, thought about taking his boys hunting and fishing, something he himself enjoyed very much.

After three months of solitary confinement, Jay was placed with another man in a small cell. Several changes of roommates were made, but after a short period he received a roommate who would be his close companion for two and a half years. "We got to know each other pretty well. We discussed every subject we could think of. He was a good listener and I talked a lot about the Church.

"In the cell next to us were two other prisoners. We learned to communicate with them through a double brick wall by using a cup as a megaphone against the wall. There was some risk of being caught, so we had to clear for each other by peering through the door or through cracks in the window to make sure no guards were around. It was difficult to hear, but we did communicate. I asked them about their religion and they asked me about mine.

"I don't know if they knew what they were getting into, but for several months I told them about my religion through that double brick wall. It is much more difficult to talk that way than it is to talk to your neighbor here."

By 1970 the treatment started to improve. The prisoners were placed in groups in larger rooms. Sometimes as many as fifty men were together and could help each other in many ways.

"One of the biggest lifts was spiritual. Much to the chagrin of the Vietnamese, we were able to hold church services. They tried to stop us—they tried to stop our choir from singing, but we held the services and our choir did sing in spite of them. We defied them, and we won.

"I was fortunate enough to be chosen chaplain for one of the rooms. I served for a year in that very interesting position. There were many different denominations in the room, and we decided that for Sunday School the men belonging to each church would take a turn explaining their religion.

"The Catholics were first because they were the largest group. They took the first two Sundays. Then in turn each of the other denominations told us about their church. When they had all had a turn, I told them about Mormonism. That took the next twelve Sundays. They heard quite a bit about Mormonism.

"I told them that all I was trying to do was give them information—history and principles. I didn't try to convert. I wasn't trying to convert anyone, I explained, because I didn't have the authority. I told them that missionaries were called and set apart.

"I hope I straightened out some misconceptions concerning the Church, and I later talked with many individuals in more detail about the Church."

After Jay had been in prison for about four years, the Vietnamese allowed the POWs to have a

Bible in their rooms for about an hour. The men copied some scriptures and pleaded for more use of the Bible.

"Finally they let us have the Bible over one night, and we stayed up all night copying sections of the book, writing on brown toilet paper. We didn't see a Bible again for two years, just before I was released.

"I learned a great lesson from my experiences as a POW. That lesson is to love and appreciate the Lord and my country. I grew to appreciate my religion more. It gave me great strength that some other men did not have. It made me appreciate having books. Oh, how much I yearned for a copy of the Book of Mormon or a Bible or some of the other books I had at home. I think I would have given a thousand dollars for some of those books, and I don't know how much for a pencil and paper," he said.

"My experience was very hard—a great test of my faith. The torture, the solitary confinement, not receiving word from my family for over three years, not being able to write to even let them know I was alive was almost unbearable," he said.

Jay's family learned at Thanksgiving time in 1969 that he was alive, when pacifist groups were able to obtain prisoner-of-war lists from Hanoi.

At Christmastime his family received two letters from Jay, indicating that he had received two packages from home and that he was relatively well. The first letter contained the news that he had not been wounded when his aircraft was shot down. The second letter contained a personal message for Mrs. Jensen and each of the three children and asked for several items to be sent.

Though the letters indicated that packages had been received, it was evident that none of the scores of letters written to him had been received.

"I did not receive a letter from my wife, Ruth—never one word. Then after five years, I received word that she had divorced me. That was a test of my faith," Jay said.

Jay endured the shock and rebuilt his faith. He had endured confinement, bad food, and heat blisters that covered most of his body and left open sores when they burst. The infection that followed was treated, after some delay, with iodine poured in the sores, much to the delight of the guards. For six years he endured the hardships and loneliness of the war prison. He had survived on hope and faith.

There was a renewal of his faith when the first 143 prisoners were released on February 12, 1973. Jay was not one of these, but the next day, in a surprise announcement, Hanoi said that twenty more POWs would be released. This was apparently a goodwill gesture in connection with the visit of Dr. Henry Kissinger to Hanoi. Major Jay R. Jensen was one of the twenty on the list.

The POWs were suspicious of the announcement of early release and balked because they thought it was a trick. It took a visit by a member of the International Commission of Control and Supervision to convince the men that their release was to be an actuality.

By February 18, 1973, the twenty men were in the Philippines for their debriefing. Jay enjoyed a steak dinner—the first in more than six years.

"I don't want anything I have to eat with a spoon," Jay said as he sat down to his first meal, thinking of all the pumpkin soup he had eaten in prison.

"I feel like I have spent six years in hell and that I have been resurrected to start a new life," he told newsmen. He added that he was anxious to get to Utah and see his family and go skiing.

A reunion at March Air Force Base was planned for February 21, 1973. Jay's parents, Mr. and Mrs.

Milton L. Jensen of Sandy, Utah, drove to the base to keep the appointment. Two sisters, Lerna Spencer and Carla Sandstrom, traveled with them. Jay's three children were flown to California, and a brother, Larry Jensen of Phoenix, Arizona, joined the family.

Jay's parents had talked to him by telephone for twenty minutes while he was in the Philippines. "He was asking about everyone before we could even find out the state of his health," Mrs. Jensen said.

Wearing a lei around his neck, a souvenir of his stopover in Hawaii, Jay shook hands with Lieutenant General William Pitt and then stepped to a microphone in front of a cheering crowd.

"Thank you for coming," he said. "You'll never know how much it means to us," he added, his voice breaking as he turned and ran toward his family to be greeted with several rounds of long embraces.

His smile was broad, his mustache trimmed carefully, and his face showed that he had lost twenty pounds. Taking the lei from his neck, he placed it around his mother's neck and almost lifted her from the ground with another hug. The reunion continued with the excitement of meeting his first grandchild, three-month-old Heidi Webster. His oldest daughter, Carrie, had married Dennis Webster while he was in prison. He tenderly held the little girl in his arms and, touching his cheek to hers, felt the joy of holding his new grandchild.

The initial excitement over, Jay and the twelve members of his family were taken to the base hospital where the visit continued. Jay stayed at the hospital for ten days for medical examination, orientation, and debriefing.

When hospital personnel expressed concern over Jensen's growing fatigue, he pleaded, "I've waited six years for this. Don't send them home."

Jay was pleased with the reception afforded him

and the other POWs. "After six years we came home with honor and to a wonderful reception by the American people. That reception proved to us, beyond any reasonable doubt, that we were not forgotten, that the American people were concerned about us and all the men serving in Viet Nam. For this we are thankful," he said.

"I had a wonderful reunion with my family. I know that my prayers for their welfare had been answered. Their prayers for me have been answered too.

"In the weeks that followed, my prayers were answered in another way, for the Lord knew what I needed and what I wanted. He sent me a wonderful companion. I met a very wonderful girl, Jan Westover of Corona, California."

Jan and Jay were married on March 30, 1973. "Not only did the Lord send me Jan, but he sent me a wonderful family, Jan's four children, Sam, 18; Lelia, 15; Andrea, 11; and Mark, 13," he said.

In late June, Major and Mrs. Jensen with four of her children and two of Jay's went on an extended vacation to New York, Washington, D.C., and Florida, and then traveled to Europe.

"I am now a very active member of the Church. I am going to school at Brigham Young University, under sponsorship of the Air Force. I expect to receive my master's degree in business. I have a wonderful future ahead of me," he said.

Embracing Air Force flight nurse, Lieutenant Sheila R. Whipkey, are Major Jay R. Jensen (left) of Sandy, Utah, and Major Hubert K. Flesher of Clarksburg, West Virginia.

Major Jay Jensen has big smile at Clark Air Force Base in the Philippines following release from Hanoi prison

Lieutenant Commander David J. Rollins

Navy, San Diego, California

Captured May 14, 1967, near Thanh Hoa, North Viet Nam
Released March 4, 1973

Chapter 12

"I Saw It All in a Dream"

Mrs. David (Jack) Rollins of San Diego, California, turned in her sleep. The nights had been lonely, and she had slept uneasily since Jack had begun his tour in Viet Nam. It was a pleasant spring night, May 12, 1967, and the morning light was already beginning to come when a dream entered her mind. But it was more than an ordinary dream; it was about Jack—his airplane was going down.

"I saw the whole sequence of the plane going down. Even the green clothing he was wearing, the water he was going into. I thought he was going to drown. The details were so clear, even the four people who came to notify me and the ward members who brought food to the house," Mrs. Rollins recalled.

Nearly nine thousand miles away, Navy Lieutenant Commander Rollins was busy with his routine. He was serving aboard the *USS Kitty Hawk* in the Gulf of Tonkin, Fighter Squadron 114. For him, a routine day was two missions; he was a radar intercept officer. His job was the management of the weapons system on an F-4B (Phantom II) jet.

Connie awoke from her dream.

"When I woke up and recalled the dream I knew it was special. I knew it wasn't just something that I had just thought up. There was such a special spirit, I just knew it was from the Lord," she said.

She got up immediately. Though it was early, her daughter Patricia, fifteen years old, was already up fixing her own breakfast and preparing to go to early-morning seminary.

Mrs. Rollins needed someone to talk to, and so, taking her young daughter in her arms, she related what had happened. "We stood in the kitchen and shed tears together. We knew it was for real, we just knew what was going to happen," she said. Her tears were dried by the time the boys were up. Richard was fourteen and Gene was ten years old. For some reason, she didn't tell the boys.

The strong feeling persisted through the day, and Connie confided in a very close friend. So sure was she of the events that would take place that she prepared the house, even replacing some things that needed attention, because "I knew there would be people coming to my home."

On Mother's Day, Sunday, May 14, 1967, Connie prepared the children for Sunday School and they all went together.

On the *Kitty Hawk,* Jack prepared for another mission—the famous Thanh Hoa bridge. The bridge, only about ten miles from shore, was a main link for Highway One from Hanoi to the south. He remembered that it was Mother's Day. He thought of Connie and the kids. They would be going to church. He reviewed in his mind his three tours of duty with the squadron and was pleased that the current combat tour would soon be completed.

His thoughts were interrupted by the signal for takeoff, and soon Commander Charles E. Southwick, of Fairbanks, Alaska, had lifted the Phantom jet from the carrier and was circling, heading westward to the target. "It was only a short flight. We could almost see the bridge from the *Kitty Hawk* in the bay—we were working that close. We were on a flak suppression mission. Heavy fortifications surrounded the bridge, and we were to silence the flak sites so the bombers would have a little more safety as they came in. We carried extra rockets that day, but our primary mission was to knock out the flak sites," Rollins recalls.

Jack's mind was soon occupied with the details of the mission. The bridge came into view, two spans, strong with angles of steel and beautiful in design. It was an Eiffel bridge, conceived by the French engineer Alexandra Gustave Eiffel, who also designed the Eiffel Tower in Paris. The Vietnamese claimed to have shot down ninety-nine aircraft at the bridge.

"As we rolled in and fired the rockets, something went wrong. The engines stalled. We weren't shot down—it wasn't a flame-out, a stall. We were unable to get power. Perhaps the rocket blasts and the debris from the rocket had gone into our engines and caused them to stall. We don't know what happened.

"There we were without engine power and our nose pointed toward the ground. We tried to get the engines started, but we just didn't have time. Every second counted. We stayed with the aircraft until we were in the treetops. There was no chance of getting the engines started so we ejected, and perhaps we waited a little too long.

"That was the wildest ride I ever had. I went out of the plane at about 200 miles an hour. In my mind it seemed like slow motion. I was able to see the plane leave and could feel and observe myself tumbling through the air.

"The parachute did not open; there wasn't time. I landed feet first in a flooded rice paddy and submerged in the mud with a terrific force. Unfortunately, I always do things with my tongue out, and I darn-near bit it off.

"I regained consciousness underwater in the mud. Though I wasn't able to function much, I did kick myself to the surface. I was afraid I would drown. After a couple of minutes I realized where I was, and I scrambled and kicked my way to a bank, thinking it would provide some cover. Actually, it wasn't any cover—it was an embankment used for a walkway.

"I was a pretty horrible sight, covered with mud and spitting blood. I attempted to use my radio, trying desperately to contact the men in the air and let them know I was on the ground alive. My radio appeared to be intact, but it wouldn't work—or maybe it was me. I had hit awfully hard and was having difficulty using my arms; I learned later that my back was broken in several places.

"I realized about this time that someone was standing above me on the bank. In a matter of moments many Vietnamese peasants were swarming around on the bank. I had landed in a heavily populated area. The flooded rice paddy had saved my life, but I knew the Lord also had something to do with it," he said.

The pilot had landed not far away, uninjured. He landed among some people and was captured immediately.

Jack was unable to walk, so the peasants put a rope around his neck and dragged him across the paddy and up the embankment on the other side. "I felt that if I didn't walk I would be choked to death, so I managed to get to my feet. My clothes had been taken from me in the paddy just before the rope was put around my neck. The people who were dragging me were quite hostile. Suddenly I saw a flash coming from the right. I turned to look and instinctively dodged, but a knife jabbed into my right shoulder. I had been stabbed. The knife penetrated into my shoulder joint, where my captors, still in a hostile mood, left it.

"The militia arrived just in time to save me from the local citizens and what probably would have been certain death. The soldiers, noticing the knife, pushed the peasants away from me, then tied me securely and led me to a nearby hut."

For about three hours, Rollins lay guarded in the little hut. He estimated the time; they had been over the target at about four p.m. and now the sun was lowering in the west. He had no watch; it had disappeared among the peasants while they were taking his clothes. The numbness in his shoulder was wearing off and he battled soreness, pain, dirt, and misery.

Rollins thought about his plight and what was to become of him. He thought about his family. A helpless feeling filled his mind as he realized there was nothing he could do but endure. And during all this pain and affliction, for some reason, he remembered that it was Mother's Day.

In San Diego, Mother's Day had been a beautiful day. The children had remembered Connie with little things. She hugged each one, but her thoughts were with Jack. The dream was strong in her mind, and though she went through the motions in a routine way, she was preoccupied, wondering when word would come.

She and the children attended sacrament meeting, where there was a good deal mentioned about mothers. She prayed that she could be strong enough to endure whatever was to come. After church the children changed their clothes and were occupied with their activities. Pat was off to fireside.

Connie felt no need to hurry. Somehow her thoughts seemed to require most of her energy. She slipped into her housecoat and some slippers and had hardly hung up her dress when the doorbell rang. It was getting dark outside.

There were four persons at the door.

Connie's eyes shifted quickly from one to the other. She made a quick mental note of identifications. She recognized Commander "Scotty" Lamoreaux, from Miramar Naval Air Station, the man designated on Jack's record to come out in case of emergency. He brought his wife, and the wife of the skipper of Jack's squadron came also. Connie was acquainted with them. The fourth person was a Protestant chaplain.

"Connie, do you know who these people are?" the skipper's wife asked nervously.

Connie's eyes shifted quickly from one to the other. For some reason she counted them—four.

"Yes," she said. "I have been expecting you for two days."

The visitors were very nervous as they told her Jack was "missing in action—presumed captured." It was an emotional time and Connie found herself sharing her sympathy with them. "It seemed as though I had more sympathy for them than I did for us.

"Later, I realized that I had many commitments I would not be able to keep. I was a counselor in the Relief Society presidency so I went to see the president, Mrs. Vernon R. Beeler. It wasn't until I got there that I realized I was still in my housecoat and slippers.

"Brother Beeler was a member of the stake high council and he gave me a blessing that our household would be calm, that Jack would know that we were all right, and that he would be safe and provided for. This blessing sustained us through the long days ahead," she said.

That night, with her children kneeling close by, she offered a prayer with deep feeling. It was a prayer that would be repeated many times in the months ahead.

In a little hut in far-off Viet Nam near Thanh Hoa, Rollins said a prayer too, as he lay securely tied.

"I needed some medical help. My tongue was bleeding profusely, and I could tell that my teeth had been shattered from the impact when I hit the ground. I was shaken up inside—I had no idea of the internal damages. A man wearing medical clothing, a white frock, and a white cap came to see me, accompanied by a female attendant. He first pulled the knife from my shoulder, cleaned a small area around the wound, and put a battle dressing on it.

"Though I was a muddy mess after being dragged through that rice paddy, I was not allowed to clean up or wash any part of my body. I would have liked to have gotten the mud out of my ears. One small boy did bring me a dipper of water, and I was allowed to wash my mouth out.

"As it grew dark I was placed in a jeep-like vehicle. I discovered that my pilot was already there. We were not allowed to speak or even see each other—we were blindfolded and kept apart. Shortly after we started, the jeep broke down, and we were transferred to a truck," he said.

They traveled all night. Rollins was in considerable discomfort as the truck jolted along on its way to Hanoi. "As it grew light the next day, we were put on display. I didn't have any idea where we were, but we were dressed only in our underwear.

"The people were allowed to come and view us. The guard determined what they were allowed to do, depending on the particular moment. Some of the visitors were allowed to throw rocks, sticks, or mud at us. Others walked up to kick or hit us. No individual act was so extremely harsh as to be really dangerous, but we could not have sustained many days of that type of treatment. We were happy to get away from the local people."

As it grew dark, they were loaded on the same truck and the journey to Hanoi continued. Despite the strict guard, the two men were able to exchange a couple of words during the two nights. Once caught, they were beaten severely. Communication was definitely against regulations. They arrived at Hanoi the second morning just before daylight.

"I suffered a great deal of pain during this time. My induction at the prison camp was annoying, but I was able to finally get cleaned up. I was sent to one of the camps called the Zoo—an old French movie studio. Those first weeks were miserable."

Those first weeks were difficult for Connie too. Things had to go on, and she was blessed with new courage. "One day, about two weeks after I was notified that Jack was down, a reporter from the San Diego *Union* called and told us that Jack had been changed from 'missing in action' to 'prisoner.'

"When I contacted the government, through local officials, they denied any knowledge of it and said it was untrue. I called the paper again, and they insisted that it was true but would not tell me their source. So we lived in limbo for thirty-one months, waiting from some word. It came two days before Christmas, December 23, 1969.

"I had been Relief Society teaching and then we went Christmas shopping. When we came home I picked up the mail that had come through the slot in the door. On one envelope, in the corner, were the words 'Women Strike for Peace.'

"I just knew what was inside even before I opened the envelope. Sure enough—it was not only a form letter that had been dictated for Jack to write, but he had also written the six lines allowed by the Vietnamese.

"It was as if Christmas had arrived two days early.

From the Shadow of Death

In fact, when Christmas day did come, it seemed like an afterthought. Our prayers had been answered!"

Chapter 13

"My World Has Stopped"

"My world has stopped," Commander Jack Rollins said to himself as he sat isolated in his six-by-eight-foot cell. He had been through the tortures of Vietnamese prison introduction. He had been branded a criminal, given a copy of the camp regulations, and stripped of everything he owned.

"I realized that everything I was going to have was in my mind. I had no money, no tools, no books —nothing. I could see why the Church admonishes us to gain knowledge. I had to live with what I had, and I felt quite embarrassed that I wasn't better equipped."

He thought about Connie, who had always been his strength—"I would be very little without her" —and he realized that if he had ever needed strength, he needed it now.

Rollins looked at his bed. It was a wooden slab similar to a barn door. One board was an inch thick, the next an inch-and-a-half. He unrolled a straw mat on the wooden slabs. It wasn't much of a mattress, he thought, as he weighed in his mind whether to put three layers of the folded blanket on the bottom or one on top and two on the bottom. He had been given the blanket as prison issue.

"It turned out to be quite comfortable. With my

broken back, I could lie with my spine next to the offset of the boards and it felt better than a flat board." He was glad he didn't get one of the beds that had built-in stocks "like the ones in which they put the witches back in Salem, Massachusetts."

The pain didn't stop, but there was some degree of comfort as he lay on the boards looking at the dirty ceiling of the windowless cell. He thought of the day he left Pioche, Nevada, where he grew up, for the Navy. Then he thought about Connie Chadburn, the daughter of a bishop. There was something special about her—special enough that he wrote letters to her after he left for the Navy. When leave time came, it was Connie he went to see.

"I wound up marrying her," he said. "It was hard to go out and have the kind of fun I thought I wanted while courting a bishop's daughter. Then my cousin, just back from his mission, came over to the house and tried to teach me the gospel. Still, I thought there were some things I still wanted to do, so I decided I would prove the gospel wrong. That was a challenge, but if I could do it, I thought, I wouldn't have any more problem with my wife or missionary cousin.

"I got a lot of help in my project. The bishop, the high council, the stake president, and a lot of my friends all decided to help me prove the gospel was wrong. After about eight months of trying, I just gave up. I wasn't able to do it. In fact, I even had a little bit of a testimony by then."

Now, as he lay in his cell, he realized that his testimony had grown since, but he also realized that he didn't have all of the testimony he might have.

He continued to think about things he had learned in Primary and Scout meetings. "I wish I had paid more attention. I guess I was more concerned about having fun with the other kids," he mused. His thoughts turned again to Connie, and he remembered with some emotion their marriage in the St. George Temple. Just knowing that she was his wife for time and eternity was a great comfort.

His thoughts were interrupted by a banging at the door. The peephole was opened, and the face of a North Vietnamese guard was pressed against it. The guard shouted a command that Jack didn't understand at first. Though it hurt to move, he got to his feet. Gradually the message was realized. The guard wanted him to bow. Remembering the torture, Jack bowed, his back excrutiatingly painful.

He recalled the humiliations and despair he felt:

"The Vietnamese knew that the American people were proud, and so they did everything they could do to degrade, belittle, or humiliate us. We had to bow to them whenever we came in contact with them. Every time they opened the little peephole to to inspect our room, when we went out to empty our waste bucket or pick up food—we had to bow each time. It was just to humiliate us. Their objective was to have us make a complete surrender.

"I got very lonely. Boy! I had been here alone so long! Then I thought about the plan of salvation and how long eternity was. I wondered what I could do about my eternal life. I thought of all the things I had been taught. I was a bit ashamed because I knew that I had been taught well but that I hadn't learned very well. Yet, I did have a testimony of the gospel.

"I prayed that I would have the desire to live the gospel. It is easy to live in a righteous way—the hard thing is to want to; so that is what I prayed for. I had to learn to do things with all my heart, might, mind, and strength. I used my memory and faith with all my heart, might, mind, and strength. I had never had to do that before, but in Hanoi I did.

"I became very ill. I didn't get any attention for

my broken back for fifteen months and then I was finally given a shot of Novocain to ease the pain. There was nerve damage that affected my stomach. The Vietnamese and my comrades thought I was going to die, I was so ill. But even then I didn't worry about family or even about dying.

"I thought back to the fact that my family was sealed to me and that in a very short time—just the span of our lives—we would be together for eternity. I hoped and prayed, with all my heart, might, mind, and strength, that I would be worthy to meet my family in the eternities."

The knowledge of the plan of salvation was a great strength to Jack, but it was also a source of anguish. "I saw my entire life in retrospect. I went over everything I had done, and I remembered many things that I hadn't done. I thought about my family a great deal, and when I got a roommate, our families became our major topic for discussion. We heard so much about each other's families that we felt we actually knew them. We talked of hopes and plans and reviewed our lives and philosophies again and again.

"We lived so close, so intimate, that we knew each other's innermost feelings. We called it 'living in each other's armpits,' because we were so close twenty-four hours a day. We could almost tell what the other man was thinking. We knew exactly what his reactions would be, what he was going to do next. We knew his habit pattern better than our own.

"When we started talking about people, we talked about ourselves. We told each other just what we thought of each other. It wasn't in anger. We just told all the good things, all the strengths and weaknesses. You kinda get to know yourself under these circumstances. We talked about our wives. I learned that I really liked my wife. Just knowing that she was my wife was a great strength."

Thousands of miles away, Connie adjusted to the news as best she could. It was not easy not knowing if she was a wife or a widow or if the children would have their father back. But she too enjoyed the comfort of the gospel.

"Not only had the Lord been so kind to let us know what would happen, but we also discovered what it really means to have the Comforter," she said. "This is something you can read about in the scriptures, but unless you really experience it, it is very difficult to explain exactly what the Comforter is. This is what we lived with, and it brought peace of mind. At a time when we discovered that the fear of not knowing is worse than knowing, we needed the Comforter to help us through.

"As a wife and mother, I had many fears. I wondered if Jack was really there, if he was well or ill, if he had been badly injured. And all the while I was trying to keep myself busy.

"The Lord was kind to me; He gave me enough problems to keep me busy. In my church assignments I went from being in the Relief Society presidency to serving in the stake Primary presidency, and I had so many commitments and meetings.

"My daughter asked once, 'Why has the Lord given us so many problems?' Things were happening to us that we had never dreamed would happen, things that never seemed to occur when Jack was at home. Of course, these were things that kept us busy and kept us occupied so that we really didn't have time to sit around and let self-pity envelope us," she said.

"I am sorry that Jack missed so many of the joys of parenthood. I think the biggest challenge was when both Patty and Richard had learner's permits and were trying to get their driving licenses. In California, a teenager must have both parents sign for him to get a learner's permit, unless one parent is dead or there is a divorce. We had neither situation—we were in limbo. For six months I struggled with the state license bureau to get the necessary permits for Patty and Richard," Connie explained.

"Richard wanted to step into Jack's shoes but did not quite have the maturity or the capability to do that. I tried to give him as many responsibilities as I felt he could handle. As he advanced in the priesthood, we gave him opportunities to call on family members to pray or say the blessing on the food so he would feel like he was the man of the family.

"He became our fix-it-man at home, and I gave him a tool box and tried to help him as he took mechanics at school. Of course, I learned right along with him. I listened for every noise in the car engine."

"I think that everyone is given problem situations. I don't think anyone really goes through life scot-free, without some type of problem. But I also discovered that it is not really the problem that you are given, but how you handle it and what you do with it, that is really important.

"Even though we didn't come out 'grade-A' with every problem, the children did learn that it was necessary for them to stand on their own two feet. We all grew in so many areas, from spiritual matters to legal details and on to the nitty-gritty types of problems.

"In June following Jack's capture, nine large crates of his personal effects were returned with the ship. When I opened them and saw the green flight suit, like the one he had been wearing the day his plane went down, I thought I would pass out. I had never seen him in a green flying suit; he had always worn an orange flight suit.

"I would have been a lost soul if it hadn't been for the gospel. We made many applications as a family, but the best one was the analogy to Christ's second coming and Jack's coming home. No one knew what day the Vietnamese were going to humble themselves and sign the peace agreement. So, we likened it to the second coming of the Savior. We listened to President Harold B. Lee at conference time when he said that no one knows when the Savior will return.

"As we waited for Jack, we had no idea what day, what week, what year it would be, and it was ironic, because so many false prophecies were made predicting the release of the prisoners. We just waited," she said.

In December 1969, when the first letter from Jack arrived, Connie and the children prepared a two-pound package to send him. Three months later it was returned, coming back through the Communist countries.

Later they were told they could send a six-pound package every other month. The children chose with care the things they thought their father would need most and things he would enjoy. Bibles, tracts, and the Joseph Smith story were also sent for the English-speaking interpreter to find. There was one in each package. Connie saw that the packages were secure and tight and filled with good things, including all of the love they could squeeze in. They wrote letters as often as allowed and waited patiently for some word from Jack. The packages and letters came back stamped "Addressee Unknown."

"One day, about April 1971, I was busy scrubbing the kitchen floor when the mail arrived. Three letters and a package had been returned. It was especially upsetting to Richard to think that they were returning our packages when we had received mail and knew he was there," Connie related.

"Mother," he said "let's call Hanoi."

"Go ahead—we have tried everything else," she answered.

Richard picked up the phone; he didn't know quite what to do, but he determined to place the call with the operator.

"I'd like to place a call to Hanoi."

There was a long, silent moment, and then he tried to explain. Connie had to come to the phone to confirm the call.

"We will speak to anyone in Hanoi who can speak English," she instructed.

"It will be a few minutes. I will call you back," the operator replied.

Richard stayed close to the phone. Connie continued with her housework with a half-hearted effort. They were both waiting for a call.

About fifteen minutes later the call came. "We have an operator in Laos. Will you accept the call?" the local operator asked.

"Yes, go ahead," they replied.

The eager smiles of anticipation disappeared as the operator in Laos explained that she had contacted people in Hanoi and when they found out who was calling, they had refused the call.

"We sat around in frustration and finally Richard said, 'Let's call Paris.'"

"'Great! We have tried everything else—let's try Paris,' I told him. So we placed a call to the North Vietnamese Embassy in Paris. We told them exactly who we were and why we were calling. They set up an appointment for us on the following Monday. We had to place the call at midnight our time, which was eight a.m. Paris time.

"When the call finally got through, one of the interpreters came on the phone and said that our call had been refused. Because we were a POW family, they had nothing to say to us."

They didn't talk about it, but the fear that Jack had died in prison was in their minds. They waited.

In Hanoi the waiting game continued for the

POWs. Each day was counted. "Some men kept careful track of time," Jack said. "It helped to occupy their minds. They could not tell what day it was, but they could tell how many days they had been in prison. I could tap on the wall and get back a report from a man three cells down from me. He kept track in his mind of every man in the cell block. We had a little celebration when someone reached one thousand days.

"Other POWs counted their military pay every day and figured out how much they would have. We had to keep our minds busy. We played mental games, taught each other everything we knew. I picked up two foreign languages, French and Spanish.

"After I had been in prison for about five and a half years the guards gave us a third-year college French-Russian language textbook. It took a while to figure out what it was, but if you work on a thing long enough you can get the answer. I now have about an eight-thousand-word French vocabulary. The average Frenchman has only about forty-five hundred words. I can't speak French because I can't twist my tongue and get the nasal sounds to come out right, but I can read French. I can speak Spanish better. I bought a copy of the Book of Mormon in French and Spanish. I have decided that I'll read French and speak Spanish."

Writing and receiving letters were a highlight for men in prison in Viet Nam.

"I was allowed to write my first letter in December 1969. I was called out one day and told to write. Some had written earlier, but at that time everyone was allowed to write. We were allowed to write again in August 1970 and then once each month. The letters were not always sent, but we could write them.

"During the first years, the Vietnamese liked propaganda letters. They wanted any statement

From the Shadow of Death

that was contrary to what our government policy was. They would offer us a reward of being able to write. They would call us from our cells and ask if we would like to write to our family. If we said yes, they would say, 'You may write to your squadron mates and tell them not to drop any more bombs, or you may write to the American people, to Senator Fulbright, and others.' Most of us did not write; even though we wanted to let our wives know we were alive, we thought it was more important to maintain our honor," Rollins explained.

"I received about eleven letters during the six years. I got the first one about August 1970. I received seven or eight between then and the next February. Then for seventeen months I didn't receive anything. This is the time that my family thought I had died because their mail was coming back.

"During this time a guard came through and handed me a picture of my daughter. He asked me if I knew the person in the picture. I did, but I hadn't seen her since she was fourteen years old. She was older in the picture. I knew my wife and children were writing when I saw the picture. The camp officials were not giving me the letters. One of my friends had been in prison for almost eight years and had not received one letter, though his family had written every month.

"The Vietnamese were trying to convince me that my wife had divorced me. They didn't tell me directly, but they kept implying it, I guess, because several of the men's wives had gotten tired of waiting and had obtained divorces. Trying to convince me was ridiculous. I knew my wife was not going to divorce me.

"I attributed my strength to my wife. I knew that without her I would have very little. With this and the plan of salvation, I had peace of mind. I discovered that others were quite fascinated with this eternal plan and the importance of the family unit and the hereafter."

In the prison camp Jack tried to live by example, realizing that actions spoke louder than words. "We talked about each other, telling what we thought about each other. The main thing people told me was about the influence I had on their lives, and this influence was not given to them by what I had to say, but by what I did. The fact that I could maintain a sense of humor and that I had peace of mind impressed them.

"I didn't worry about my family. I mentioned them in my prayers and wondered what they were doing. I felt that my priesthood and the Comforter were what caused me not to have worries about my family. I knew they were being taken care of.

"It wasn't necessary to preach, only to live as we believed. We were so close in prison that our actions became our religion. Our cell mates knew us right down to our innermost thoughts. They knew what kind of man we were. It didn't do any good to put some religious principle on a pedestal and not live them. A person was known by his principles. Others could see the effect a principle had on his life. If they liked what it did, then they could accept it. It was not like the outside world where you see people only on the surface, and things that are said sometimes project an image. A POW's thoughts and principles were completely known; there was no facade.

"We did put forth points of the gospel doctrine as we talked. We had group discussions where we explained our religions to anyone who was interested. Quite a number of men heard the Mormon story. We had church services, at first alone, and then, as we came together, in groups. After we were put together in November 1970, we had group meetings," he said.

Jack became the first chaplain in his building, serving for five months. There were fifty-seven men and the assignment was rotated. Jack was chosen because the men recognized that he had a good knowledge of the gospel and the teachings of Christ.

"We would begin with a prayer and a scripture. We had put together all of the scriptures we could remember. We had a choir of three or four men, but it had to be very quiet, because we were not allowed to make noises.

"One humorous thing: I worked for four years trying to come up with the fourth verse to 'Ere You Left Your Room This Morning,' a hymn that I felt was especially appropriate in Hanoi. I finally made up a verse, only to discover later that there are only three verses to the song. I have the only fourth verse, mostly parts of the other three verses put together. I was really glad to finally get a hymn book," Jack said.

"It is difficult for me to say what role prayer played. I felt I wasn't on the best of terms with the Lord before I was captured, and in that environment, I didn't want to make any promises. My prayer was for a desire to live the gospel, to live in a righteous way, and for strength to carry out that desire.

"I think my prayers were answered. I was given the strength to sustain the ordeal. I have a little different outlook on prayer now than I had before I was captured. I think I am a little more willing to let the Lord's will be done.

"Prayer was really a comfort to me. I found myself praying, not so much in formal prayer night and morning, but throughout the day as I felt the need for a little brief communication, or a little 'thank you,' or a little 'help me, Lord.' Over the six years my prayers became sort of a way of talking with my Father in heaven. My formal prayers were that the Lord would forgive me of my bad thoughts and actions.

"There was a time when one of my very closest comrades, a man for whom I have a deep love and affection, stopped me and said, 'You know, you're going to be consumed by your hatred.' That made me stop and think. I probably would have been completely consumed had he not had the love and friendship to tell me to take a look at myself. He was a fine Lutheran brother. We had many discussions over the years.

"This hatred was probably caused by the living conditions. From then on, I would start the day by asking the Lord to help me not to hate. I think I was able to overcome that. I came out of my experience without any animosity. I do have some reservations and some feelings that I would like to remove, but I don't have hate for the experience itself. I am happier about that than most anything," he said.

"To the best of my knowledge, there were nine Latter-day Saints who got into the prison system alive. I met three of them while I was in Hanoi. We were not allowed to communicate for the first years, but we were able to say a word or two as we went from cell to cell, to another cell block, or out in the yard.

"One of them would quietly say, 'Hey, what is the seventh Article of Faith?' In six years, we were only able to put together twelve Articles of Faith. As soon as I got to the Philippines and contacted Colonel George Kiser, the branch president at Clark, I wanted to know which one I had missed.

"I almost cried when I reviewed the Articles of Faith. I had left out the most important one. I won't say which one it was, but it was the most important one to me. I lived by faith—not only faith in God, but also faith in my fellow Americans and my fellow prisoners."

Most of the POWs had someone they could talk to, a confidant. Several came to Jack to talk. This may have been their only contact—they had nothing else in common—but when they needed help, they felt they could come to him. "We sustained each other and maintained faith in our fellow POWs, our God, and our country. That is what got us through," Jack explained.

The POWs lived according to "The U. S. Fighting Man's Code," which grew out of the Korean war when, for the first time, American soldiers were subjected to the Communists' systematic program to exploit them.

One of the articles of the code states: "As a prisoner of war, I will keep faith with my fellow prisoners. I will give no information nor take part in any action which might be harmful to my comrades." This was a very meaningful statement to Jack.

"We had guidelines from our government, which said, 'I will resist to the utmost of my ability.' We believed that any information that was given that was not extracted by undue torture or duress was a direct violation of that code. We freely admit to having given information, but I feel that any information that was given that was not forced from the POW is, indeed, wrong and a violation of the code. This is a personal opinion. I did not volunteer any information. I think that the code is good and should stand.

"The code provided me with fortitude. I am a career military man and had served almost twenty years when I was shot down. I am of the old school and believe that if you have rules, they should be enforced. I think the code held up well. Oftentimes the senior officer clarified and amplified the code to fit the condition in which we were living."

Jack was a senior officer for a one-year period for a small group of men. After the POWs were put together in 1969-70, wing and squadron commanders became the senior officers and provided the leadership.

"The average fighting man did not have any information that is classified. The Vietnamese were understandably interested in what the next target might be, but the most insidious thing was their demand for propaganda material. I was tortured many times because of my political beliefs. When I refused to say that the U.S. was an aggressor or that I had committed actual criminal acts, I was subjected to punishment.

"One time they kept me awake for eight days just to make me write a statement that I was being treated in a lenient and humane way. After eight days I wrote the statement, and I later apologized to our camp commander for violating the regulations."

Chapter 14

The Needle Maker

Cell time was almost twenty-four hours per day for American POWs in North Viet Nam during the early years. Camp regulations forbade talking and wall tapping, and precautions were taken to keep the men from seeing each other.

Commander David Jack Rollins was generally allowed to leave his cell only to empty his waste bucket, bathe, or face interrogation. "We were sometimes allowed to wash every day, and then at other times I know how the buffalo hunters must have felt at the end of winter—they must have been as dirty as we were. About six weeks is the longest I had to go without getting water to bathe.

"We were given a liter of water in the morning and a liter in the afternoon—about two quarts a day. We could do anything we wanted with it, but most of the time we drank it all. So we got very dirty. After you get so dirty you can almost peal the dirt off. We tried.

"We did get to shave. At first I was given a razor to use about every six weeks, but later I got to shave twice a week. We got a haircut about once a month. During the last year I was one of the camp barbers. I became quite good with a razor cut."

Interrogation was a diversion, but it was not always a welcome diversion. One day Jack was called by the interrogator, who "put me on a stool and ran through the usual ritual."

"How are you today?" the smiling Vietnamese asked.

"I am fine."

"What is your name?"

"Commander David J. Rollins," he replied, knowing that they already knew his name because they had sent for him.

"Are you married?" the interrogator asked, nodding his own head because he already knew the answer.

"Yes," Jack said, shifting position on the stool.

"You must miss your family?"

"No." Jack always said no because they couldn't understand that; it would upset their ritual and they wouldn't know what to do next.

After regaining his thoughts, the interrogator continued in very good English, "And now [this was the real purpose of the interrogation], what is the best cigarette in America?"

This was a surprising question. Jack thought for a minute, trying to figure what was going on. He didn't know that there was that much difference in cigarettes to matter to the North Vietnamese.

He hesitated too long.

"Aha! See, in America you do not know—but in Viet Nam, everyone knows which is the best cigarette," the interrogator said with unusual pride.

Jack was amused and said to himself, Of course everybody knows there is no choice. There is one best grade and one worst grade, and everybody know which is which. The same with soap and most everything else. They have no choice in anything they do. They can't understand why we can't even rank our automobiles as to which is best.

Being interrogated was not a very satisfactory diversion from the four walls of a cell. Oftentimes it ended in a beating or some other punishment. "Usually it was just a beating," Jack recalled. "The beatings were very similar to a mugging in an alley. Four or five men just surround you, slugging, kicking, and hitting. Some men did get their eardrums ruptured from repeated kicks and hits to the head. I had the front of my face caved in and some ear damage, but they were careful not to permantly mark us. They used things like rubber hose.

"We had what we called our 'ten most wanted' list. I had one guy who could fill the top three spaces. I think that during some of these I survived on hatred. I had to overcome that and tell myself many times a day not to hate.

"Probably the worst torture was emotional and psychological. A person could recover from the physical torture, but the emotional stress never left. Many men were in solitary confinement for periods of three to four years, a few up to five years. One man was moved to an area where we could not make any contact with him for over seven months.

"It was necessary to establish communication with each other during this period of isolation. We converted every noise we could make into intelligent communication, and though we faced severe punishment for being caught, we communicated at every opportunity.

"With my metal-smithing background—for many years I was an airplane mechanic—I was able to manufacture some tools and make some pen points. We made ink out of everything imaginable—ashes, brick dust, vitamin pills, food, the dye from our clothes. When we would get new clothes, we'd soak out the dye and evaporate the water to get color to make ink. We lived on ingenuity," he said.

"One of the best things we used to make ink was the medicine they gave us. We were given a medicine very much like tincture of violet to treat the fungus we all had. It could be diluted and used for ink.

"Pens were made from bamboo sticks, or in some cases I made them from a tin can smuggled from the kitchen in our clothing. With these homemade pens, we had to write one letter at a time and to write larger than we would with an American pen, but, by golly, some of the metal pens I made worked as well as the Vietnamese pens," he explained proudly.

For twelve years of his military service as an enlisted man (he was commissioned in 1960), Jack had worked as a structural mechanic. He had fixed aircraft and had a good knowledge of metal. In the prison camp he made a knife from a nail by rubbing it on concrete. With this sharpened nail he could scribe the metal, then break it, hone it down, and clean it up on the concrete.

The POWs were constantly on the lookout for metal or any other useful item. They would work for a week or two to loosen and extract a nail from a board. They needed needles to patch their clothing or in some cases to do some needlework, such as the American flags that they made and displayed.

"I managed to acquire some copper wire. Once I took a section right out of the Vietnamese electrical system and another time from the public address system. I would break off a piece of wire about an inch and a half long and grind it down on the concrete until it was sharpened to a point. Then I'd take a small nail and sharpen it to a point and drill a little hole through the end of the wire needle. I must have made approximately 100 needles. Some of the men wore them as lapel pins when we were released.

"I got to a point where I could make a needle in a couple of hours. I had a really good nail and could get a needle polished up and ready to use during a nap period with no problem at all. We would pass the needles in a drop area, either where we bathed or picked up our water. After 1970, when we were really quite proficient in needlemaking, we were allowed out of our cells a little longer, so passing things was no problem," he said.

The prisoners would steal sticks and bones to clean their fingernails or use as toothpicks. To hide the needles or toothpicks from the guards, who made weekly inspections, the men would dig holes in the walls, make slots in their bed boards, or stick things up in the air vents. If any of these small items were found, a punishment would follow or, in later years when the prison attitude changed, a good scolding would result. The prisoners would apologize and go right on with what they were doing, but would use more care and caution in their activities.

Jack became known as "Mr. Fix-It." The prisoners would bring projects to him and he would go to work on them as best he could. "I made a cookstove. We used it to cook the animal fat that we'd get in our food. We would render it down and then light it in a tin can with a wick.

"I made a chess set out of a clay made from bread and ashes and dried into a hard finish. I had played a little chess and was familiar with the pieces. The set I made was rather modernistic. Others made some very fine sets and other fine pieces of sculpture. We would pass every bit of information along. We learned from each other," Jack explained.

"One Christmas we had a complete Nativity scene. We decorated our rooms and made wreaths and little boxes. Glue was made from the bread. Kool-Aid that we received in our packages from home was used for color. With paste made from bread and the brown toilet paper, we could make almost anything with papier-maché. All of this was done after the fall of 1969. Up until that time, we were very restricted. Even then we were inspected once a week, and if anything was found it would be taken away. It got to be very discouraging.

"Some guards were tender-hearted and some were cruel. One guard we called 'The Court Jester,' because he had a sense of humor. He couldn't stand to watch torture. He would leave the room.

"To my knowledge, only one American hit a Vietnamese. This was at a quiz and the POW just got fed up, stood up, and smashed the Vietnamese in the face. He received severe punishment for a long time.

"One standard punishment was called knee time. We had to kneel on the concrete floor with our hands raised vertically. I was caught many times for making things or hiding them, and this was my punishment. The longest time I was on my knees was three days. I was almost insane by then—it was about all I could take. The concrete was so rough that after several hours of kneeling, there was no skin on my knees. If they caught me with my arms down, they would beat me. We had to cheat; there was no way we could maintain that position. I have actually had a guard stand with a bayonet in my back and have passed out from having had to remain so rigid. After I passed out, they revived me and started over again. Their idea was to make us repent of our crimes. I can't begin to count the times I was forced to submit to this knee treatment. The last time was in October 1969. They stopped the torture abruptly about that time."

This turning point in the treatment of the POWs has been attributed by many to the pressure of public opinion. Others feel internal politics or the peace efforts of the United States helped bring about improved conditions in the Vietnamese prisons.

With the decrease in torture came an increase in the quality of food. Jack described his first meal as a bowl of pumpkin soup. "When I landed in the rice paddy, after our plane went down, I almost bit my tongue off. I had to hold it behind my teeth to keep it in place. Because of this I did not receive anything to eat. I couldn't have eaten anyway. By the time my tongue had healed enough for me to eat I was very, very hungry.

"Then they gave me a bowl of pumpkin soup. It wasn't really soup—it was boiled pumpkin. The Vietnamese told us it was good for a headache; they really thought it was. It seemed to me that it was a headache to have to eat pumpkin soup for six months. I thought that pumpkins were just used for jack-o-lanterns, but they started serving us the soup in April and continued to the end of the pumpkin season in October. Then they served us cabbage. I used to like cabbage, but after I had eaten cabbage for hundreds of meals in a row, I lost my appetite for it. We received some rice or bread with each meal and with the exception of about ten meals, we always had soup. Sometimes there were noodles or beans or potatoes in the soup, but usually we would get greens. We called them weeds. We got weed water from three different kinds of weeds, including one that looked like the old pig weed that we pulled from the garden. Another weed, which we called kerosene greens, looked like chard, but oh, it was bad! Sometimes the weeds were fried.

"By 1969, the prisoners had lost a lot of weight and looked very much like walking skeletons. Malnutrition was setting in, and some of the men were getting beri-beri, scurvy, and other diseases. I had weighed 213 pounds when I was captured and I think I got down to about 150 pounds.

"Our diets were sometimes supplemented with what we called starch cubes. The last year we received a cereal bar for breakfast two or three times each week. Sometimes they were chocolate and sometimes they were plain, but they were really quite good. They were a combat ration of some kind, either Chinese or Vietnamese. We also were given milk, but never the same day as the cereal. We were too hungry to save the cereal until the next day to have it with milk.

"We were given French-style bread, like a poor-boy sandwich, canned fish, and sometimes dried fish. The Vietnamese raised fish everywhere they possibly could, even in the tank that held our bath water. We ate the whole fish, scales and all. We even ate the bones.

"By the time I reached the Philippines I weighed 162. Now I weigh 204, and the doctor has told me to take off fifteen pounds. He must be crazy!"

Medical attention was sparse in the POW camps. Jack received no medical attention for the first fifteen months. "I had undergone a rather severe beating and was unable to walk; I was in a great deal of pain all that time. In 1969, I developed pneumonia and almost died. Then, for the next two years, I received a considerable amount of medical attention. It was to keep me alive, not to cure me. I was even offered an operation in 1970, but I declined. I wasn't sure what they wanted to do; they tried to tell me they could fix me by cutting.

"I was also given tremendous injections, both intravenous and intramuscular. And as my diet improved, my health improved steadily, and by the fall of 1971, I was able to function quite normally.

"One humorous thing happened about this time. When I started to pick up weight, my shape changed. I had been size 34 waist when I went to Viet Nam, but now I needed size 36. By then Connie was able to send packages and the clothing was too small. The next time I was able to write a letter I wrote, 'Send my underwear to fit a yard waist.'

"The U.S. intelligence people (our correspondence was examined for information) assumed that

From the Shadow of Death

I must be working in the yard, and they suggested something to wear outside. The clothing I received was still size 34," said Jack.

With the improvement of food and medical care, there was also improvement in communication. The American prisoners in Hanoi heard a news broadcast almost every day. Of course, it was Vietnamese news, telling one side only, and with it stories of all four thousand years of Vietnamese history plus all the bad things that were happening in the United States.

"We heard about drug problems, sex problems, floods, hurricanes, and earthquakes, and anti-war activities. We didn't hear anything good like the U.S. men landing on the moon or the new developments in the automobiles.

"In October 1972, we were able to piece together enough information, from the way the Vietnamese emphasized different points, that we knew release was eminent. By the time they told us officially, the climax was past.

"We knew the order in which we had been shot down, and we had agreed to come out in that order. I was number 188 and my pilot was number 189. The prisoners were separated by the Vietnamese and placed in areas according to their shoot-down dates. The first and second groups to be released were kept at the Hanoi Hilton.

"The situation relaxed a great deal as the first group left, and we tried to get the guards to tell us when we would leave. Since they would tell us nothing specific, we surmised it would be about two weeks after the first group had left.

"The morning we were scheduled to come home, we got all ready and were fixing our food. One of the Vietnamese came to our officer in charge and told him that we must make more coal balls, which were used to cook with. (The prisoners made the coal balls from coal dust and water.)

" 'You don't need more coal balls—we are going home,' the Air Force colonel said.

" 'I got to cook meal,' the cook replied.

" 'We don't need the meal—we are on our way out,' was the reply.

" 'I don't know about that. I know I need to cook. I need coal balls,' the Vietnamese answered.

"There was a strange look on the colonel's face, but the men were assigned to make the coal balls. We didn't leave that day, or the next or the next. It was five days before we were released. That waiting was an emotional experience.

"The camp commander, who was watching us leave, noticed that one strap on my shoe had broken. The strap was made of innertube and the shoes were made of tires. He didn't want me to go out into the world with a broken strap, so he ordered a new one.

"We had another anxious moment when they took us to the airport. We were taken in little camou-flaged buses, and I was in the next to last bus. We could see two planes on the field, but they were soon loaded with the men in the first buses and we were left waiting. 'Wow,' I thought, 'they have really blown it.' The Vietnamese couldn't speak English, so they couldn't explain the delay. Much to our relief another plane soon arrived, and we were on our way to the Philippines."

The debriefing stop in the Philippines added to the excitement, as did the prospect of facing life as a free man. For Jack, prison had been a real test of endurance and faith.

"I acquired a whole new prospective while I was in that cramped cell. Now that I was free, I wanted to compare a lot of those things with how I felt out in the world, associating with other people." His thoughts were filled with mental images of Connie and the children, and this presented new emotions. He was finally on his way home!

In San Diego, Connie was having her share of excitement too. "I was in bed about one a.m. when the casualty assisting officer called. He said Jack was on the third plane out of Hanoi and that it would land in the Philippines at 2:14 a.m. I thought of the analogy we had made with the Savior's coming and wondered if that is the way he would come, perhaps with an announcement by our prophet.

"What a thrill to know that I was going to see him on television in just an hour! Six years of emotion just tumbled out. It was the most beautiful sight you can ever imagine when I saw him coming down the ramp. I thought of the many things that had gone by and the catching up that we would have to do after six and a half years."

Patricia watched the homecoming from her apartment in Provo, where she was attending Brigham Young University. Richard was at the Naval Academy and had gotten the wrong information and missed the landing, to his deep disappointment. CBS, however, arranged for a film clip to be sent to him, and he viewed the event the next day.

"During those lonely years I had done some deep thinking," Connie said. "I wanted to have things right for Jack's return. I had even been released from presidency positions in the Church and assigned as a librarian in the ward so the pressure wouldn't be too great.

"I had always felt that the Church must always come first, but after reading an editorial in the *Church News,* I discovered that the family was the most important and came first. I knew that when Jack came home his readjustment and transition back into family life and society would be top priority."

Connie and all three children were at Miramar Naval Air Station near San Diego to meet Jack. She shook like a leaf as she threw her arms around Jack. It was a beautiful sight.

Gene was dressed in smart new slacks and sweater that had been purchased for the occasion. Richard, proud, was dressed in his midshipman uniform, and Patricia had a cast on her leg from a recent accident. Dwarfed beside the giant plane, the five walked slowly away—there was so much to say, so much to do. A new life was beginning.

"We had a very spiritual and joyous reunion," Connie said. "We couldn't have asked for a better reunion."

Jack recalled, "When I returned, my wife asked me some very strange questions about what I was wearing the day I was shot down. In tears, she explained to me about her dream. It was humbling to me. She saw me in an unusual uniform, and it was true: I had been wearing Marine fatigues, which she had never seen me wear. This experience added to my testimony."

Gene, who is teachers quorum president in his ward, recognized what the gospel had done for his family during the years his father had been gone. "When he left I was in Primary, about nine years old. In the next few years I had a lot of help from Mother and many others. As the years went on, the gospel really helped me out. I am now sixteen years old, and I have discovered that there is a lot more than just sitting around and worrying about myself. I have a friend who, with the help of the missionaries, has been listening to the gospel, and he was recently baptized. I think we need problems to grow. My family situation has helped me to grow strong and to grow in the gospel. The Lord has really blessed our family."

There were some adjustments for Jack and the family.

"I have had to learn a new language—there are

so many modern words," Jack says. "Probably the biggest change is in men's fashions and long hair. And there have been changes in automobile styles. I used to be familiar with every style of automobile, but now I have to ask Gene which is which as we drive along.

"There have been changes in moral standards, and a lackadaisical attitude about responsibility and unity. When I left, our motto was 'United We Stand' —we banded together for a common cause. When I returned, it seemed as though many wanted to take out and not put in—an attitude of 'you do your thing and I will do mine.' I think 'our thing' should be to keep the greatest nation on earth strong, and if we are in different directions, we can't be united."

Jack has been flooded with requests for stories. His initial press conference was brief. When contacted by the *Church News* he declined to discuss his experiences for two months. "I wanted to see if the values I had developed and my prospectives were going to remain the same over a period of time. I wanted to know that these things stayed with me while I was out in the world.

"Now, after three months, I am pleased to say that my definition of honesty, for example, is still the same. My definitions of loyalty, responsibility, integrity have all remained the same."

"I also had many fears about how my ideas would work out and how our family relationships would develop. I came back to a wonderful family. My wife has given me all the support imaginable, and my wonderful children are contributing to society rather than taking from it.

"We do indeed enjoy the gospel of Jesus Christ. I have had an opportunity to compare my principles and belief in the gospel with the beliefs of others, and it is rewarding to have had an opportunity under duress to compare the thing that brought us through that duress: faith.

"I am just about the proudest man in the world that I am who I am. Everything has worked out for me," Jack declared.

Lieutenant Commander David J. Rollins, left, heads for
Freedom Gate in Hanoi after handshake with Colonel Emil
Wengle, special assistant to Assistant Secretary of Defense
for Public Affairs

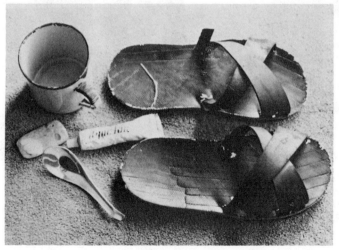

Lieutenant Commander David J. Rollins
photographed cup, spoon, soap,
toothpaste, and sandals he brought
home; a needle he made in prison is
shown on the heel of one sandal

Lieutenant Commander David Rollins is welcomed home by his wife, Connie, and his three children, Richard, Gene, and Patricia, at Miramir Naval Air Station

From the Shadow of Death

Major Jay C. Hess

Air Force, Bountiful, Utah

Shot down August 24, 1967, fifteen miles south of China border
Released March 14, 1973

Chapter 15

"I've Got to Get Out of Here"

Captain Jay C. Hess struggled to lift his face from the dirt. It took all the strength he had just to twist his neck, all of his concentration just to wake up. He tried to focus his eyes. He could see a young boy crawling on his hands and knees. There were soldiers and women and children coming up the hill where he lay, only semiconscious. Captain Hess was lying on his stomach on a jungle trail in North Viet Nam. His parachute had billowed down about him. He struggled, but faded again into unconsciousness.

Only moments earlier the forty-two-year-old Air Force captain had been piloting a sleek F-105 aircraft. His plane was one of twenty in the formation. They flew in flights of four. He was number four in the first flight. It was three p.m. August 24, 1967, fifteen miles from the China border, northeast of Hanoi. He had just dropped his bomb. This was his thirty-first mission.

"In the plane I really didn't know if I was hit or not. I felt a thud, like you might expect if you drove a car through a guard rail at sixty miles per hour," Captain Hess recalled. Almost immediately the airplane caught fire. Flames roared from front to back. The fuel was burning, fanned by the high speed of the aircraft. "This can't happen to me, not me," he thought.

Then things happened in rapid succession—the fire, the high speed, the forces of gravity. Automatically his hand reached for the ejection handle. That was the last thing Captain Hess remembered until he struggled for consciousness and spit dirt from his mouth.

The extreme speed and forces of flight had rendered him unconscious as he floated from the flaming aircraft. He didn't guide the parachute; it just floated downward in the gaze of waiting soldiers. He touched the ground, limp and unaware, crumbling on his face.

With great effort he opened his eyes. "I must get up," he thought, but before his wobbly arms and legs could respond to the message of a groggy mind, his captors jumped on him. He remembers the commotion, the strange and excited language. He felt no pain, he had no injuries.

"There seems to be some concern to protect me from any violence that might occur," he thought as he began to realize the miracle of his safe landing and felt the protecting spirit that accompanied his capture.

"There was a commotion and some quick decisions, made in excitement and anger, by the Vietnamese. I received some slight injury, right after or during my capture. I don't know whether it was accidental or intentional. I don't know whether it was a bullet or a stick, but something brought blood from an injury on my neck and head. They started to take my clothes and shoes off, but they stopped for some reason, and I put them back on," he said.

When his mind began to clear, the realization came to him of the whole miraculous thing, of being in an airplane, going so fast, being unconscious, not even remembering the ejection, and getting on the

From the Shadow of Death

ground without injury. The chain of events seemed almost impossible.

Tears swelled in his eyes. He knew that someone was working for him. "It was the simple faith of my children," he said to himself, feeling close to that divine guiding Spirit. With his flight suit and boots back on, and at the direction of his captors, he began to walk.

"We walked for a couple of hours and reached a cave. I was given some medical treatment for the wound. They offered me food right away. Then I was questioned about who I was and where I was from." He realized that he was very much alone. A young, but impressive, Chinese man served as translator.

As the evening approached, Captain Hess was taken by jeep to various military units in the area for war rallies, where he was shown off. There were speeches and shouts for victory and jeers for the captured airman. It was a humbling, even humiliating experience for him.

"I tried to explain that I was just trying to help them, to show them a better way to live. It even seemed silly to me at the time. But I hadn't approached the problem with any hate for the Vietnamese. It was a matter of trying to make their lives better. I was completely unsuccessful in convincing them of my reason for being there," he explained.

The night drew on as Captain Hess was displayed at camp after camp. He had no rest. His mind was filled with baffling thoughts of what to do—what could he do?

"During that first day the thought of escape was immediately on my mind, but only one time did I consider it as a possibility, and then the opportunity was so brief that I missed it. It was one of those moments that was to gnaw on me in prison as I thought about all the ifs.

"I was riding in a jeep after I was captured. There were two in the front seat and four of us in back. I was untied at the time. I still had on my shoes and clothing. It just seemed like a possibility that I could take a pistol out of the soldier's holster and overpower the men in the vehicle, and then just run into the jungle. We had two vehicles in our convoy, and it was only for a moment that the other jeep was around a bend. I hesitated for just a moment. It was just a thought. I don't think I would have made it to freedom, but there was a possibility. I have thought of it often," Captain Hess said.

It was nearly dawn when the truck ride ended. Captain Hess had ridden for several hours, from about midnight to perhaps four o'clock in the morning. There was a short wait, well guarded, but lonely, before he was flown to Hanoi by helicopter. The night was hot.

A two-day interrogation period followed, then a break, and then more interrogation. It was a pattern that was to last for more than two months.

"The first break they gave me was on Sunday. It was the first day I had been left alone, and that is when my deep serious reflections began. My concern for my wife and family was upmost in my mind," he said.

"I've got to get out of here before that blue Air Force vehicle pulls up in front of my house and gives my wife the bad news," he thought to himself. He was helpless. The blue vehicle, with chaplain and driver, would make several stops at the Hess household before he would return. There would be three long years of uncertainty for his wife and family. It would be more than six years before he would again hold them in his arms.

From the Shadow of Death

Chapter 16

"Above All, I Seek for Eternal Life"

As he stood naked against the gray walls of the old prison, alone and stripped of his clothes, Captain Jay C. Hess was left to ponder. He wasn't really alone; his captors were never far away. Their eyes and their guns were upon him. But it was a lonely experience and the fact that he had lost his freedom was becoming a reality to him.

He pondered. Though he was physically tired—he had been without sleep the whole night—his mind turned over and over the events of his capture: the smoke-filled cockpit, the echo of the voice from his radio—"you are torching, you are torching"—the struggle for the ejection handle. He couldn't remember finding it.

He remembered being on the ground. There were shots and shouts and overpowering Vietnamese. It was only now, as he stood naked, that the reality of a miracle—he was alive—came firmly to his weary mind. It was obvious to him immediately, when everything else was taken away, that the most valuable possession he had was the promise of eternal life.

"Everything is gone," he said in a whisper. "I am separated from everything that counts—my wife, my children, my home."

The loss of his clothing seemed insignificant. It

came as a blow to him how much time he had spent thinking of a new car and trips, and how nice it was to have this and that. Suddenly, with all of his possessions gone, he felt the significance of the hope of eternal life.

"I can stand the loss of anything, but it would really be a tragic loss to be without the possibility of eternal life. That is the greatest gift," he said to himself.

The real value of eternal life was well established in his mind those few minutes before he was interrupted by a guard, who motioned to a pair of shorts tossed down for him to wear; they were only a borrowed possession. He examined the shorts, felt the material. That first day he wondered, "Will these be the clothes I'll die in?"

He was taken to a cell with a boarded window and an iron door. The small light burned, casting shadows on the wall. There was a straw mat on the floor—his second borrowed possession.

It was nearly three weeks before the standard issue of clothing and personal supplies was given to him. The issue included two sets of long clothes, two sets of short underclothes, sandals made from a rubber tire, a mosquito net, a tin cup, a bar of soap, a toothbrush and toothpaste. "I never realized how great an instrument a toothbrush was until those weeks without one." The mosquito net was valuable too. POWs never went to sleep without putting up their mosquito nets.

Alone, hauled out and interrogated, then alone again. That was his life style. This was a period of much praying, and from prayer came complete assurance. There was misery, but no fear. There was discomfort, but no anguish.

Jay had read the Doctrine and Covenants just before he was shot down, as part of a project to study all the scriptures as quickly as he could. The passages were fresh on his mind. "When Joseph Smith was in prison he offered some prayers for relief, and the answer the Lord gave him was that the ordeal would last for just a 'moment'."

Jay remembered the words of the scripture, "My son, peace be unto thy soul; thine adversity and thine afflictions shall be but a small moment." (D&C 121:7.) From this scripture he gained strength as he offered his own prayers.

These first days were filled with religious motivation. Jay thought often that the time he spent alone, those first forty days, were days of preparation and seasoning for what was ahead. He thought of the Savior's forty days in the wilderness, as he himself was experiencing all kinds of temptations, alternately with hours of meditation.

Many things came back to his mind, things that he had been taught, words and phrases and verses that had sunk in: "Don't give up, keep trying," "Press on," "Though the way be full of trials, weary not." There were hundreds of these memory bits that surfaced during the time he was alone in the prison cell.

He remembered the stories of faith that he had been taught since childhood—of Daniel in the lions den; of Meshach, Shadrach and Abednego in the fiery furnace; and of Job.

"I thought I could do anything, but I learned from this that I didn't have the kind of faith that those men had, that I just couldn't get up and walk through the walls or have the door fall off like Paul the Apostle did when he came out of prison.

"I had hoped for that in that prison cell. Mountains can be moved with faith, and if they can, then I could walk out of jail, which I wanted desperately to do. But I couldn't. It seemed, maybe, I wanted it too much. Maybe I had something to learn there.

"I found out that it takes a great deal of courage

and faith to try those things. I never realized the amount of courage it would take to try and act like that I had strong faith, but I would like to have had more," Jay said.

This time period, when he was alone, was very significant. Jay continually reflected on his values, his life. He would think back often and examine the crossroads in his life.

"I could see that I had not recognized some of the real crossroads. I could see many ways that my life could have taken a different course, like when the instructor in college suggested that I might be interested in chemistry of soils. It maybe would have been interesting and taken me off into a whole new area. It became clear that simple things like that were crossroads. The eternal road was the important one, however, and there was a great amount of prayer," he said, explaining that this was part of the mental exercise that was necessary for his well-being.

He thought of his family and of his church assignment as group leader in Thailand, a position he had had little opportunity to serve in before he was shot down. He thought of the things he liked.

The Sound of Music came to his mind. He had seen it three times during the previous year. His children were just the age of the children in the musical, so now in his cell he drew a parallel.

"A few of my favorite things," he said to himself. "When the dog bites, when the bee strings, when you're feeling sad—think of your favorite things." He did just that. He thought of his favorite things.

He thought of Farmington, Utah, where he had grown up. He dwelled on that subject for a whole week. It was one of the thought projects that he assigned himself. During the next week he thought about the school in Farmington he had attended. He remembered the people and what they were like, the experiences, the playground, the winter that made the hills so slick it was impossible to climb them. He thought of places he would like to go. These optimistic mental exercises helped his outlook and made those difficult days easier.

"The hymnbook," he said. "I will think of the hymnbook. We never went to a meeting back home but what we would sing hymns. Then I just sang the words; now I have a reason to believe them. 'Come, Come, Ye Saints'—that's a powerful hymn. 'No toil or labor fear—and should we die, it is going to be a lot easier; but if we get out of here, we are going to make the music swell.' " He smiled at his original words.

Sundays were special days for him. They had always been important, and now they were more important than they had ever been before. That first Sunday in prison he made a decision. "I will dedicate Sunday to the Lord for thought and prayer. It will be his day here just the same as it should be anywhere," he decided.

He partook of the sacrament a few times by himself, recalling the words of the prayers as best he could. Later, he discovered that he had remembered only one word wrong in one prayer.

When he received his first roommate, Konrad Troutman, they planned simple services together on Sunday. Jay had been keeping track of the days. When his roommate, who had been shot down only two weeks before, questioned his date, Jay, who had been there for about two months, was concerned, and then pleased, to find that his mental calendar was correct.

Before the week ended, two more POWs were assigned to the room, making a total of four, and they were moved to another camp. Jay discovered others could use his help in taking care of their spiritual needs. One of the two new roommates,

Navy Lieutenant Mike McGrath, from Colorado, was anxious for religious activity and suggested they hold services. At first they were simple, but as the camp population grew and as conditions became better, bigger and bigger meetings were held. Jay served for a time as room chaplain, then later the wing commander appointed him wing chaplain. He often gave spiritual guidance to other men who came to him, frequently talking to them about their families. Many were impressed with the LDS family home evening program. "I will send you a copy of our family home evening manual when we get out of this place," Jay would promise. "We can realize now just how much we have neglected our families in the past."

Jay thought of his children often. His youngest was three years and his oldest boy was in elementary school. As the days slowly passed, he tried to envision them growing. In his mind's eye he would see them go to school and progress in the Church. But when the first pictures came, three years after he was captured, he hardly recognized his children.

"Hey! This is someone else's picture. The Vietnamese have switched pictures or something," he said. Almost everyone in prison had the same experience.

"Oh, no, I can see it now, they are my kids, how they have grown," Jay said after he had studied the picture and gotten used to the idea. It was three years again before he got the second picture, and he had the same experience. "Wow!" he said. "That's Cameron. When I left he was in elementary school; now he is 6 feet 4 inches tall."

His youngest daughter, Heidi, had written him a letter in her own handwriting. "Dear Daddy," the letter said, "I am soon going to be baptized and Cameron is going to baptize me."

"On, happy day," he said with a chuckle of

satisfaction. "Just to see that handwriting, her own handwriting. Why she was just a baby, only three years old, and now she is going to be baptized."

Jay stopped and realized how much time had passed. "Eternity is for ever," he thought. "That is my anchor, eternal life."

He thought it curious that the music of the Mormon Tabernacle Choir came to his mind so often. He would remember it especially on Sunday mornings as he thought of his home and family. He didn't find out until four years later that his wife was singing with the choir.

"I would have been so happy to have known that she was in the choir," he said looking back. "I wonder if perhaps that is why the tie was so close, why the broadcast was so impressed on my mind."

He could hear Elder Richard L. Evans saying, "Within these walls . . ." and he said to himself, "Yes, within these walls," as his eyes scanned the dull, dingy plaster of his prison cell. "If only I had a Bible," he said. "It has been more than three years since my special project to read all the scriptures. Like anything that is rare, the Bible is appreciated more," he said softly. When at last the prisoners were allowed to have a Bible for half a day on Saturday, the Vietnamese provided a pencil and paper so they could copy some scriptures.

Jay sat with the pencil in one hand, the Bible in the other. "How I have missed a pencil. What an amazing tool," he said, as he started to copy to Sermon on the Mount. "I will write the parable of the Sower also, and the first chapter of Genesis and the thirteenth chapter of First Corinthians, which deals with faith, hope, and charity, and some other scriptures that will be most valuable.

"Three years without seeing a Bible," he thought to himself. "I hadn't realized the great value of the Bible. It's amazing; the language is so beautiful," he noted, realizing that the POWs had built up a manner of speech all their own and were limited in their vocabulary.

"These simple truths are so meaningful. I will make it a point to memorize everything I copy," he said. Most of the scriptures he did memorize. He was more than glad later when an inspection of his cell resulted in a loss of the copied scriptures, so painstakingly written by hand. "I can remember most of the Sermon on the Mount," he said, and recited it with little hesitation.

Some prisoners had their own Bibles. The POWs were not all treated the same. It was part of the system; the Vietnamese had different treatment for different prisoners.

"There was a long break when we had no Bible, then a time when one was available for half a day, and then there was a complete change in the program, and we actually got a Bible for our room. I had access to it for all of one night. What a choice experience, just to have it in my possession. I thought how often a Bible had been available, and I had not read it, and now I had one for a whole night," he said, for once happy that the lights were left on all night.

Jay could feel the strength of the scriptures. He could feel the courage of the Savior and the prophets. "I am sure that the Savior is the source of courage. That is the thing that prepares a person. Learning true principles doesn't take an outstanding experience or some magic moment," he thought.

The moral courage, the solid faith Jay had was apparent to those who shared a cell or a prison room with him. "Tell me the Mormon story again," a roommate would say, and Jay would, with delight, tell the story of the Church and bear his testimony. He had done it many times. "I enjoy that story more and more every time I hear it," one roommate responded.

"I wonder what will happen to this man. We have been so very close. I wish we had a full church organization so I could show him the whole thing. Well, I have told him. He has heard my testimony, and perhaps sometime in the future, sometime when the Vietnamese won't be hammering at us, trying to destroy every value we have, the truth will become apparent," Jay thought.

Evidence of anti-war demonstrations and lack of support for the U.S. government was often presented to the POWs. In just two weeks after a demonstration, they would get movies with sound tracks. The North Vietnamese never lost a battle, never had a casualty. The prison officials used everything they could to break the prisoners down; they did everything they could to keep their own people motivated.

"They did things so much like the Church that it scared me. They have their kids sing about Ho Chi Minh; we teach our children to sing about Joseph Smith. They sing about their armies; we sing 'Hope of Israel, Zion's army.' In the Church we try to motivate people; the Vietnamese are masters at motivation. The difference is the purpose," Jay said.

The contacts Jay had with other LDS men while in prison were very limited. He felt their strength and hoped they felt his. "If it is just one word a year, it is something." He thought of the brief conversations, once or twice during his imprisonment, when he met Larry Chesley or Jay Jensen in the courtyard or during a move. It was against the rules for prisoners to talk to each other during those first years. Even with cell mates, conversation was secret, spoken in very low tones.

The days passed, and the time came when it appeared that there might be an opportunity to write a letter home. Jay was excited. He weighed in his mind the things he would like to say. "What will be the most important? What can I write that will be of more value than anything else?" He thought back of the day—months and months ago—when he had stood naked in the prison yard.

"The thing I want most to tell my family is about eternal life. That is the thing that is of most value. But there are also the basic simple things that are always taught in the Church that are important too—attendance at church, temple marriage, a mission. They are the steps along the way to eternal life. These are the things I will write about in my first letter."

He thought to himself, "Will this sound so spiritually strange to the Vietnamese censor that he will not allow the letter out?" He weighed the situation. It was worth a try. Jay wrote the letter many times in his mind. He worried—would it fit in the space allowed? He composed it again with fewer words. It would sound like a telegram.

There was excitement when he was escorted to a room, given pencil and paper, reminded of the restrictions—write only about health and family.

He knew just what he was going to say, but a rough draft was required first so it could be censored. What remained could then be rewritten for mailing.

"Dearest Marjorie, Cameron, Heather, Warren, Holly, Heidi. Above all I seek for eternal life with all of you. These are important; temple marriage, mission, college. Press on . . . set goals, write history, take pictures twice a year."

These few words, written by the now *Major* Hess on a small piece of paper, about four by five inches, carried the message that brought new hope and tears of joy to his family in Bountiful, Utah. A story appeared in the *Church News* about that important message of hope. With it was a photograph of the family. This photo was later sent to Major Hess in Hanoi.

"It was the best picture that any of the prisoners ever received, so clear and good. There were tears in my eyes when I saw it. It was the first I knew that the letter had gotten through." There were other letters, but none so significant as that first letter.

Jay thought again of the pencil he used to write the letter. "A pencil is so necessary to communicate, to organize and to direct your thoughts. It is a wonderful thing."

The day he left the prison Jay Hess again assured himself that eternal life is the most valuable possession. "How can I impress this idea on others, especially my children? I must take them a gift. My nephews and nieces and others in the family, they need a homecoming gift. A pencil," he thought. "When you live in a world where you have no means of writing, you learn to appreciate a pencil. It was a big loss to me not to have a pencil.

"If my children can appreciate being without means of writing things down, then maybe it will help them understand the significance of the loss of eternal life. I will put on those pencils an 'EL' to remind them of eternal life as they use the pencils. I will tell them about eternal life when I give the pencils to them.

Chapter 17

"At the End of the Storm Is a Golden Sky"

The telephone rang.

Mrs. Marjorie Hess, wife of Air Force Major Jay C. Hess, who had been a prisoner of war in North Viet Nam for five and one-half years, answered it.

"The phone had rung all morning," she said, "but as soon as I heard the operator ask about the number, I knew it was Jay." Marjorie had been expecting the call, but she didn't know when it would come. Even since a Mr. West from Hill Air Force Base had called her at a quarter to two one morning and told her that her husband was being released, she had waited for that call.

"That seemed like the longest time in my life, even longer than the time when Jay was gone. Of course, the six years were longer, but it's funny what time can do. The days you are anxiously waiting for something can seem endless."

Major Hess had just been repatriated with the third large group of POWs released from Hanoi. He was calling home from Clark Air Force Base in the Philippines. "He said, 'I don't want you to talk for a minute,' and then he recited to me the beautiful words of the song 'You'll Never Walk Alone.'

"The reason he recited the song," she explained,

"was that on the Sunday before he was repatriated a choir of prisoners had sung the song in prison. He said he could feel a lot of the bitterness of the men leave them in this wonderful service, so he wanted to repeat the words to me as he first contacted me and heard my voice.

"The words, particularly 'At the end of the storm is a golden sky,' were very moving to him. At the end of this long wait, there is a golden sky—that's the way he felt. It was very moving," she said, as tears welled up in her eyes.

"To hear his voice after six years was absolutely indescribable. It sounded exactly the same to me as I remembered it. But I didn't shed any tears, no tears. I had shed so many before that I often wondered what I would do when he called, and my family had wondered if they would be there when the call came."

It was a long five and one-half years for Mrs. Hess and her family of five children. Cameron, their oldest, was just eleven when his father went to Southeast Asia. When he returned, Cameron was nearly seventeen.

There were problems and heartaches while he was away. Grief struck the family over the Labor Day weekend in 1970 when their house in Bountiful, Utah, caught fire and the family barely escaped with their lives. "My daughter woke up as the smoke got to her first. She ran into my room and woke me up, and as I went into the front room, the flames were leaping up to the ceiling. We got Cameron up from downstairs, and he said, 'Mother, when I woke up I couldn't see my hand in front of my face bacause of so much smoke.'

"His room was next to the family room downstairs, and the family room had a chimney, which funneled the smoke from the upstairs. The fire was caused by a faulty fireplace chimney, which permitted the smoke to smolder behind the paneling until it broke into open flame.

"I grabbed a hose and started to spray water on the fire. A policeman soon arrived (we have a volunteer fire department in Bountiful) and said to get out right away because the roof could go any minute. We all got out and went across the street to the neighbors."

There, the family huddled together and helplessly watched their house burn. "I had many questioning thoughts that night, but everything is all right now," Mrs. Hess reflected. A fireman told Mrs. Hess that if they had stayed in the house another few minutes, they would have all died of smoke inhalation.

There were always a lot of nagging problems, like frozen pipes and clogged drains. "But in times like this, you do what has to be done." There were decisions to be made—never-ending decisions. There were times of sickness, and there was the waiting.

"Over the years I wondered, Why does it have to be so long? Anybody can endure something so long, but six years is such a long time to wait."

Major Hess was shot down August 24, 1967. "We had a feeling before he left that something would happen. I knew there were a lot of men going down that week. Jay was the thirteenth to be shot down that week.'

A short time later two men arrived at her home from Hill Air Force Base in northern Utah to tell her the news. "I had just come home from my first Waiting Wives group meeting where Elder Marion D. Hanks had spoken. I was just getting ready for bed, and the doorbell rang. It was about 11:30 P.M. I asked who it was, and a man answered, 'The chaplain from Hill Air Force Base.' Immediately I knew something had happened.

"After putting on a dressing gown, I opened the door and exclaimed, 'Oh, you're not going to tell me that Jay's dead!' And the chaplain replied, 'No, but he has been shot down.' There were two men and I invited them in. I don't know what have been the reactions of the other women, but I wanted the men to leave so I could be alone, which they did shortly. I found out later that the man with the chaplain was LDS. I should have recognized that, because when they walked in the room I felt a spirit that I could not discern immediately. It was there because that man held the priesthood."

For nearly three years, Mrs. Hess did not know if her husband was dead or alive. "However, I never thought of Jay as being dead from the moment they came to my door and said he had been shot down."

During April Conference in 1970, she received word from personnel at Randolph Air Force Base in Texas that her husband was alive. "I was singing at conference with the choir [Mormon Tabernacle Choir], and a call came in on that Friday. The children just told the caller that I was not home.

"On Saturday, I came home after the first session of conference and I told the children that if he called again to get his name and number. I had to run to the store, and in that ten minutes that I was gone, the man called again.

"I called back and got the information from the committee of liaison, the group in New York that handled the letters for prisoners, that Jay's name was on the list released by Hanoi as being a prisoner of war.

"I asked immediately to have a telephone number I could call, and I called and talked personally with the president of that organization. I told her that I had the press after me for a statement, and

I wanted to know how much validity I could put into the fact that he was a prisoner of war.

"She said, 'You can believe it's true, and you will have a letter from him in a few days.' I wondered how long those few days were going to be. The next day, I had a call from her, and she said, 'We have just received two letters from your husband, and they'll be on their way, or they're already on their way now.'

"I called the Post Office and the airport and said if the letters came in the middle of the night to call me and I would come after them. Well, as it turned out, they came two days later around noon when our mail was delivered by our Bountiful Post Office.

"The first letter I received started out with all our names. And he said, 'Above all, I seek for eternal life with all of you.' He told me later that he had wondered many times if I had ever received that first letter. He's very emotionally moved by the fact that I was able to get that letter.

"And he has given me—well, every letter we've had from Jay has been very strengthening and uplifting, always looking for the good, never the bad experiences or the hard times."

Mrs. Hess tried to fill the loneliness with other activities. She went on three trips with the Tabernacle Choir.

"We tried to have as many family nights as possible. We bowled, we went to movies. But to be honest, it was difficult toward the end, to really be in a very happy mood. In fact, my mother-in-law, Jay's stepmother, has said to people that she knows, 'Marge is a different girl,' and I was. It was not that I was always morose, but that it was constantly on my mind that Jay was a POW.

"I wondered what he was doing, how they were treating him. If I could have just dismissed those

From the Shadow of Death

thoughts from my mind, it might have been easier. But I just could not do that. My husband was in a prison in North Viet Nam. I had to hear the news every night. I had to know what was going on.

"During the entire time," Mrs. Hess added, "the thing that kept me going was the gospel. I once received a call from a woman who asked me to speak in her area. I told her that I was not physically up to it. That was last fall when I was expecting Jay to be released. She asked me a question, 'Tell me how through all of this, you've been able to stay faithful to your husband, and to keep your faith strong?' She said that everything around her was crumbling. The only answer I could give her was, 'The gospel has carried me through. It becomes so all-consuming.'

"I had down times. I was sick a lot. I doubted people because of human weakness. I doubted myself many times, but I never doubted the gospel— ever. The gospel brings all things into perspective. What I had to do years ago was make up my mind what I wanted. Jay was worth waiting for, and if we wanted to be together in the life after this with our families, then it was a matter of just waiting."

A week before her husband was released, Mrs. Hess attended a meeting in the Ogden Tabernacle, which she felt helped her to understand why she had to wait so long.

"Lynn McKinlay spoke about the life of Job. It was a beautiful experience. He described how Job was covered with boils, and said that he had to wait until those boils were ready to be lanced. He put emphasis on the waiting, that things have to be done at the right time. I felt as if he was talking right to me. I knew that was the reason why I had to wait so long.

"Sometimes the Lord teaches us that we have to wait for things in order for his works to go on as he knows best," she emphasized. "It may sound odd, but I look on this whole experience as a great blessing. It wasn't a blessing to have Jay away, but while he was gone, I developed and learned so much. The things I've learned have made me a better person. I feel it was for a purpose. It's helped me to understand things better. I have more empathy for people. I feel the Lord touched me with his finger, so to speak, and that I have been able to learn many great things."

Huge crowd attends Farmington, Utah homecoming given for Major Jay C. Hess upon his return from Viet Nam prison

Major Jay C. Hess and family salute the flag during homecoming ceremony at Farmington, Utah: left to right, Holly, Heidi, Captain Leonard Moon, who conducted the meeting, Warren, Major and Mrs. Hess

Major Jay C. Hess reports POW experiences to
Elder Boyd K. Packer of the Council of the
Twelve of the LDS Church

Major Jay C. Hess
ponders question at
press conference
held at Hill Air
Force Base, Utah,
following his return

Major Jay C. Hess is honored at testimonial dinner attended by Governor and Mrs. Calvin L. Rampton of Utah and Elder Marion D. Hanks, Assistant to the Council of the Twelve of the LDS Church

Charles Willis

Civilian, Pocatello, Idaho

Captured January 31, 1968, at Hue, South Viet Nam
Released March 27, 1973

Chapter 18

The Tet Offensive

The quiet of the night was broken on January 31, 1968, by the hail of mortar shells landing in the ancient capital city of Hue, South Viet Nam. An occasional mortar shell or a little skirmish of Viet Cong guerrillas had become almost routine during the past weeks for the people of Hue. But this was the Tet holiday, the Lunar New Year, and the North Vietnamese had declared a truce—there was to be no fighting.

That false security was shattered by an intensive burst of mortar shells and the movement of Viet Cong forces through the streets.

It took only two seconds for Charles "Chuck" Willis, civilian manager of Voice of America in Viet Nam, to bounce from his bed to the sandbag bunker he had built next to it.

"That one was close," he said to himself as he looked at his wristwatch. It was 2:30 in the morning.

He was joined a second later by his assistant radio engineer, Candidio "Pop" Badua of Baguio, Philippines.

They didn't see any immediate danger. This had been going on for months, and the bunker would provide the safety they needed. Chuck had added the bunker to his bedroom the same time he had protected his receiver and transmitter stations with nearly a million sandbags ordered from Japan. The receiver was four miles west of town, the transmitter four miles east of the city, and the office home for Voice of America was in downtown Hue.

In the next few minutes the house took several hits, and the shells kept coming. That morning more than three thousand 61 millimeter mortar shells of Chinese make fell in the area.

The two men sat in the dark, the prospect of sleep now gone. They thought about the transmitter, but it was protected by troops and mines and was well fortified.

About four o'clock in the morning the house took a direct hit, exploding into the room. The air mattress that Pop was sitting on was punctured, and the sound of the escaping air caused the two men to look at each other. "As the air went out of the mattress and Pop starting sinking, he put his hand out to catch himself and found blood on his hand. He thought he had been hit and was a bit shook up about it. It turned out to be my blood. I was so frightened that I didn't even feel the pain. I didn't discover the wounds on my leg until later when the dust settled," Willis related.

"The dust and smoke was so strong that we had to breathe through a blanket. The cordite (powder) fumes were burning our eyes.

"Within about an hour the shelling slowed, the dust settled, and we could hear voices." Crawling across the floor, still not dressed, Chuck peeped from the window and could see literally hundreds of guerrilla and National Liberation Front troops walking past the house. They were walking in broken ranks and not paying any special attention to the house.

"We could not tell what the voices were saying, even though Pop understood Vietnamese very well. The voices were mixed together. We did, however,

From the Shadow of Death

understand the intentions of the troops. They were all armed with guns and hand grenades and rockets."

Crawling back to the bunker, he checked his gun, an automatic weapon, called a grease gun. There were guards outside, four guards next door, and within three blocks, there were tanks and other heavy equipment at the military compound.

Chuck called for assistance. "I am sorry, Mr. Willis. We have tanks, but we have no drivers. It is a holiday; there is a truce and everybody is away," was the answer to the request.

Twelve miles away an American Marine task force was pinned down by more than 15,000 National Front for Liberation (NFL) troops. At DaNang and Saigon heavy Viet Cong attacks were underway.

The seven-day truce the Communists had proclaimed for Tet was later referred to as being clearly a hoax and a fraud. It was the beginning of the bloodiest week of the war up to that time, with 983 allied soldiers killed. Red casualties were 13,195. The battle for Hue lasted four weeks.

"About six A.M. a group of the Viet Cong separated from those walking past and surrounded my place. We immediately went to the bunker again, with the hope that some assistance would come. I had not bothered to dress, but my clothes were laid out ready for a quick departure.

"The mortars stopped, and we sat quietly. I took the safety off the grease gun. I was prepared to shoot anyone who came in the doorway. In the next couple of seconds I noticed the door being opened from the hall. I was ready with the gun. I heard someone at the other door, and I realized the only thing I could hope for was to shoot the first one. No one else would enter. They would just toss in a hand grenade and that would end both of us. So at the crucial moment of deciding whether to fight or surrender, with a hope of later getting a better chance of escape or rescue, I disengaged the gun, put it under the air mattress, and threw some blankets over it.

"I asked Pop to go out and surrender. I planned to get dressed before I had to go out. There was a small pistol in my trousers that might come in handy. Slowly Pop went out the door, speaking in Vietnamese. The guerrillas rushed in and forced me to remove my trousers, and within ten minutes we were taken from the house.

"I realized that my leg had been wounded as we were forced to walk to the stadium, only a block away. There we were lined up against the wall. It was obvious to him that he and six others, including his engineer, had been selected for execution.

"One Catholic man started saying his Hail Marys and praying very hard. I figured it was the end, but at that exact moment a North Vietnamese officer, dressed in a very neat khaki uniform, wearing a side arm, sun glasses, and a hat with a nice little Viet Nam star on it, ordered the guerrillas to lower their rifles. He talked to them for a few minutes and then ordered them to take us to Hanoi for interrogation.

"It was decided that we could go by boat. Hue is near the China Sea, about fifty miles south of the DMZ. We walked all night barefoot to reach the sea. We were exhausted by morning and were unable to leave by sampan because our Navy was pounding the beach with everything they had. Nothing was moving along that beach area. We struggled through three days of horrifying bombing, strafing, and shelling by the Navy.

"They gave up the trip by boat and told us we would walk to Hanoi. I had no shoes, I wasn't even dressed, and we had very little food. My arms had been tied all the time and they were swollen.

Even my hands had swollen so much that my wedding band was covered. I worried about blood poisoning because of the tightness of the ropes.

"They took Pop and me, the two of us, with five guards, and started north. There were no roads. Sometimes we traveled in a small boat; sometimes we tromped through the jungle. We walked for five days, still tied with rope and with no shoes. We walked through rice paddies for hours, squashing down in the mud. I stepped into a soft hole and fell forward. I was unable to cushion the fall with my hands tied behind me. I went face first in the mud and severely strained a ligament in my leg, which later gave me a great deal of difficulty and almost cost me my life."

Limping from the rice paddy, the group crossed Highway One, followed the railroad tracks, and then went into the mountains, traveling only by night. In the daytime they would hide in thatched huts or squat in the jungle.

Chuck was covered with mud, his feet were cut and swollen, the pulled ligament in his leg was extremely painful. He was cold and hungry. "As we moved into the mountains, I collapsed with fatigue. One of the guards, kicking and pulling, tried to get me up, but I couldn't move—I had had it. My leg was bleeding from wounds, my arms were bleeding and swollen. My tendon had begun to swell and was twice the size it should have been," Chuck said, figuring he couldn't take any more.

The guard cocked his gun. Chuck watched, unable to muster strength to resist and expecting to be shot. The VC showed no mercy. He had the gun pointed at Chuck's head. Pop came to his feet, jumped in front of the gun, and dragged Chuck to his feet. Pop was a small man, but somehow he found the strength.

"I was able to bury my face between his shoulder

blades, and he would give a tug and pull me as I hobbled along. We went on like that for another hour and then collapsed, but by that time we were far enough away from the danger area that the guards let us rest.

"They gave us food, rice, and vegetables, and we rested and slept for about five hours. By that time it was morning, and since we were under heavy jungle cover we could move during the daytime.

"For three days we traveled day and night, just resting when we couldn't make it anymore. We had moved westward across the narrow neck of South Viet Nam to the border of Laos. We came into the camp of thirty-two Americans who had also been captured in Hue and were being held there because most of them had been injured and were in bad physical condition."

This transient POW camp remained in the jungle for eight days, mending their wounds and gaining strength for the march to the north. Chuck's arms were untied, and the swelling decreased.

The larger group of thirteen prisoners, under guard, started toward Hanoi, walking forty-five minutes and resting five. "During the break we spent the time picking the leeches from our nearly naked bodies. They were the blood-sucker type and were smaller than the tip of my little finger, but after they got on, they would swell with blood to twice the size of my thumb. We had no way of getting them off except to pull them off, and each time a little bit of flesh would come with them. These little spots, of course, soon became infected and gave us a lot of trouble.

"We slept on the ground, with no blankets. It was during the very rainy season. It is a wonder we didn't all get pneumonia."

At that time the group was increased to about twenty-eight prisoners. Communicating as best they

From the Shadow of Death

could in a secret way, they planned their escape. As the prisoners were marched along the narrow jungle trails, those who were strong and healthy took the lead and moved out as fast as possible. The injured and weak prisoners moved slowly and thus stretched the line out as far as possible.

Two men were selected to escape. They were enlisted Army intelligence men, trained in escape and evasion. As the jungle train curved back and forth and the line got longer and longer, and the two men found a time that they could slip away unnoticed by the guards and made good their escape. They reached safety about two days later.

"The guards did not find out about the escape until that evening when we had our meal. They were very angry and said that two of the remaining must pay the penalty—for every one that escaped another prisoner would be shot.

"We had two women with us at this time, Dr. Carlson, a Quaker with the International Volunteer Service (IVS), and Sandra Johnson, a teacher from Rhode Island.

"These two women were selected to be shot. Dr. Carlson, about 35, attractive, dressed in a skirt and blouse, and Sandra, who was 25 years old, wearing a dress and barefooted, were taken aside, and preparations were made for their execution.

"As we waited helplessly, a high-ranking North Vietnamese officer came into the area. One of our members, a Canadian named Marc Cayer, ran over and started talking to the officer in French. The officer understood. Explaining that the girls had nothing to do with the escape, Marc volunteered to be killed in their place.

"The officer seemed to be touched by the speech. He made a radio call, and as a result it was decided that the women would not be killed, but sent back to their families."

Chuck then advised the two women that they should memorize the names of all the prisoners so they could tell the authorities when they got out. "We have been warned that we must not tell the authorities anything or that none of you will reach your destination," Dr. Carlson said.

"Then call my wife collect in the Philippines. She has worked for the FBI and will know how to handle a sensitive situation," Chuck said. They agreed, and Sandy memorized the names very quickly.

The group was divided, and Chuck and twelve other men continued through the jungle to the north. They traveled for fourteen days, crossed the DMZ, and went on to the area of Vinh Linh in North Viet Nam. The war was raging, and the bombing was so fierce that the group was unable to go on. In fear, one of the North Vietnamese made radio contact ahead but was unable to get permission to proceed. The bombings went on day and night as the weary prisoners huddled for protection.

"All of a sudden the sky caved in. It was March 15 [1968]. Two jets came with rockets and bombs. The rockets were everywhere, and all six bombs hit our camp. I was sharing a bowl of rice with the agricultural adviser from Hue, Tom Ragsdale of the IVS, when a bomb hit in our camp. Tom was killed instantly and I received fragments in my hip and leg. Several of the VC were also killed.

"When night came, we dug a grave for Tom with our rice bowls. We laid him in the shallow grave and covered him with soil and rocks, erecting a wooden cross made from a small tree." The twelve captive Americans had a short graveside service, conducted by Chuck, who had the civilian rank equivalent to an Army colonel, making him the ranking member of the group. The weary and

From the Shadow of Death

battered POWs bowed their heads in prayer as Chuck said a few appropriate words. Tom's body was located about four months later by American forces. Seeing the cross and recognizing the name as American, they removed the body. Positive identification was made, and the remains were returned to his home.

"After Tom was killed, we walked for another day and then were put on trucks. For thirteen nights we traveled. We went into Laos and back into North Viet Nam and eventually arrived in a camp near the border of Laos.

"We were put in small bamboo cages, three feet wide, five feet high, and five feet long. They were woven so tightly that we couldn't see daylight through them. We could not stand up or lie down.

"This was a very trying time. My wounds became infected, and maggots began to eat the dead tissue. I worried about blood poisoning and would drift in and out of consciousness.

"They kept insisting on interrogating me. They wanted me to admit that I was a psychological warfare agent, that I had come to kill their women and children, and that I was a clandestine operator using the Voice of America as a front to carry on a subversive war."

"I refused to admit these crimes they accused me of, thinking that if I admitted them, they would assassinate me. After about a week of this, I didn't have my real mind—I couldn't even think straight, yet they kept interrogating me. They would ask me if I had reformed my mind. I would tell them no. The next day, it would be the same questioning over again," Chuck said.

"Have you reformed your mind yet?" the interrogator asked. "I have reaffirmed my mind quite well," he responded. Chuck had said *reaffirmed* and the Vietnamese thought that he had said *reformed*.

"Now we are getting somewhere," the interrogator said and offered a cup of tea to the startled prisoner.

Chapter 19

Lizards for Company

The next day Chuck received medical help. The bomb fragment was removed from his hip, and his other injuries were treated. That was March 28, 1968.

Once the Vietnamese were satisfied that Chuck had admitted to their charges, he was given a penalty. Taking out a little black book, the interrogator thumbed through the pages and said, "The people's penalty for a psychological warfare agent in our country is one year in solitary confinement, with two feedings a day and no association."

Chuck was put back in the cage, where he remained until July 3, 1968. "I had thought I would be killed if I admitted to their charges. Instead, I was then taken to a maximum security prison, built by the French and called Camp 77, located twelve miles south of Hanoi. I was interviewed by the Vietnamese when I arrived."

"The people of North Viet Nam are kind and human," the prison officer said. "Since you have already spent three months in the cage, you will not have to serve those days over again. You will only have to serve nine months in solitary confinement at this prison to complete your sentence."

"That was the last daylight I saw for nine

months. There was no conversation; I couldn't even speak to the guard.

"I had three unmatched boards to sleep on, a ragged mosquito net, blankets, and my own sanitary bucket in that dungeon-like cell. The room was six feet by six feet with a twelve-foot high ceiling. At the very top were two vent holes about four inches square. The door was heavy wood, with a peep hole about four inches high and eight inches long that had a sliding panel on the outside. There were two locks, one in the door with a key about eight inches long, and a bar that fit on the outside with a padlock.

"The guard would bring my food to the door, which was opened by the turnkey, and would place the food inside. An hour later, they would come back to pick up the bowl. They gave me red rice, boiled cucumber, squash, or pumpkin. There was no fat, no oil, no meat.

"There was no medical treatment. My hip became infected and started to drain, but it finally healed up on its own.

"The only association I had was with a lizard that came in the little vent holes at the top of the room. I named him Herman. He was a nice guy and we got along very well. I would talk to him—well, actually, he turned out to be Hermina and had baby lizards. I had a whole roomful of lizards before it was over.

"The lizards were quite a bit of company, but I could only see them for a couple of hours in the morning, when the sun shone through the vent holes twelve feet above.

"Once a frog came in when the door was opened during the rainy season. He just hopped in when they put the food in. We were good friends until he ate my pet spider.

"I tried tapping to contact the other men in the

prison, but the walls were so thick that we were unable to make communication effective. If we shouted to each other it would cost us a meal. I spoke to the turnkey one day, asking for some medication—I had very bad sinus trouble. Because I spoke to him, I didn't get any food that day. I didn't receive any medication, so I never asked again."

To keep his mind occupied Chuck worked mathematical problems in his mind. He found quadratic equations very entertaining, especially when he got the right answer.

"I built a house for my family—I thought a lot about them. I built a boat and worked on many other projects.

"I would reminisce over the years, like a continued story of a soap opera. I would start remembering what had happened to me when I was six years old and would take it up with myself for that morning. In the afternoon I would work on math or other projects. I had studied math and engineering," he said.

Chuck remembered back to 1947 when he had met the little Mormon girl from Idaho. She had earlier signed up for the WAVES during World War II, and since her birthday was the same date as when the WAVES were organized, she was sworn in on their birthday. The press made a story of it. The war ended with VJ Day before she was inducted, and she was discharged before she could even get going. That was a disappointment to her, so she applied for a job with the FBI and was working in Washington, D.C., when he met her.

In this dungeon cell, he remembered their marraige and the birth of their first son, Charles Riedel, in Tampa, Florida. Chuck had been in the Air Force at that time, and he remembered those days with Strategic Air Command.

Their second son, Howard James, was born in

Alaska, where Chuck worked for the Federal Aviation Agency at a transoceanic transmitter site.

During the lonesome night hours in Alaska, he listened to Voice of America broadcasts. He was impressed with what he heard and with the idea of projecting the American image on a peaceful basis to other countries.

"I felt I could contribute a little to the betterment of mankind by working for Voice of America, so I went to Washington, D.C., and in three days I had signed on the dotted line."

Following a year of training, he was assigned as receiver site supervisor of the relay station in the mountain city of Baguio, Philippines. On a hot July 12, 1965, he arrived for his new assignment. His family accompanied him. Less than two years later, on January 12, 1967, he was assigned to Hue, South Viet Nam.

"I wasn't very happy about my husband's assignment to Viet Nam," Mrs. Willis said. "I thought there were other people who could have done the job, but because of his special ability he was chosen.

"The first news I had of any invasion of Hue was in January 1968 when the teletype was cut off. The VOA office called to say it was out, but that was not alarming because it had gone out before. When it didn't come back on for several days, I began to suspect that there was more to it. There were other women with husbands in Viet Nam, and one by one they received word from their husbands, but there was nothing from Chuck. There was not a word until March 27, 1968.

"I waited from January until March 27 for any word about Chuck. The word I got was that he had been seen March 4 alive and well as a POW. Again in April I heard that two women who had been released reported that they had seen him and that he

From the Shadow of Death

was having trouble with his feet, but was otherwise well.

"It was nice to know that he was alive and well. That was the only word I had about him until the end of 1972 when Navy Lieutenant Markham Aigon Gartley reported a small bit of information," Mrs. Willis said.

Gartley was released with two other POWs, Navy Lieutenant Norris Charles and Air Force Major Edward K. Elias, on September 17, 1972. A special ceremony was held in Hanoi, and the men returned in a twelve-day trip by way of Peking, Moscow, and Copenhagen. Gartley had been a POW for four years, Charles for nine months, and Elias for five months.

"Lieutenant Gartley said that he had a room-mate who knew of a prisoner in camp by the name of Charles 'Pop' Willis. I knew it was true because of the way it was put. Pop Badua was the Filipino engineer who was with my husband, and the names had become mixed. Pop was there and was released with the first group along with another Filipino.

"It was a long wait. At first, I was told that they would not hold my husband because he was a civilian, but as time went on, we began to realize that he was being held."

Mrs. Willis and the two boys left the Philippines on June 1, 1968, and returned to the United States by boat, a trip requiring twenty-one days.

"We came back to Pocatello, Idaho, where my mother lived, and then took a trip east to visit Chuck's folks and also Red Cross officials in Washington, D.C. We wanted to find out where we could write so Chuck would receive the letters.

"We were given the names of several groups. I wrote through the Red Cross and twenty or thirty other addresses and several other countries, but he never received any of my letters, and I never received a letter from him during all the time. No letter was ever returned, but a Christmas package I sent in 1968 was returned, in August 1969, in perfect condition. It had never been opened, but was stamped on the outside, 'Refused by the National Liberation Front,' " she explained.

There was little compassion for Chuck in his dungeon cell. "There was one guard, an elderly man, who used to come on Sunday morning. He would not speak to me, but he had some feeling of compassion. He would shake his head in a sympathetic way.

"I prayed—we all prayed or we would not have made it through," he said. "There were eighteen cells in our block. There were many times that some of the prisoners back there would go out of their minds. They would scream. I could hear them banging around and slamming their bodies against the walls of their cells.

"These were the most trying times for me. I would be awakened in the night when one of the prisoners would start screaming. It would catch on and go from one cell to another. One man would start, and this would cause another to go over the edge and he would start. Soon there would be four or five of them yelling and screaming. I would find myself standing in the middle of the floor, with my fists clinched. I would shout every mean and hateful thing I could say to make myself angry. I couldn't be quiet and peaceful; I just had to blow off steam. I had to explode or I would lose my mind," he said.

Chuck was kept in solitary confinement at Camp 77 for nine months and then moved over to the other side of the prison where he shared a room with three other Americans. One of his roommates was Captain Floyd M. Thompson, who had been a captive for nearly nine years. He was captured March 26,

1964, while serving as an adviser to the South Vietnamese. The other two men were Lewis Meyer, a fire fighter at the Navy storage department in Hue, captured February 1, 1968; and Lawrence J. Stark, manager, U.S. Navy Supply, DaNang, captured February 1, 1968.

"The four of us lived in one room fifteen feet long and eight feet wide with iron bars for a door. We found the bars made the room uncomfortable— the heat came in during the summer, and the cold came in during the winter.

"We had two waste buckets in the room. Each day they were set just outside the door for the trustees who worked at the prison to empty. We discovered that we could use them for communication. After the buckets had been taken by the trustees, they were mixed with other buckets and we did not get the same buckets back. We found that we could pass messages by squeezing some rice and making a paste out of it. With the paste we would stick a message to the bottom of the bucket. Sometimes it took two weeks to get an answer from just three cells away.

"The guards found out about this system of communication, and some of us were punished for it. But there was some excitement, looking on the bottom of the buckets every day to see if there was a message."

"We were given a four-post bed with board slats and a rice mat for a cover. I had developed large calluses from lying on my left side because of the injuries on my right hip. The calluses became very hard and crusty and would crack and bleed. I would have to peel them by layers.

"Conditions were much better in this room than in solitary confinement, and we lived here for more than two years. At this time we were never allowed out in the compound, though we were taken one day each month for interrogation.

"I had a scare during one of those interrogations. The Vietnamese asked me about a man that I had a slight acquaintance with, but had forgotten until they recalled him to my memory. He was a man that my wife had known in Pocatello before we were married, a man she had gone out with years ago." Chuck explained.

"Did you know your wife is running around with this man and having an affair?" the interrogator asked Chuck.

"Oh," Chuck answered, "that's all right as long as they are old friends."

The interrogator was not only startled, but he was shaken. The technique that he had used to anger Chuck had indeed been reversed. He just sat there and looked at Chuck for five minutes before storming from the room with such anger that the guards came rushing in with fixed bayonets.

"They stood very rigid with their bayonets pointed at me, and I looked right back at them. Finally the interrogator came back into the room. He shook his head and said, 'I don't understand you Americans.' I understood his technique. It was to make me angry and catch me off guard. It was like a battle of wits to see who could pull what on whom."

On December 12, 1971, Chuck was again moved. This time he went to a prison camp north of Hanoi, near the China border. Here the cells were built in a continuous long row, with a seven-by-twelve-foot courtyard built in front of each cell and a nine-foot wall, covered with barbed wire on top.

There was a table, chair, bed, and water closet in each room. The water tank was fed by a mountain stream using bamboo tubing. The water closet was a hole in the floor with two-foot blocks.

"This prison camp was an improvement. But one day a typhoon passed over, and a dam in the mountains broke, flooding the camp. Within fifteen minutes the water was knee deep in my cell. The toilets all back flushed, and still the guards would not let us out. I was on the high end of the cell block. The water was much deeper at the other end. Before it was too late, the guards finally took the men at the lower end out and then proceeded up the row.

"We were still in solitary and unable to talk to each other, so they had to take us out one at a time and put a bamboo blind in front of us so we could not see each other. The water continued to rise. It was quite an experience to be locked up with the water getting higher and higher—like 'The Pit and the Pendulum.'"

When the peace feelers started, there was some concern about the health of the POWs. Many of them were starving and in very bad condition.

"I had beri-beri and scurvy. All of my teeth were loose, and my eyes and legs were swollen. Following an inspection of our camp, I was given twenty-eight shots of vitamin B-1 in a period of about a week. They gave me a bag of three hundred multiple vitamin tablets. They even sent a camp officer, by bicycle, into a village about five miles away to bring back limes and lemons to feed us."

The North Vietnamese instituted other prison improvements as the peace talks proceeded. POWs were shifted, mostly to Hanoi, and privileges were added, such as having books available and having recreational opportunities.

"When I got to the Hanoi Hilton, January 27, 1973, they were passing out magazines and books to read. As they passed out the books, the handed me a copy of the *Ensign* magazine. It was the June 1971 issue with the conference talks in it. I read it from cover to cover and passed it on to Colonel Benjamin H. Percell of Columbus, Georgia. He was a very religious Southern Baptist, who had made a small chalice and covered dish for his sacrament each Sunday. He wanted to take the magazine home with him, but they would not allow that. There were some interesting talks concerning the young people, their marriage, their family, and their obligation to themselves, their country, and their religion. Colonel Percell wanted to pass the ideas on to his young people.

"I have no idea how the magazine got to Hanoi," he said.

Many strange and interesting things happened in the Vietnamese prisons.

"Monica, a German nurse, was in our camp at one time. The guards had given her a kitten, and it had grown to be a good-sized cat. Its life had been a prison life, and it would visit each cell, wandering back and forth in search of a handout of food. We didn't have much and we didn't share much, but when the cat came around we gave it a little to eat.

"Monica made a collar for the cat. We called him Mew, the Vietnamese word for cat. We would put messages in the fold of the collar. He was a very good mailman. If he visited my cell one day and I put a message in the collar, chances are I would get an answer back in three days. Mew made his rounds pretty regularly. The guards never did catch on to what he was doing."

At the Hanoi Hilton the American prisoners taken in South Viet Nam were kept separate from other prisoners. When he arrived at the Hanoi Hilton, Colonel Theodore W. Guy of Tucson, Arizona, who had been captured March 22, 1968, was in charge of the military prisoners and Philip W. Manhard, an employee of the State Department from McLean, Virginia, who was captured January

31, 1968, was in charge of the civilian prisoners captured in South Viet Nam.

The civilian portion of the camp was not run on a military basis, but rather according to democratic vote system. If something had to be done, Mr. Manhard asked for a vote and then represented the prisoners with the decision to the camp commander. On many occasions Chuck, who was second in command, accompanied him. When Mr. Manhard was freed with the first group of POWs, it became Chuck's responsibility to take command.

Almost daily he had contact with the camp commander, Mr. Mao, and his assistant. They both spoke English, and with the little bit of French that Chuck could speak, they communicated very well. A fairly good relationship developed.

"I had a birthday party at the Hanoi Hilton. I had been working with the camp commander and was very displeased with the conditions at the medical ward. I had also been in the mess hall to see how the food was prepared and had some suggestions for improving the sanitation there. The commander had heard that I intended to speak to the people of the world about how the Communists treated human beings. I had made the statement months earlier in the hope of getting better food, but I only got into trouble. They wanted me to write down what I was going to say. I refused and was severely interrogated. I was given civilian clothes and sunglasses and taken to Hanoi incognito to the foreign office, where I talked to one of the central committee.

"He said that I only needed to submit an outline of what I was going to say so they could fill me in on their side of the story. I refused.

"So my reputation had gone before me, and because I was the senior officer, they were making things as pleasant for me as possible under the circumstances. I was given a birthday party. They gave me special treats and talked about the Voice of America. They offered gifts, which I refused unless they would give a gift to every man.

"I explained that if they wanted to know what I was going to say, it would be available in the near future, as soon as I got out. They wished me a long life, lots of happiness, and good health and sent me back to my cell.

"Because I had lost so much weight—fifty-one pounds—I was given triple rations. We had the opportunity to play ping-pong, and I did have a contest against the guards one time. They were too good for us," he said.

Chuck had been to downtown Hanoi three times. Once he was taken with four other men to be shown the damage done by the B-52 raids.

"We had contended that we didn't think the Americans would bomb the hospitals, churches, and downtown. They told us we were lying, and to prove their point they took us on a tour.

"We were given civilian clothes and taken to Hanoi and the outlying area. I saw that hospital that was so much spoken of as having been destroyed. One end of the building was damaged, but 95 percent was standing and still in use. The pictures they took only showed the damage.

"Another group of us was taken on a tour of downtown and to the museum. The museum was open to the public, and there were other people there. We were in civilian clothes, and I am sure there were also guards in civilian clothes.

"It was very unlikely that the Vietnamese citizens would try to do any bodily harm to us because they are so repressed by the military and secret police that they would not dare to make trouble," he said.

Chuck had been scheduled to leave Viet Nam with the second group, but because he had made such a point that the sick and wounded should be the first to leave, the camp commander asked, "Would you let one of them go home in your place?"

"I had already talked to the men, and I knew I was right in answering, 'There is not a man in our camp who would not gladly give up his place to let one of the injured and sick go home.' "

There was no response to the conversation, and Chuck was sent back to his cell as they continued to process him for his trip home.

He had in mind a friend, Captain Theodore Gostas, a Wyoming man who had been captured in Hue on February 1, 1968. At the time, Gostus had twenty-eight abessed teeth and was emotionally troubled following seventeen sessions of torture at the camp with the cages. He needed immediate help, and Chuck had asked that he be sent home immediately with the next group. There were eight others who were also suffering and needed attention.

"Two days before the group left, the camp commander took me out of the cell and put Captain Gostas in my place. Several others were also changed." Chuck was moved to the last man on the list of the captives to come out.

It was raining in Hanoi the last day that Chuck spent in prison. The POWs were called at six A.M. and taken from their cells to the compound area. Standing at one end of the hall, they were ordered to strip to the nude and leave their prison clothes.

Their skinny bodies were pale from lack of sun, but their bones protruded less than they had a few months earlier, for they had enjoyed double rations in a forced-feeding program.

The men left their pajama prison garbs in a pile on the floor and at a command walked to the other end of the hall and picked up new clothes for the trip home.

The sizes weren't exact, but it was "good to get some decent clothes," Chuck thought.

"We were given leather shoes, manufactured in Hanoi, of a modern style with blunt toes. They were fairly nice. We were given boxer-type shorts and a tee shirt, both made in Russia. Our socks were cotton knit, from China. The trousers were pale green cotton, and we had a white short-sleeved shirt, made in Hungary. We wore a windbreaker jacket made in Austria.

"We each had a haircut before we left. We didn't know that long hair was the style or we could have come out that way.

"One of our men had been a barber, and he managed to get an old pair of rusty clippers, a pair of scissors, and a comb from the guard. We lined up and got haircuts. I still owe for mine; he was taking verbal IOUs.

"The camp commander decided to allow all of the men in my compound to have a gift, and most of them received what they asked for. I accepted a comb for my wife that had been made from a B-52 and also a recording of a cultural show that had been given the night before."

The men waited for two hours because of a disagreement over procedure. It was three hours before they were picked up in the bus.

"We left the Hanoi Hilton by the front gate and got on a bus. There were thousands of people there to see us go. There were hundreds of soldiers in the area. The people were cheering and smiling, and some little children waved at us. An elderly women threw a rock at the bus.

"We crossed the Red River to the airport. They held us behind the hangars for another two hours while more negotiating went on; there was still a possibility that we might not go.

"They gave us each a loaf of bread, a drink, and

a can of meat. It was only eleven A.M. and I couldn't eat all my food. I carried the bread to the Clark Base hospital where it was examined and found to have very little nourishment.

"When it was time to go, we lined up. There was a tent for the dignitaries with microphones set up in front. My name was called out and I moved up and repeated my name, made a right turn, and met my escort, Mr. Lawrence, from the State Department. He took me to the airplane," Chuck recalls.

"As I went up the ramp of the aircraft, the first thing that stared me in the face was a pretty Air Force nurse in a miniskirt. It was the first one I had seen, and I didn't think it could be true. When I got on the plane, I saw that the other nurses were dressed the same, except the head nurse. She was wearing the old-style uniform. That nurse in a miniskirt was my first cultural shock."

Following the short debriefing at Clark Air Force Base, Chuck was flown to Bethesda, Maryland, because it was close to his agency and convenient for his family. He arrived home March 30, 1973.

On the tenth floor of the Bethesda Hospital his wife and two sons waited. Mrs. Willis wore an orchid sent by President Richard M. Nixon. From the window they could see the helicopter, lit by floodlights, as it landed in the night.

There was a crowd in the lobby. Photo flashes were going off as Chuck made his way to the elevator.

Peeking around the door were the boys, now taller than their father. "He's coming. He's coming," they shouted as he turned down the hall.

In a moment there were hugs and kisses and six years of hellos.

Howard, his youngest son, a four-year seminary graduate, said, "I hugged and squeezed him until I felt things start to crunch. He looked so thin from how I remembered him that I don't think I would have recognized him if I had seen him on the street. His cheek bones were really prominent; he was so thin."

Chuck looked up at his towering son, Robby, who had gotten the news that his father was coming home while he was working out on the trampoline at Brigham Young University.

Soon the room was filled with relatives. Chuck's parents were there and many others. It was an exciting time to catch up on all that had happened and make plans for the future.

Chuck received the Award for Valor, the highest award given to an American civilian, on May 24, 1973. Three days later, he was promoted as a foreign service officer, a civilian rank equivalent to that of a military general.

Chuck did as he said he would: he made a thirty-minute broadcast for Voice of America. The message has been translated into twenty-three different languages. The world will hear what he has to say.

This building was residence and office of Charles E.
Willis at the time he was captured during Tet offensive
in 1968

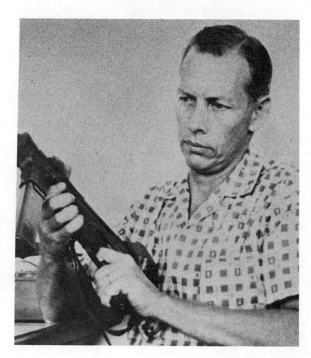

Charles E.
Willis was
armed with
automatic
weapon,
known as
grease gun,
but decided
against firing
at captors

Charles E. Willis addresses citizens during homecoming
celebration at Washington, North Carolina

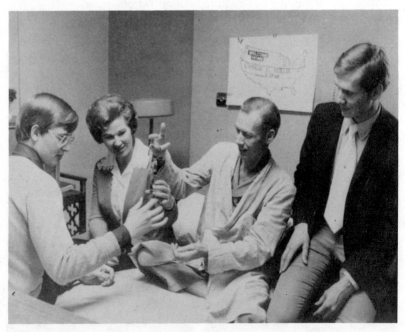

Charles E. Willis shows POW bracelets to his family: left to
right, Howard, Mrs. Willis, Mr. Willis, and Rody.

From the Shadow of Death

Mrs. Charles E. Willis is happy to have her husband home; she received no letters from him during his five years as POW

Charles E. Willis smiles with two sons, Howard, left, and Rody, who have outgrown him during his five years in Viet Nam prisons

Charles E. Willis received "Award of Valor," highest civilian award, for his courage and stamina as POW

Commander Dale H. Osborne

Navy, San Diego, California

Shot down September 23, 1968, near Vinh, North Viet Nam
Released February 12, 1973

Chapter 20

The Man Who Wouldn't Die

Two sleek A4F Skyhawk fighter bombers streaked across the Vietnamese sky. The late afternoon sun was dimmed by the gray overcast sky that threw a dullness onto the green landscape that was already turning brown and red as the fall season began.

It was September 23, 1968, the time about three P.M.

Navy Commander Dale Osborne, then thirty-five years old, a native of Salt Lake City, was at the controls, his large six-foot-three-inch frame filling the cockpit, his skillful hands controlling the plane as the powerful jets pushed against the humid sky.

The two planes coasted into the mission area, a water-borne target, just north of the city of Vinh, midway in the panhandle of North Viet Nam. It was an armed reconnaissance flight, and the roar of the motors had been diminished as the planes·swooped in.

"It was a bad day, visibility about five thousand feet and overcast. As we coasted through the area, the flak got quite heavy. I was in the rear and above the section leader, and it appeared that they started to use barrage fire. I told him to break. The shelling was getting heavy. I saw the target

193

as I pulled into the clouds to escape the fire, and estimated my rocket run position," Commander Osborne said.

A moment later, his Skyhawk broke from the cloud cover over the target. "I made my rocket run and was pulling off the target, climbing with all the power I had." The high-pitch whistle of the jet shot across the countryside, telling the message of the pilot: "Let's get out of here."

The anti-aircraft fire increased, the puffs of black smoke leaving telltale signs of the exploding shells. One of those shells found its target. It hit the cockpit of Commander Osborne's plane. "I didn't know what happened; I was knocked unconscious," he said.

The plane, now out of control, its wounded pilot slumped over the controls, wobbled in the sky and continued with great force through the air. As the shell exploded in the plane, shrapnel flew in every direction. One piece hit Commander Osborne's chin and lodged in the roof of his mouth. It was like a prizefighter's blow to the chin— Osborne was out.

"I came to sometime later. I don't know how long I had been out. Suprisingly calm, I thought, 'Where am I? I tried to see, but I couldn't; my vision was impaired. Everything was black. I could smell smoke now in my oxygen mask. I knew I had to get out, the plane would crash any second.

"I reached down with my right hand to pull the ejection handle. My hand wouldn't work—I couldn't use it. I couldn't see what was wrong; it was a terrible feeling. The fear of crashing filled my mind. I didn't know how long I had been out or how high the plane was. I felt numb all over. I reached down with my left hand, wrapped it around my right hand and gave a pull. I remember

From the Shadow of Death

the canopy leaving the airplane, and I started up the rocket rail and passed out again."

The plane went on, damaged and unguided, to crash in the countryside or the sea. How long it flew—how far it went—is something Osborne will never know.

The wounded pilot, his parachute opening automatically, floated down without his guidance. How far he floated or how long it took, he did not know. "When I came to I was lying on the ground, struggling to breathe. I realized that my bail-out bottle was out of oxygen."

Automatically, he tried to remove the mask. He fumbled with helpless hands at the fittings. By now some of his vision had returned, and through blurry eyes he looked at his right hand. It was shattered at the wrist, bones sticking out, just barely hanging to his arm. He tried to use his left hand. It had been broken during the ejection or upon hitting the ground.

He was bleeding from his mouth. He could feel with his tongue that his teeth had been knocked out. They were lodged in his head, and remained so during his imprisonment. In desperation he nosed his face into the ground to scrape the oxygen mask from his mouth and nose. He spit, he breathed, and as he did, he blacked out again.

He had not landed unnoticed. The North Vietnamese started to gather around. At first they looked upon him in fear. He was not a pretty sight. They approached with caution, not knowing whether he was dead or alive. Soon there were nearly twenty people surrounding the downed airman. One was brave enough to touch him. Someone took the watch from his broken wrist. Someone else grabbed his helmet. When he came to again, his clothes were being ripped off.

"They found my survival radio and wanted me to speak into it. I couldn't understand what they said, but I supposed they wanted me to call the other aircraft back. I remember shaking my head negatively, and then I became groggy and passed out." The scavengers continued the process of looting the unconscious pilot. Piece by piece they stripped him down to his shorts. Some of the bloody clothes they threw away.

They surveyed Commander Osborne, his wounds, his unconscious condition and the loss of blood. He would die, they thought. They slowly, one by one, walked away.

"When I woke up again I could see the Vietnamese walking away. They were about seventy-five yards away. They had just left me there. They figured that I wasn't worth bothering with, and they knew that I couldn't go anywhere. Realizing my precarious position, I started yelling and waving one arm."

Osborne craned his neck to see better from his ground position. With anxious eyes he watched the Vietnamese pause as he yelled. They hesitated a moment, and then encouraging each other, they started walking back.

The events were dim in the mind of Commander Osborne. He thanked the Lord for their return to help. He began to realize that it was a miracle that he was alive. It was a miracle that he had come to just long enough to pull the ejection handle. It was a miracle that he had survived the unconscious landing.

The Vietnamese placed him on a stretcher. He had not realized that his legs were badly wounded, or that his body was punctured nearly fifty times with shrapnel.

"I woke up that night in a bamboo hut. It was dark now so I knew some time had passed. I was in extreme pain. I was lying on my stomach. Twisting my head, I could see two medical people wearing white smocks doing something to my left leg. This was the first time I knew anything was wrong with my leg, and it felt as though they were stripping all the skin from my ankle and foot. The pain was severe. I started screaming and pleading for some pain killer, some morphine or something. They just kept going and I passed out again."

Commander Osborne slept. Hallucinations filled his mind. The next day passed and he was still uncounscious. The medics left, but others watched as he lay on the ground of the large hut.

"When I was clear again," he said, "I found a couple of young girls looking after me. They were about nineteen years old and very pretty. They were fairly nice to me. They would feed me rice and give me tea, never as much as I wanted, but at least they were doing something. My legs were both bandaged. They were not broken; it was shrapnel damage. There were two large holes in my left leg, most of the left calf was gone, and there was a large hole in my thigh.

"It was also a miracle that I had even survived the shell explosion in the cockpit, that no vital organs were hit."

For several days, he lay on the dirt floor, near death. He was very weak from the injuries and from the loss of blood. He passed from consciousness from time to time, as the two girls cared for him.

The hut was quite large—a family residence. The family slept on table-like beds at the other end of the room. They were frightened at first, then curious as the dramatic events unfolded. First, they watched from a distance, somewhat concerned that their house had been taken over. As the days passed, they came closer and introduced themselves to the American pilot. First an old man and an old lady came up. Commander Osborne could not understand the language, but he could get the message that they were making themselves acquainted with him. Then two young couples and several children and even the babies were introduced.

As the news spread in the village that an American was in the hut, individuals and small groups of the citizens came to see him. "Some of the visitors looked down on me with pity, some with animosity, a few even kicked me, and others stared apathetically.

"The girls continued to help me. I could not use my arms or legs and they had to do everything. They would help me to the bathroom, which was quite embarrassing—the whole family was around watching. But I had bigger worries than embarrassment, and I was grateful for their help.

"I was having hallucinations much of the time and I kept trying to buy my way back to Manila. I asked the girls to help me. I asked for a pencil and paper and wrote as best I could with my left hand, which was in a sling, a message to the disbursing officer on my ship. I wanted him to send me fifteen hundred dollars for medical expenses. I signed the note and gave it to the people, thinking if I could get some money, I could get the medical attention I so badly needed. If they would just put me on a plane to Manila I would be glad to pay for that too.

"I worried a great deal about my family at that time, and I prayed a lot, but I had a hard time concentrating on anything. My mind would wander."

Time was unaccountable for Commander Osborne. But sometime later they put him on a stretcher and on a truck. The bouncing and turning of the truck offered only a background for his already twilight condition. He couldn't know how

From the Shadow of Death

far he traveled, or in which direction. He was taken to a small hut.

He did know he was thirsty—he needed water. He did know he was cold—he needed clothing.

The treatment got progressively worse. Osborne received no attention. He wished that the two young girls were there to care for him, but he was alone, lying on the floor, a wooden board for a bed. The pain continued.

Osborne devoted all of his energy to just staying alive. He could feel himself growing weaker and weaker. "They stopped giving me water for some reason. The bandages were getting dirty; I knew that I needed attention. I could feel I was slipping, and I wanted very much to see another American, just anyone.

"Most of my thoughts were with my family, what they were going to do if I died and how it would affect them. I prayed very hard. It was good to have someone to talk to.

"I kept seeing my wife's face as we had kissed and parted. 'Don't make me a widow,' she had said. I thought of that all the time. I wasn't thinking of my condition as much as I was thinking of my family."

There was no way to be comfortable. He shifted his head from side to side in anxious anticipation of help. He listened for every footstep that approached the little hut. He watched every shadow that passed the open door. He watched with hope, but they did less and less for him.

He slept a great deal. It was one way to escape the thirst and pain. One day he awoke to the noise of a spade digging in the ground near the hut. He could hear the sound through the earth; his ear was on the dirt floor of the hut. Twisting his head and focusing his eyes, he could see a man digging a hole in the yard. The realization—

like a slow curtain of a theater opening—hit him: "They are digging my grave! I could see them digging it, and I knew it was for me."

Osborne watched with disgust. His determination not to die became stronger. They seemed in a hurry to finish the hole. Some of the dirt they carried inside the hut, something Osborne could not understand.

"One night I woke up and they were lowering me into that hole. I could see the deep sides as I looked up at their faces. I started yelling."

The ropes jerked quickly, and he was pulled again to the surface. In his unconscious condition they had thought he was dead. With short steps and excited conversation they carried him back to the hut.

Osborne's mood was not for sleep, yet he was so weak he knew no night or day, but only periods of consciousness alternated with periods of sleep. "I awoke once to see an old man at my side. He looked concerned, but I had grown very suspicious. He spoke words I could not understand, and unfolding his hand he offered me a string of beads with a cross on it. I would not take it; I thought it was more to do with my dying. I wouldn't die, and I cursed the old man so he went away.

"I have thought since that it was a bad show on my part. He was a Christian, and I suppose he was trying to offer me comfort the best way he knew how. I thought he was trying to harass me. The thing I needed was a drink of water.

"They offered me food periodically, but it would be some old bread or something that I had no appetite for. My tongue started to swell and my lips were cracking and hot. I fevered, and my thirst was even greater." Soon after the grave experience, Osborne started to travel again. He was anxious to be moving north; he hoped things would be better if he reached Hanoi.

He was taken from the stretcher and placed on the back of a flatbed truck that served as ambulance, bus, and cargo truck. The soldiers and citizens took advantage of any transportation that was available.

"As the truck started to move, I had no way to hold on. My arms and legs were useless and I was just lying on the bed of the truck. The roads were really bad, I guess from bomb craters, chuckholes, and the rainy weather. I still had no clothing, and as the truck lumbered along, I bounced up and down. For hours we rode. Large holes started wearing in my back. My shoulder blades became raw. An open sore developed on the back of my head. My hips and buttocks were worn away in large areas. The open sores became inflamed and very painful. I thought at one time I was being made to lie on boards with nails sticking through them, but later I realized the pain was caused by the raw wounds.

"We came to another hut, where I stayed for three or four days. It was raining a lot, and I was extremely cold. I still had only the same old dirty shorts on—nothing else. I wanted something to lie my head on because of the sores. I was so cold that I just lay shivering on a wooden table.

"A medic came in and looked at me. He took the old bandages from my legs. They were caked and dirty. He showed a great deal of animosity toward me. He spoke sharply, was rough in his work, and did not put another bandage on my leg.

"The place was filled with flies, cockroaches, bed bugs, mosquitos, and who knows what other bugs. I was trying to do my best to keep the bugs out of my open wounds. I would call for the medic whenever I was conscious. He did not wrap my wounds that whole day. I woke up that night and found a rat eating on a wound that hadn't been covered. I tried to kick it away with my other leg."

He didn't feel like sleeping, but he had no strength to stay awake. Even the pain of the raw sores against the rough boards was not enough to prevent sleep.

"Sometime during the night I had to go to the bathroom very badly. I woke up out of a dream and I had defecated all over the table. The filth was getting in my wounds and on everything else. I was greatly alarmed. Then I discovered that it acted as a lubricant for the wounds on my buttocks and back. It stopped the friction between me and the boards so I rationalized that it wasn't so bad after all," he said.

He was shivering with chills and fever and was later told by a Vietnamese doctor that he had malaria. "I would wake up screaming. It upset the Vietnamese and they would come in to quiet me. Sometimes they beat me and told me I had to be quiet. I would apologize and tell them that I would be quiet—that I was having nightmares. I was getting dirtier and dirtier every day."

Osborne felt he was getting closer and closer to Hanoi and that he must hold on. Surely there would be help there. It had been a miracle that he hadn't been buried alive and now it would be a miracle if he didn't die from infection. He studied the room, being careful to move slowly to guard against shocks of pain. He knew nothing but pain now and he was looking for anything that would give comfort.

"In the corner of the room I could see some clothes. I was concerned about how cold and dirty I was. I figured that perhaps if I could get some of the clothes over to where my table was, I could get them on and keep warm.

"There was an old pole in the place, and I managed to get it and work it between my legs and arms, and after a great deal of effort I fished one of the pieces of clothing to where I could get it. It was a little tee shirt, much smaller than I thought it would be."

The pain had been difficult and the effort exhausting, but there was a hope and a renewal of courage for the accomplishment. Slowly, carefully, he started to put the shirt on, sliding it over his head. Carefully one arm was moved to the sleeve. He was a large man, and the Vietnamese shirt was small. Cramped, struggling to get his arm through the sleeve, he found it impossible. To add to the problem, he couldn't get his arm out. He was hung up in the shirt, one arm sticking up in the air. There was only one thing he could do. He started yelling.

"Soon a medic came in. He cut the shirt to where I could get it on and then he put a bandage on my leg and washed my face.

"The next day they put me on a truck again, and we started heading north. At night we would stop at a flak site or military camp. Again I was getting extremely dirty from rolling around in the mud on the ground when they would put me off the truck.

"I began to stink quite badly. People even stopped coming around me. They finally got a blanket to cover me. I guess the blanket was to keep the smell down, but for me it provided some warmth.

"As the truck jogged along, the blanket would work its way off. Rather than come to the back of the truck and put it on, they would take a stick and push the blanket on. No one would come near me.

"One night we were going along on the truck. It was raining, and I was wet and cold, but I drifted to sleep. When I woke up I found myself in a ditch at the side of the road. It was dark, still raining, and very cold. I think they had just dumped me off the truck.

"There was no one around. I knew I was in another predicament. I could see a light in a building about two or three hundred yards away. I knew that if I just stayed there in the ditch I wouldn't make it. I was worried about pneumonia because of my run-down condition. I still had the tee shirt on; it was soaking wet.

"I started to crawl toward the building with the light. I could not use my hands or feet, so I crawled on my elbows and knees. I would go a little way and pass out or get so tired that I had to quit.

"There were a lot of puddles along the way. Sometimes I would drink a little water from them, but I worried about the consequences. I tried to get the cleanest water, but I don't know how I could tell.

"It took me most of the night to reach the building, but I finally crawled up the steps and collapsed. Shortly after I arrived at the building I heard a police whistle. A Vietnamese fellow came wandering by, dressed in shorts, blowing his whistle. I guessed he was calling reveille to whoever was in the building. In a few minutes soldiers were hustling around.

"When they saw me, they became excited. I guess they were wondering what to do with me. Soon they got a little straw mat and put me on it behind one of the walls. After a while they took me in a room and changed my bandages, and I received a blanket. That blanket was one of the greatest joys of my life.

"But still I was thirsty. By this time I was completely desiccated. I had quit eating several days before. I suppose I hadn't eaten for a week or more. Because of my craving for water, I had just lost interest in eating. There were offers of food, but I didn't want it. I just wanted water—water that I never received."

Osborne stayed in that place for quite some time. He became nervous because he was not moving north to Hanoi. He knew he was getting weaker and weaker, and it was all he could do to keep his eyes open. "I was afraid they were just leaving me there, waiting for me to die. I kept indicating to them through sign language and every way I could that my wingman had seen me captured and knew that I had been taken prisoner. This was false, because I didn't know anything about the man I was flying with. He didn't see me or know what had happened to me, but I wanted to make sure that they thought I had been seen. I thought it would improve my chances for survival.

"One day I was taken into a room, known as a quiz room, and was lain on a table. A few minutes later about fifteen Vietnamese officers came in and formed a semicircle around me. They didn't say a word to me or to one another, they just stared at me. I got the feeling that it was some sort of inspection, that they were deciding about me.

"It took every ounce of energy that I had to make it up to my elbow and force my eyes open and I started staring back at them. They looked at me for three or four minutes and then just left without saying a word. I collapsed back on the table. It had been a great effort just to raise myself.

"Sometime after, perhaps an hour or two later, they came in and carried me out to the roadway, hailed a truck, and threw me on the back of it."

Chapter 21

"He Saved My Life"

Commander Osborne felt some security from the blanket that covered him as he bounced along on the truck. Where he was going he did not know. He was conscious so little of the time, and the keen sense of direction that he had enjoyed as a pilot had long since disappeared.

He did not have the energy to pay much attention to the sounds that surrounded him. The roar of the truck and the bounce of the flatbed were all that reached his senses.

Unnoticed were the sounds of a city. The traffic, the people, the commerce could have all been heard had he been well enough to listen. A train whistled in the switchyard. The smell of the countryside was gone and in its place were the odors of the city.

Somewhere along the way the blanket had been pulled over his head, barring his vision. When the truck stopped he was carried, the blanket still over him, into the place called Hoa Loa, pronounced Wallow, or Hell Hole, and known to the Americans as the Hanoi Hilton.

"I could feel them carrying me with bouncing steps. I didn't know where I was. Once placed on the floor, I was left alone for a considerable time."

The North Vietnamese had difficulty knowing what to do with him, his injuries were so extensive.

This was no hospital; this was a prison. He was more bother that he was worth.

After some time, Osborne, the newest prisoner of war—they would call him a criminal—was again picked up and carried, into room 18 in New Guy Village. The blanket now was pulled from his face.

As he lay on the floor, a North Vietnamese who spoke English came in and began talking to him. Soon the interrogator was yelling and ranting, his temper shortened by the inability of Osborne to answer. "You killed several Vietnamese soldiers when you were captured," the interrogator shouted. "You must sign this paper apologizing for your crimes and sins, for killing our honorable soldiers."

Osborne struggled to make sense of what the interrogator was saying. He was beyond the point of arguing or resisting, but he did shake his head, and through his dry lips denied that he had killed anybody. "You did," the interrogator shouted. "Yes you did, and if you don't sign these papers you will be sent back to where you were captured and the people will take care of you."

The message sank in the mind of Osborne. The agony of the trip back was more than he could bear. The thought boggled his mind. The interrogator continued to yell, but Osborne, concentrating on what he could say, trying to reason out his position, praying for that needed strength, heard little of the yelling.

Lifting his two useless and broken hands, Osborne said, "Look, how could I shoot anybody with both of my hands broken?" The interrogator thought for a moment. It was obvious that this prisoner couldn't sign anything either. Picking up the papers that had been placed on Osborne's stomach, he marched from the room.

"I stayed in that room for two days and two

nights before I received any further attention. I was having a lot of hallucinations. The second day I was there they brought me a teapot full of water and a little cup. I didn't bother to try to pour water in the cup. I just took the spout and lifted it to my mouth and drank. I think I drank the whole thing in about five seconds."

The empty teapot dropped at his side, Osborne again went to sleep, and in his sleep his mind turned to hallucinations. "I remember I made a call on a telephone that wasn't there. I dialed each number just as though it were there, and I called the hospital. I told them I wanted to be admitted at six o'clock in the morning. I made my appointment, and then called a cab. I told the cab driver to pick me up at 5:30 A.M. so we would have plenty of time to get to the hospital. I had the whole conversation with people who weren't even there. It was just as realistic as could be and related mostly to my being at the Balboa Hospital in California.

"Some of the hallucinations that I had were quite comical, but they were very real. Sometimes I would be at the hospital, and I could even smell the alcohol and the ether. The doctors were there and just as real as could be, and then all of a sudden—bang—I would be back in that stinky prison room again.

"They didn't give me much help, but they didn't give me any physical torture either. They did use some psychological torture on me. They brought in a large board. It must have been four feet by four feet. It had a spinning wheel in the center of it and a light on each corner, and there was a buzzer on it. Throughout the night, without notice, the lights would start flashing, the bell would ring, and the spinning wheel would go around and around, its bright colors blurring as it turned.

"That light gadget didn't bother me in the least.

I was too far gone, and besides I felt some security in that place because at least there was someone who cared for something. I felt some security in a spiritual way too, because I had no explanation for some of the things that had happened along the way, and why I was still alive. I felt strongly that someone was watching over me, and that I wouldn't die."

He still longed to hear an American voice. He needed some encouragement. After two days he was put in a room with Commander Brian Woods of Lemoore, California.

Under normal circumstances, he would have been placed alone in a cell, but he needed attention. The Vietnamese could not give him that attention. If he were going to die, let him die with one of the other prisoners. If he were to be fed, someone else would have to feed him.

The interpreter had explained to Woods that they had a prisoner with a broken arm who would be put in for him to take care of. Woods had been shot down two weeks earlier. He was pleased with the prospect of a companion. The two weeks of isolation was enough to prove that it wasn't a pleasant life; it was almost unbearable. There was little he could do to prepare the cell for a roommate, but he was glad for the arrival of another prisoner.

Osborne, in the meantime, was given some medical treatment before he was to go to his cell. A doctor and a medic checked all the wounds and bandaged them. A splint was applied to his left hand. This broken wrist had been set earlier in his captivity—where, he could not remember—but by the time he got to Hanoi the splint had been worked away and he was using his hand, awkward as it was.

Osborne looked at the doctors with an anxious face. He wished he could communicate. He had been given the idea that his left leg and right arm would have to be amputated. He had picked the bone pieces from his wrist, and one look at the wounds on his leg had left him convinced that, indeed, they would have to be removed.

He worried about infection, gangrene, and crude medical care, but thought he had better prepare himself for the worst. As the doctor worked over him, Osborne was unsure of what would happen next. The doctor put a thermometer in his mouth. He had a fever—he could feel that himself. There would be no operation while he had a fever.

They took him to the cell where Woods was imprisoned. Two men carried the stretcher in and placed it in the corner where Woods had expected they would. There really wasn't any other place.

Osborne had been given a new pair of long prison clothes. His towel and other issued items were placed on top of him. His eyes slowly moved around the cell until he sighted Woods. To Osborne, on the floor, Woods looked tall. Actually he was only five feet six inches tall.

Their eyes met; they studied each other's faces. Osborne was pale, hollow cheeked. His cracked lips smiled. Woods smiled back. It was the kindest smile, the kindest face Osborne had seen in a long time. That kindness extended over the weeks and months as Woods nursed and fed the helpless Osborne.

Woods was small in stature. Osborne was six feet three inches tall and had weighed about 180 pounds when he was shot down. Osborne was a Mormon, reared in Salt Lake City; Woods was a Catholic. They were both in the Navy.

Woods looked down at the barely conscious Osborne. He was dirty—filthy—and as close to death as anyone could be. Only the new bandages were clean. Woods, now nurse, began to take inventory. Hardly knowing where to start, he began by talking. The first days of conversation were mostly one way, but

From the Shadow of Death

the voice of an American, a friend, was comforting to Osborne.

When food was brought to the cell, Woods literally forced Osborne to eat. First, just a sip, then a spoonful. Osborne had no interest, but he needed strength. Woods talked to him, words of encouragement as he fed him, much as a mother teaches her baby to eat. The process was performed with great tenderness.

It was a different story when Osborne needed the bed pan, which was the usual bucket, kept in the corner of the cell. His helpless hulk, now weighing about 145 pounds, had to be lifted and maneuvered by Woods, who was quick to admit that he was not the nurse type. When it was over, despite the labor and agony, they both had to smile.

Osborne was bathed from a bucket of water. Woods tried to figure out scientifically how he could keep the water as clean as possible, gently washing with the rag provided and then rinsing the cloth and moving on.

They prayed for each other. They talked about God and religion. "I know a lot more about the Latter-day Saints now than I did before," Woods said.

From time to time the Vietnamese medic came to the cell to change the bandages. It was not often enough, and the bandages were caked and hard. The process was so painful that Osborne would pass out. He received penicillin shots, and the wounds were cleaned with alcohol.

"I could often hear the soft Hail Marys as Woods petitioned the Lord for me. He did all sorts of praying; he did a great many things for me," Osborne observed. "He saved my life. I know what a great friend he was."

On November 18, 1969, Osborne was taken under cover of darkness to a hospital somewhere in Hanoi.

"They operated on my right hand. There were a lot of bone splinters still protruding from my wrist. I had been picking them out myself. It was pretty grim and smelly."

The shattered bone was removed and his arm set, resulting in a shorter arm and no use of his right hand. He was returned to his cell the same night.

"I received a second operation in the spring, on April 18, 1969. They picked me up after dark, when no one could see me. They took me from the cell, put me on a truck, and drove me to the hospital downtown. I wish they had not done the second operation. I feel I would have had a better chance for repair at a Navy hospital in the United States.

"I started getting up and walking around on a crutch in the spring of 1969, and my health improved from day to day. I threw my crutch away that fall and was able to get around pretty well."

Conversation was the big thing those first days in the cell. They talked about Lemoore, California, and Salt Lake City, Utah, their home towns. Osborne had graduated from East High School in 1951 and was a Pi Kappa Alpha at the University of Utah, graduating in banking and finance in 1956. "My roots are very deep in Salt Lake City. I grew up in the Tenth Ward."

Osborne shared the worries he had about his mother in Salt Lake City. His father had died in 1965, and his mother was nearly seventy years old. He did not know until his release that Mrs. Osborne had left her home on Westminster Avenue and moved to California to stay with her sister.

The two prisoners talked of their careers. "I got a craving to be a pilot when I was just a little boy," Osborne said. "My brothers were in World War II as pilots. In fact, my older brother was shot down over Belgium, and he was missing in action for a year. It was very hard on my mother. I don't think she had much confidence in the MIA status. It really broke her up. Then my brother was confirmed as having been killed," Osborne said in a sad tone, thinking of his own condition.

"I don't know how my mother could take another missing in action. It's more than she should have to bear." Osborne's name was released on a list of POWs on Thanksgiving Day in 1969.

For entertainment the two POWs talked about pleasant things. "At first we made up guessing games like Who Am I? or Ten Questions. We would think of all the flavors of ice cream and list them in our minds, and then we would start on all the makes of automobiles. We talked about our plans and what we would do when we got out.

"We played Monopoly without a board or any of the cards or the play money. We would roll the dice by using the fingers on our hand. We would just say, 'one, two, three,' and hold up some fingers and that is the way we got the roll," Osborne explained. "Yeh," Woods said, "Monopoly was Dale's game. He knew the board. I wasn't sure which square was which, and I didn't know where I was landing. I had to take his word for it. I think I paid some extra rent a time or two, but it was fun and helped to pass the time."

The two men had become great friends. In the fall of 1969 they changed rooms and another man, Major Goble James, was put in with them. The three were together until the spring of 1970, when Woods was moved out and three other men were brought in.

The moves in prison happened without much warning. Woods, in an understanding way, extended his left hand to meet Osborne's left hand, and their eyes met. They had been together for two years.

"See you around," Woods said.

"Thanks for saving my life," Osborne replied.

Chapter 22

For Him, the Battle Goes On

Osborne was hobbling around by Christmas of 1969. There were still a lot of problems, and he wouldn't be running any races, but he had come a long way.

By the spring of 1970, however, the medical care that Osborne had been receiving greatly diminished. Maybe it was the politics of the war, or perhaps the whim of the North Vietnamese changed the policy at the prison. Or maybe it was just the transfer of a medical officer in the compound, or maybe it was further up. "The medical care went to pot. The wound on the calf of my leg had not completely healed, and it became infected and opened up.

"There was no flesh on my calf to aid the healing. When it reopened the pain was severe, even more intense than when I had received the wound. A green jelly-like fluid started to run out of my leg. I don't know what it was, but it got all over everything. It was on my clothes, on my blankets, and dropping on the floor. It was a mess."

Four other men now shared the prison room with Osborne. They did all they could to help, but without medication or bandages it was a difficult situation. To substitute for bandages, the men conserved the brown toilet paper that was rationed to them and made a compress to absorb the discharge. The cellophane wrapping from a home package was used to complete the bandage for the infected leg.

Because of his physical condition, Osborne was not tortured with the rope as most other prisoners were. "I was—quote—fortunate—unquote—because I had some amnesia associated with my shoot-down, and I used that as an excuse whenever I was called in for an interrogation.

"I would just say I didn't remember anything about the mission or the aircraft, and I finally convinced them that it was true. Some of the things that they asked me about I could remember, but I gave the same answer—'I can't remember.'

Although Osborne didn't tell them anything, the Vietnamese made every effort to tell him something. "We got Vietnamese study books and propaganda books and even a Russian book. This Russian book was of special interest to me because I knew a little Russian. I had taken a course at Pensacola College while I was stationed there as an instructor. It gave me a good chance to review."

Like most prisoners, Osborne was transfered from camp to camp. "It took me a long time to get used to the work camp. I had a different idea about what a camp should be. I was at the Plantation and the Zoo, similar camps and both in the Hanoi area. Some of the buildings were old army buildings that had the windows boarded and cemented.

"Shortly after Christmas of 1970 we moved into a large room with about fifty men. We were able to have church services every Sunday. We took turns conducting the meeting and tried to have someone of a different denomination conduct each week. I had a chance to talk about my church.

"When the men found out I was a Mormon, they wanted to know more. There was a great deal of interest in the Church. Most of them had heard strange stories about the Church, and I found that many of them didn't even think we were Christians. It was a surprise for them to find that we used the Bible," Osborne explained.

About this time they received a Bible in their room. They were able to keep it for about three weeks, passing it back and forth among the twelve men in Osborne's compound. In the dim light of his prison room Osborne stayed up late at night reading the thin pages. He read the stories of Adam and Abraham and memorized all of the names from Adam to Solomon.

Twice he read the entire Bible from cover to cover. He memorized scripture after scripture, spending most of the day with the Bible. In it, he discovered peace of mind.

Bible reading was a far cry from the propaganda literature. Osborne found comfort in his study and started to read the book for the third time. Then without warning or any known reason, the Bible was jerked away by a guard. During the following months, Osborne taught a Bible class from memory.

Prison life gave plenty of time for evaluation. "I went over my life several times. I realized a lot of things I had done wrong in the past, things that I probably would not have realized if I had not been in prison.

"I discovered some strengths too. I evaluated my whole life and as I did, I recalled many things with which I was very pleased, the way I had handled certain situations characterwise.

"I did become aware of a lot of shortcomings that I am trying to overcome. I know I am going to appreciate life much more than I would have if I hadn't been a POW. I made no resolutions; I didn't feel I needed to. I knew what I wanted to do. It was a real soul-searching experience," he said.

From the Shadow of Death

At times, life in a POW camp is very lonely, but there were also times when a man would wish he could be alone. "We were very close together. It got to be a problem at times. Everybody recognized that. It is a challenge to live with a woman as man and wife, let alone be confined to a room for such a long period with another man. In prison we had our disagreements, even some heated discussions, but what could you do? You couldn't just get away from each other for a while. You had to look at each other and smile. I think we did really well. We never came close to any violence, just disagreements. I think the POWs handled the situation in a marvelous way under the circumstances."

Some of the pangs of loneliness, doubt, and fear were removed when letters arrived for the POWs.

Osborne received his first letter in April 1970. He had been allowed to write his first letter six months earlier. He was sure that his family would not recognize his handwriting. He had to use his left hand, and that without practice. The letter he had written in October arrived home on Christmas day. It had taken nearly three months to be delivered.

Word had been received by his family that he was a POW on Thanksgiving day in 1969. He received about a dozen letters that year.

In the fall of 1970, a delegation from Europe came to the camp. Osborne, who had not usually been shown off to visiting groups, was forced to meet the party from Europe. He felt like a caged animal in a zoo with people looking at him and making comments.

"You are free to ask questions," the camp commander said, inviting the visitors to speak up. The questions were stupid, Osborne thought. Not only that, they were slanted. Of course the food wasn't good, the place was miserable, the medical treatment bad, and the prisoners weren't criminals.

The camp commander was irate when Osborne answered truthfully. "You are the blackest of all criminals," the commander retorted, and told Osborne he would receive no more mail. The commander kept his word; there was no more mail for Osborne.

Communication among the prisoners was fairly good despite the restrictions. And after 1970, when the men were grouped together in larger rooms, they were able to have more association with each other.

They started a system much like the American Indians or other cultures that had no written language. It was a system of stories or chapters to acquaint new POWs with what had happened in the past, to preserve the stories of bravery and endurance and the facts of injustice and repression.

Dale Osborne was one of the chapters in the spoken history of the prison camps. Told and retold, the story of his courage was known throughout the various camps as men were shifted and transferred. He was the hero's hero. His was the story of courage that gave new hope to other prisoners.

"I think courage is just inborn. I think anybody in the same condition, in the same position, would have done the same thing. Several times I felt like turning over and going to sleep, but I kept thinking of the one thing that my wife told me before I left when I kissed her goodbye—'Don't make me a widow.' I kept seeing visions of her as she spoke those words. Rather than going to sleep, I would grit my teeth and try to stay awake, to keep living. I think that vision of her face was a big factor—her and the children and my mother."

Day by day the men built courage in each other. Just as the story of Osborne was told and retold, so were stories of other POWs. Major Jay C. Hess was known as the prisoner who never got angry. "I never met Hess," Osborne said, "but I did hear about him. I did meet Jack Rollins the last year we were in Hanoi and we talked a great deal about the Church."

"I was always sorry while I was there that I didn't know more about the doctrine of the Church, because I had so many questions asked of me. People were interested in the Mormons, and they wanted me to discuss it with them. I did as well as I could, but I was always sorry I hadn't studied more. Of course, I never realized I was going to be in the position I was in. You never know when you are going to be a missionary," Osborne affirmed.

"I was just dying to get hold of Hess or Chesley while I was in prison. I had so many questions I wanted to ask them about the Church. I finally met Chesley at Clark Air Force Base. I also met Colonel George Kiser. He was a dentist and the branch president there. He came by and left me a copy of the Book of Mormon—something I wish I had had during my prison years."

Rumors of peace started to move through the prison camp in October 1972. There were hopes, but the POWs had learned to go easy on hope. The rumors dwindled, and so did the optimism of the prisoners.

Then the B52s started their raids.

"We took new hope. It was one of the happiest times in my life. We were all overjoyed and felt it would help end the war. We were optimistic, but could hardly believe it when we were told of the cease-fire. I had some idea it was coming when I was moved to a special compound for the sick and injured. My leg had been feeling better, and I took the bandages off the morning of January 29, 1973. I was pleased about that, but I couldn't get too optimistic about the things the Vietnamese were telling us about the peace agreement. I was afraid to let myself believe for fear that something would happen and I would have another letdown. I had been let down so many times.

"That afternoon, the twenty-ninth, the real word came. We found out we were going home."

The Navy officials felt that Osborne was a stretcher case and wanted to carry him from the plane that brought him to San Diego. He insisted on walking, his head high, his left arm held stiffly at his side in military fashion. His right arm, more than four inches shorter than the left, hung at his side, the hand without movement. He ignored the dull pain in his left leg. He had learned to live with it.

He smiled as the damp warm breeze blowing off the waters of North San Diego Bay hit his face. The smile was sincere, but it lacked the teeth that were still embedded in his head.

He would be at the San Diego Naval Hospital for a year or more, the doctors working to repair his right hand, to remove the wad of skin and flesh that remained from the operation by the Vietnamese. There would be shrapnel to be removed and operations for his left leg. These operations would take time. There would be pain; there would be plenty for Osborne to endure yet.

"I may never fly again," he said with a sad tone in his voice. "I guess I will return to school to receive my master's degree from United States International University."

There would be lessons, study, endless therapy, and pain. He must continue to battle discouragement with the same courage and endurance that sustained him in North Viet Nam. Many challenges would await him. The battle goes on; it isn't over yet for Commander Dale Osborne.

Commander Dale H. Osborne flew for the Navy with
skill and pride; when shell exploded in the cockpit
he was injured but was able to eject from the plane
before it crashed in Viet Nam

Navy Commander Dale H. Osborne leaves Air
Force C-141 jet transport at Travis Air Force
Base, California, after being released from
Hanoi prison

Captain Lynn R. Beens

Air Force, Kaysville, Utah

Shot Down December 21, 1972, over Hanoi, North Viet Nam
Released March 27, 1973

Chapter 23

The Eleven-Day War

"Peace is at hand," Special Presidential Adviser Henry A. Kissenger announced to an anxious world on October 26, 1972, after he and the North Vietnamese delegation in Paris had just hammered out a nine-point tentative cease-fire agreement on the Viet Nam War.

The next day, Defense Secretary Melvin Laird announced that the United States had halted the bombing of North Viet Nam above the twentieth parallel, which put Hanoi and Haiphong in the off-limits area.

The U.S., however, failed to meet Hanoi's deadline for signing the draft agreement. October 31 came and went without an agreement. Two days later, Hanoi said there would be no further talks with Kissinger until the U.S. signed.

The war, meanwhile, dragged on.

On November 20 Kissinger and North Viet Nam's Le Duc Tho began a new round of talks, but it lasted only five days. On November 25 the talks broke off without agreement.

On December 4, six weeks after he said that peace was at hand, Kissinger began negotiations with Tho again. But many Americans wondered if peace would ever come. Negotiations in Paris, which had been turned into a propaganda contest and a patience duel, had been going on since May 1968.

Nine days later, on December 13, the talks broke off again without explanation, and on December 16, President Nixon stepped up consultations among his chief diplomatic and military advisers, trying to decide what course of action should be taken.

That course was reported to the world on December 18, when it was announced that the U.S. had lifted the bombing restrictions which limited air operations of North Viet Nam to the panhandle area below the twentieth parallel.

The bombing blitz, around-the-clock saturation bombing of North Viet Nam—later referred to by U.S. servicemen as the eleven-day war—began.

The costliest day of the entire war for the U.S. Air Force was December 21, when three B52 bombers were shot down. United Press International reported, "U.S. military authorities today announced the loss in combat of three more B52 bombers, raising the total downed since the resumption of the full-scale air raids over North Viet Nam to six.

"Two of the huge bombers were shot down near Hanoi early today and another crashed in Thailand, the U.S. Command said. The twelve crewmen aboard the B52s down near Hanoi were listed as missing while the six in the bomber downed in Thailand parachuted to safety.

"Military spokesmen said the three latest B52s downed in combat were shot down by Communist gunfire. In keeping with American policy, U.S. military spokesmen did not disclose the extent or effect on the raids, which Hanoi earlier called the fiercest of the entire Viet Nam war.

"Other sources said almost every American warplane in Indochina was engaged in the raids, which they said were concentrating chiefly on targets north of the twentieth parallel. Some sources said this meant about 600 warplanes, including one hundred B52s."

More than one thousand U.S. jet fighter-bombers and 147 waves of B52s struck North Viet Nam between December 18 and Christmas Day, the U.S. Command reported on December 27. On Christmas Day, the bombing was stopped for thirty-six hours. During that week's raids, the most intensive of the entire war, forty thousand tons of bombs were dropped—double the explosive power of the atomic bomb that fell on Hiroshima.

World reaction was quick. Protests came from major political capitals of the world—from Moscow, Peking, Hanoi, capitals in both eastern and western Europe and from the domestic front.

The North Vietnamese delegation in Paris said, "The Nixon administration . . . has multiplied raids by B52s and various other types of aircraft with a view of razing to the ground Hanoi and Haiphong and numerous other areas of North Viet Nam." Administration officials said privately that the President wanted to put pressure on Hanoi to break through the impasse at Paris.

During the first week of the blitz, **B52s** struck at least fourteen times within ten miles of Hanoi, and some hit within a mile of the city's center. The bombing was costly to the U.S. Eighteen planes, including twelve B52s, were shot down, and seventy airmen were reported missing during those first seven days.

On December 29, President Nixon ordered a brief New Year's Day pause in the bombing. It was the eleventh day since the blitz started. The next day the President ordered the bombing of North Viet Nam halted, but it was too late for Captain Lynn Beens, an LDS navigator from Kaysville, Utah. He was shot down and captured on a B52 raid over Hanoi on December 21, the costliest day of the war for the Air Force, and a sad day for the Beens family.

Chapter 24

"I Wish I Had a Camera"

The day was December 21, 1972.

Three giant B52 bombers were shot down that day in combat in Southeast Asia. Two were shot down near Hanoi, and the official report said that all twelve crew members aboard both planes were listed as missing.

One of those twelve crewmen was Captain Lynn Beens, a twenty-six-year-old elder from Kaysville, Utah, who was a navigator on the lead plane that day.

"We took off from Guam right after midnight," Captain Beens recounted. "It was my first mission over the north, but I had had sixty missions flying over Viet Nam itself. It was about an eight-hour trip from Guam to North Viet Nam.

"We usually flew in a three-ship formation, the lead ship navigating, and the other following. We were normally the lead ship because our pilot was a lieutenant colonel. The ranking people were usually in front.

"It was a busy trip over. Certain checks had to be made on a schedule checklist to make sure all equipment was working. I was so busy going over the list that I didn't even get around to eating my lunch, but everything went as scheduled right up to bomb release.

"Once we got over Hanoi, we got a lot of activity. They were firing at us, with a lot of missiles and Triple A's and everything. But everything was just right by the checklist. We had released our load and had actually made our turn away from the target, which was a railroad complex."

"A missile's coming!" yelled the co-pilot.

"My heart sank. A million thoughts flashed through my mind. I knew if we were hit and couldn't stay with the plane, that I could just figure on being caught because we were right over Hanoi itself. It is a densely populated area right around there. The terrain is flat with villages and rice paddies around.

"I was sitting downstairs, without much to do but to listen to the co-pilot call the course of the missile. It was coming right toward us. The co-pilot called the missile up all the way, up to a point where it disappeared under the belly of the airplane."

The missile slammed into the tail of the plane, and immediately the giant ship started into a dive. "We lost control immediately," Beens recounted, "but there were no fires or holes in our crew compartment."

"Bail out!" the pilot yelled.

Captain Beens continued, "Each regular crew member has an ejection seat. If you're upstairs, it's a matter of squeezing the trigger; downstairs you have a handle to pull. I was in a downward seat, so I went out the bottom of the plane. There's some kind of charge in the seat and once the handle is pulled, you're out of the airplane in less than a second. It is unbelieveable.

"The seat and all are thrown out of the airplane, and once you're out, the seat has a separator that kicks you out and you freefall. I went out at 26,000 or 27,000 feet. I had never made a jump before. We had had training in para-sailing, but the real thing is different.

"Ejection is violent. There are a lot of forces besides the speed of the airplane. In the dive, we were probably going 630 or 640 miles per hour when I went out. That's fast in that size of airplane."

Captain Beens said he felt very blessed that the ejection was safe. "I can't say lucky, because I don't think it was luck. I ejected. I did things wrong in my ejection, but I came through it. When I went out of the airplane, I lost my helmet, so I didn't have any oxygen. I knew it was really cold up there because when I got down to the lower altitude, I could feel my fingers warming up a little bit. It was a long way down, but happened so fast that I really didn't need the oxygen."

Captain Beens was in a freefall until about 14,000 feet, when his parachute opened up.

"Once I got in the 'chute, I couldn't see the airplane or anything, or the other 'chutes. I had the feeling that my crew hadn't left. I thought to myself, 'What if I was the only one that left the airplane and everyone else is just sitting up there!'

"And even after I was captured, and couldn't find any one of my crew, I kept having that feeling. It kept gnawing at me until I had been in camp for awhile and saw the name of our pilot on a medical record. Then later I saw him, and I knew the others had left the plane."

Coming down, Beens lost track of time. "It seemed like forever. I was coming down in the 'chute, and I remember thinking, 'What if I had a camera, what a picture I could get.' There were missiles going off, there was anti-aircraft fire, they were shooting flares in the air, and the rest of the planes were going by. I could see the bombs exploding on the ground—and all this together. I wished I had a camera."

But Beens was soon jolted back to reality as bullets went whizzing past him from ground fire. "It was really scary. I was curious where I was going to land and what chances I had of escaping, but first I had to get on the ground. There are things you have to do like employ your survival kit. I was pretty much in shock from the time the pilot told me to leave the airplane until after I was captured. Everything I accomplished was something I had learned on a checklist, emergency procedures that we were taught to follow automatically.

"I couldn't really see the ground when I came down through the darkness. I could see the fires burning and the bombs going off, but there was a thin cloud cover, so I couldn't see where I was going to land until I came through the deck. Once through the deck, I saw the city of Hanoi spread out below me."

He landed in a rice paddy. "I was covered with mud from head to foot. Immediately upon touching down, I took my 'chute off and started to run for a nearby ditch. I was going to try to get away. I figured if I could get in the ditch, it would give me some cover. But there was no chance for escape. I was quickly surrounded by people—maybe twenty or thirty, all armed, but they weren't violent.

"When they came up to me, I put my hands up, and they proceeded to take what they wanted—my watch, my ring, my .38 pistol. They stripped me to my garments and tied me up. I never saw my clothes again. I was watching the people in front of me while the clothes disappeared in back of me.

"They had trouble taking off my survival vest, and I just reached down and unzipped it for them. With my flight suit, they had a real tough time. The zipper had broken in ejection and had become stuck, so they just ripped the suit off me. They didn't waste any time.

"They were all civilians. I didn't see any uniforms anywhere, yet they were armed. I was surprised at the artillery they had. Once I was on the ground, there were no shots fired.

"I had one sock on and one sock off. They made me run to a bomb shelter, sort of like a subway. Every time I slowed down a little, one guy who could speak a little English kept saying, 'quickly, quickly,' and pushing me on. He'd give me little jabs to keep me moving."

Once inside the shelter, the man who spoke a little English started to interrogate Beens, but to no avail. "He was having a rough time with the language," Beens said, "and I just kept saying, 'I don't understand.' So he stopped."

Securely tied, Beens stood alone with his thoughts. He wondered about his family—his wife, Kristine, and his three-year-old daughter, Rebecca. She was too young to know why her daddy had left, and why this Christmas he would not be home. He was scared of what might happen to him being held captive by civilians. It was cold and he stood undressed, shivering.

"Soon the military showed up," Beens recounted. "They were interested in what airplane I was flying. I felt I would be a lot better off if I didn't answer at all. We went through name, rank, and serial number to begin with, but they weren't even interested in that. They just wanted to know what aircraft. The same question over and over again."

"Answer our questions or you will die," they demanded. When that failed to work, they tried a softer approach. "Answer our questions and you will be home with your family soon."

Beens continued, "They just went back and forth with the interrogation, without getting anywhere."

When daybreak came, they blindfolded him and

From the Shadow of Death

marched him out of the shelter. "I was still just dressed in my garments, but they were pretty well ripped up because the people had been so violent taking my clothes off."

When he left the shelter, he was met by a group of angry people. Although he was blindfolded, he could see out the bottom of the blindfold. He saw the feet of people lined up on both sides of the narrow walkway.

The next thing he saw was a pair of feet jumping out on the walkway. Then he felt a blow. The pain shot into his head from his chin. The man—"I have no idea who he was"—jumped out and knocked him to the ground. "The guards, who were holding me by the arms, just dragged me up again. There were people yelling all over. I couldn't tell what they were saying, but from the tone of their voices I could tell they weren't friendly. I was glad that I was in the hands of the military. I was a lot more afraid of the civilians than I was of the military."

Beens was taken to a truck. He was glad to get away from the angry citizens. "They took me to another place and asked me the same questions." "What plane were you on?" they questioned. Again he refused to answer. He was then put on a different truck. His parachute, survival kit, and everything that had been gathered up was thrown in the truck with him.

The truck rumbled through the streets of Hanoi on the way to the Hanoi Hilton. The trip took less than an hour. "I must have been on the outskirts of the city," he said. As the truck jogged along, the blindfold on Beens fell down around his neck. He looked around. He was approaching the prison.

"As I got to the gate, a man in civilian clothes snapped my picture. He had one of the larger Vietnamese cameras, a single lens camera, I remember. I don't know why he shot the picture."

Through the courtyard, the truck inched its way, and then into another courtyard. Beens looked at the prison, and one of the things that made an impression on him was that all the roofs were red tile. It's funny how little things like that make such an impression on a person.

Chapter 25

"Thank You for Flying Those Missions"

"They took me from the truck and placed me in a cell. A short time later an interrogator came in, and I gave him my name, rank, and serial number. They put the blindfold back on me and tied me up again. It was similar to what is called the rope treatment, but not so severe. It was a matter of tying my arms around behind me, cutting off the circulation. But my elbows were not tied together, as some of the prisoners' had been.

"They left me tied, and would come back every so often and ask the questions again. This went on till early afternoon. I lost all feeling in my hands. I could touch my hand and not feel that I had touched it. Any struggling that I did just tied me up tighter.

"I don't know what time it was in the afternoon, but once when they came back I went ahead and answered the questions. I gave them the aircraft I was from, and some other answers just to satisfy them. But they still didn't untie me. This really irritated me. I had given them an answer, and they had still left me tied up."

A short time later, two men came back into Been's cell. "I don't know if it had been minutes or an hour since they had left me," he said. The one man, who hadn't been in the room before, told the other, a guard, to untie Beens. All feeling in both his arms and hands was gone.

"They wanted me to write a statement for a news release—a message to my family, or a statement that I was captured and was in good health. The message was to be released over Radio Hanoi. I told them, 'I can't write.' " The men went away. Beens lay in his cell, exhausted, hurting, and scared.

Finally, a man came with some clothes. "They brought a long and short pair of pajamas, and said, 'Put these on.' " Beens was given a size forty-two pair of pants. They were reddish purple and gray and much too large.

"I just put them on over my garments. I wore my garments all the time I was in prison, even though they were badly torn and dirty. No one ever said I could or couldn't. They just didn't seem to care.

"After I dressed, they put me in a jeep and took me down to make a radio broadcast. This is the first time I saw any other Americans, and then I only got a glance at them. There was a whole string of jeeps carrying men who had just been captured. They were going to the radio station and then back to the camp, and I got a glimpse of some of the other men there."

The jeep carrying Beens stopped in front of the radio station. He wondered what they would want him to say. As he walked into the building, he was very apprehensive. "But there were no pressures. They asked me if I would like to make a statement that I was there. It wasn't propaganda. They wanted me to say I was shot down on such and such a date flying over Hanoi, and how I was being treated, and whether I was in good health or not. And then I could give any message I wanted to give to my family. I thought it was an opportunity to let somebody know I was there."

Been's wife, Kristine, learned of his fate only hours after she learned that he had been shot

From the Shadow of Death

down. "Two officers came to the house about 3:30 in the morning on December 21," Mrs. Beens reflected. She was living with her parents in Kaysville, Utah, at the time. "They gave me a written letter that they had to read, about Lynn being missing in action. It just said that he was missing, and any details would have to come later.

"I had a sick, sick feeling. Any military wife knows that when you get two officers in uniform whom you don't know coming to the door, there is trouble. My mother answered the door, and they said they were looking for Mrs. Beens. I knew exactly what had happened. It was just awful."

That morning Lynn's name was placed on the prayer list in the Salt Lake and Ogden temples. His family had placed their trust in the Lord.

"Late that afternoon, I got a call from the casualty department at Randolph Air Force Base in Texas, telling me that they had received Lynn's press release. They told me that they assumed it was reliable, and that we could assume that he was a prisoner of war. The man who called read the statement that Lynn had given on Radio Hanoi, and later on I got a copy. Lynn said that he was okay, and that he wanted to tell his family that he was all right and it was just a matter of waiting.

"I know that our prayers were answered. I know that is the whole reason we found out so fast that Lynn was alive. At that time he was the only one of the entire crew whose fate was known. I thought, 'This is not just luck,'" she emphasized. "We were really blessed."

"The broadcast was a simple matter," Beens said. "All the newsmen were gathered out in front with a bunch of microphones and lights inside. I just walked in the door, up to the microphone, and said I'm so and so, my social security number is such and such, and I was shot down. Then I turned around and walked right out again. There were no questions asked or anything.

"The Vietnamese seemed to be worried that there were so many people missing in action. They probably felt pressured to let the world know we were alive. But I don't know; it was just those in good health who went down to the radio station. If you weren't injured or anything, they would take you down there."

After the broadcast Captain Beens was returned to the prison camp. "When I first arrived back, they started to put me in a room where another man was already sitting. They took me right back out, and put me in a room by myself."

The room was about twelve feet by twelve feet, and in one corner on the floor was a set of planks, three feet by six feet. That was his bed. The room was one of the few in the entire compound that had windows. The one in the front opened into the courtyard, and the one in the rear opened into the kitchen. Both had shutters which could be opened and closed. Also in the room was a table and a chair for the interrogator.

Beens opened the shutters very slightly on the rear window, so as not to be noticed. He observed that the kitchen was an area where the Vietnamese cleaned their fowl. He saw a lot of feathers, wings, and legs thrown in a pile. It was not a particularly inviting sight, so he closed the shutter and went to the other side of the room. He opened the other shutter slightly and looked out on the courtyard, but it was empty. He noticed the red tile roofs of the buildings. Once in awhile a guard walked across the courtyard, and Beens watched every step.

Unexpectedly, he heard the key in the door. He quickly closed the shutter. In walked a Vietnamese with Beens' first prison meal. "It was some kind of soup, with noodles in it and, I think, some cauliflower. But I had a hard time eating it. In fact, I had a hard time building up an appetite at all. I ate because I knew I had to."

The next day Captain Beens was moved from this cell to a cell two doors down. "And I lost my windows," he said. The following day he was moved again, this time in with another prisoner, Mike Martini, from California. "We were put on dishwashing detail, and we washed dishes for some other people in the camp, as well as for ourselves. It wasn't too bad. It gave us a chance to get out of our cells once in awhile."

Beens said he was told that he was in a section of Little Vegas. Here he spent Christmas. "I could never keep track of the days, but my roommate kept a calendar. Christmas was much the same as any other day except they served a little bigger meal and then that evening the guard brought a little sack with cookies and candies for each prisoner.

"They said it was a gift from the Catholic fathers downtown. Somebody said that the Vietnamese were on good terms with the Catholics. When they brought in the goodies, they told us, 'If you hadn't come over here and bombed, you wouldn't be here now. You would be home with your families.' "

Two days later, Beens moved into Heartbreak Hotel with six other prisoners. "They put a squawk box in the room, and we were subjected to a constant barrage of propaganda on the war."

On January 18, 1973, Beens was moved to the Zoo, another prison compound in Hanoi, which at one time had been a French movie studio. "There were eight of us, and we immediately began cleaning up the camp. It was really dirty, partly because of the bombing nearby. There were piles of rubble and broken plaster all about. Once we got it cleaned up, they started moving prisoners in. We ended up with twenty-six people in our building, six in each of three rooms, and eight in another room. I stayed there the rest of the time I was in prison."

Sundays were special days to the men at the Zoo, but they were the days the prisoners got out of their cells the least. "We were out to eat and wash dishes and then right back in our cells," Beens said. That was the pattern until the last three or four weeks, when the Vietnamese permitted them to get together with the prisoners in the building next door and hold a church service and sing songs. "We usually sang 'My Country 'Tis of Thee' and 'Onward Christian Soldiers.'

"We had a Bible just about the whole time we were there. Once we got in a group of eight, they gave us a Bible. We had it all day long. We also had a pencil and propaganda paper. There was one pencil per room."

While in prison, Beens gained a real appreciation for a knowledge of the gospel, since he was asked many questions he couldn't answer. "It bothered me while I was in there. We would be reading the Bible, and we would come up with questions among the group. There were three Catholics and one Mormon, and I really felt at a loss because they were putting questions to me that I couldn't answer.

"That was one of my resolutions—to go back and learn more about the Church. It is surprising how many questions people can ask you. You realize how little you know or how ill-prepared you are to answer."

Beens and his Catholic friends continued this process of questioning and learning for the rest of the time they were in prison. "We usually went to bed around eight in the evening, but sometimes we would stay up until midnight talking about religion."

The experience Lynn Beens went through gave him new perspective and insight. "I thought many times how fortunate I was to be alive. I realized there were many things I needed to do, and things I needed to repent of," he admitted. "And I was so grateful that I was getting a second chance to do just that.

"Although I had never done anything seriously wrong, I thanked my Heavenly Father that I did have a second chance, that I was allowed to come back and do things as I should.

"In Guam I had fallen to a point of inactivity when we were flying most of the Sundays. There was a church on the other side of the island, but we had no transportation, so I didn't get over there very often. I might have been able to go more often if I had tried harder.

"My prison experience really changed me. It built my testimony and made me realize that I was very thankful for the gospel and, more than anything, for my temple marriage. It was very comforting because I knew if I didn't see my wife again or if I didn't make it out of there, I could still have her and my child in the hereafter if I was worthy. My religion was really a comfort to me."

When Captain Beens was to be released, Mrs. Beens had a traumatic experience. "It was the night of December 21 all over again," she explained. "I knew that Lynn would soon be coming home, and I expected a phone call telling me when. This one night, I was up with my dad watching TV. About one in the morning I heard a car pull into the driveway. I looked out the window. My heart sank. I saw a colonel sitting in a staff car.

"It was like it wasn't real. I wanted to scream. I started crying. I thought my husband had died. All I could think of was that he was dead.

"The man came to the door. When he saw me, he said quickly, 'Now wait a minute; I have some good news for you.' "

And it was good news for Kristine Beens and her family—Lynn was coming home.

"I really hesitate including myself with the prisoners of war," Captain Beens said after it was all over. "We were there just three months, and we came back and have enjoyed the glory and the benefits. We are simply the survivors of the eleven-day war, but it makes the experience seem really worthwhile when you talk to some of the old POWs and they come up and say, 'Thank you for flying those missions.' Apparently, it meant a lot to them."

Captain Lynn Beens
responds to questions
of the press as he
arrives in Salt Lake
City after release from
Hanoi prison camp

Rebecca Beens is
handed to her father,
Captain Lynn Beens,
by her mother, Kristine

Captain Lynn Beens receives big hug from his mother when he arrived at Salt Lake City International Airport after prison release

Captain and Mrs. Lynn Beens receive exciting welcome from large crowd assembled in front of Kaysville, Utah, city hall for homecoming ceremony

Young people are anxious to hear Captain Lynn Beens tell about parachute drop from B52

From the Shadow of Death

Captain and Mrs.
Lynn Beens pose
with President
Richard M. Nixon
for picture, snapped
by a friend at the
President's party at
Washington, D.C.

Captain Lynn Beens
explains to Starli
Christensen
oversized
pajama-type
clothing that he
wore in prisoner of
war camp

The Hanoi Hilton

Chapter 26

"Hell-Hole" in Hanoi

Jay Hess lay on the hard bed in his cell early one morning in prison. He was in the Hanoi Hilton. He was a prisoner of war, but the North Vietnamese had branded him and all the other prisoners as criminals.

Jay was in a small room with a boarded-up window, but at the top there was a small crack where the boards did not completely cover up the window, and from his bed he could look out and determine whether it was day or night.

"I lay there waiting for it to become daylight," Jay recalled. "It seemed like it was a very long night, and yet the gong had gone off, which meant it was time for me to get up, but still it was not light outside. The daylight approached without my really being aware it had happened, because I was deep in my thoughts.

"Suddenly I noticed the sun was up. I just said within myself, 'Oh, good morning, sun.' " Through the small crack, he saw that the sun's rays were shining on the leaves of a tree in the courtyard. He could see only a few leaves on the top of the tree.

"As I looked at those leaves, I could see that the sunshine had changed their color from green to transparent yellow. Inside the leaves, I could see the veins that carried life and strength. I could clearly see the structure of those leaves."

During the days that followed, Jay watched the leaves. They became as a friend to him, and he spent much time studying them as he lay on his bed. It gave him something to think about during those long, lonely days in prison.

"One day as I was watching the leaves, I noticed that they had started to turn red. Then they turned brown, and then fell noiselessly to the ground, leaving the tree bare. I thought of that tree as a sort of symbol of the many lives it had seen in that prison in North Viet Nam." The tree, like a silent sentinel, perhaps had seen hundreds— or even thousands—of lives affected by the war through the years, as it stood watch over an area of the main prison camp.

The main prison was the Hoa Loa, pronounced Wallow or Hell Hole. It was nicknamed by the Americans the Hanoi Hilton, not out of affection but because it was necessary to have quickly re- cognizable identification of people, places, and things in the communication system they devised.

The Hanoi Hilton was not the only prison in or near Hanoi. One POW put it this way: "There is a shortage of everything in North Viet Nam except prisons." There were the Zoo, the Plantation, Camp 77, and others. Each became easily identifable to the Americans.

The Hoa Loa was built by the French in the heart of Hanoi when the French were in control of Viet Nam. It covers a city block and is surrounded on all four sides by busy streets.

"There are basically three different sections in the Hanoi Hilton," explained Jay. "There was the Unity Section, Little Vegas, and New Guy Village." Little Vegas included cell blocks with names like Desert Inn, the Stardust, Thunderbird, and the

Mint. "There was no way I know of to communicate between sections, unless someone was moved from one to another," he said.

Larry Chesley talked about the prison: "Many Vietnamese were incarcerated there during the French domination. The Vietnamese made their own little modifications for us, however." The rooms were small and depressing. Most of the windows were boarded up from the outside, and there were no provisions for heat in the winter or ventilation in the summer. In the door of each room was a small peephole that was covered from the outside.

Escape was almost impossible, according to the POWs. "There was about as much chance as the sun coming up in the West," explained Jay Hess.

"The prison had walls four feet thick, and then there was a space and then another wall with wire on top of it, and, of course, guards were all over," Larry said.

"I heard while I was in prison," he continued, "that there had only been one successful escape in all the years of that prison. It was a pretty famous one back some time ago. A group of Vietnamese got out through the sewer system some way."

Jay, however, talked about one escape he was aware of. "You probably heard about a couple of escapes. I was living in the room next to one of the men. There was considerable discussion about the escape plans, and there were lots of different opinions. Finally, the plan was approved, and an attempt was made.

"They got out of the room first of all, which is a major problem. It is a very difficult thing to get out of the room. They managed to crawl across an open court in full view of guards and managed to get out of the prison. They were hiding downtown when they were recaptured."

"We did have some men escape from the Hanoi prison, two different pairs of prisoners," said Jack Rollins. "One of the men was killed when he was returned. We believe he was tortured to death. There was some very brutal torture after that escape."

Each of the incoming prisoners was forced to read the camp regulations, which branded him as a criminal. Jack brought home a copy of the regulations, which had been posted in English on the walls of the Hanoi Hilton.

The regulations were dated February 15, 1969, and stated, "In order to insure the proper execution of the regulations, the camp commander has decided to issue the following new regulations which have been modified and augmented to reflect the new conditions. From now on the criminals must strictly follow and abide by the following provisions:

—The criminals are under an obligation to give full and clear written or oral answers to all questions raised by the camp authorities. All attempts and tricks intended to evade answering further questions and acts directed to opposition by refusing to answer any questions will be considered manifestations of obstinacy and antagonism which deserves strict punishment.

—The criminals must absolutely abide by and seriously obey all orders and instructions from the Vietnamese officers and guards in the camp.

—The criminals must demonstrate a cautious and polite attitude to the officers and guards in the camp and must render greetings when met by them in a manner already determined by the camp authorities. When the Vietnamese officers and guards come to the rooms for inspection or when they are required by the camp officer to come to the office room, the criminals must carefully and neatly put on their clothes, stand at attention, bow

From the Shadow of Death

a greeting and await further orders. They may sit down only when permission is granted.

—The criminals must maintain silence in the detention rooms and not make any loud noises which can be heard outside. All schemes and attempts to gain information and achieve communication with the criminals living next door by intentionally talking loudly, tapping on walls or by other means will be strictly punished.

—If any criminal is allowed to ask a question, he is allowed to say softly only the word 'bao cao.' The guard will report this to the officer in charge.

—The criminals are not allowed to bring into and keep in their rooms anything that has not been so approved by the camp authorities.

—The criminals must keep their rooms clean and must take care of everything given to them by the camp authorities.

—The criminals must go to bed and arise in accordance with the orders signaled by the gong.

—During alerts the criminals must take shelter without delay; if no foxhole is available, they must go under their beds and lie close to the wall.

—When a criminal gets sick he must report it to the guard who will notify the medical personnel. The medical personnel will come to see the sick and give him medicine or send him to the hospital if necessary.

—When allowed outside for any reason, each criminal is expected to walk only in the areas as limited by the guard-in-charge and seriously follow his instruction.

—Any obstinacy or opposition, violation of the preceding provisions, or any scheme or attempt to get out of the detention camp without permission are all punishable. On the other hand, any criminal who strictly obeys the camp regulations and shows his true submission and repentance by his practical acts will be allowed to enjoy the humane treatment he deserves.

—Anyone so imbued with a sense of preventing violations and who reveals the identity of those who attempt to act in violation of the foregoing provisions will be properly rewarded. However, if a criminal is aware of any violation and deliberately tries to cover it up, he will be strictly punished when this is discovered.

—In order to assure the proper execution of the regulations, all the criminals in any detention room must be held responsible for any and all violations of the regulations committed in their room.

—It is forbidden to talk or make any writing on the walls in the bathrooms or communicate with criminals in other bathrooms by any other means.

—He who escapes or tries to escape from the camp and his (their) accomplice(s) will be seriously punished.

In spite of the severe regulations against communication, the prisoners devised a code by which they were able to communicate by tapping on the walls. It was a "block code" that consisted of five horizontal squares and five vertical squares. The first square, both horizontally and vertically, was for the letter *A*; the next square horizontally was for *B* and so on. Because there were only twenty-five squares in the block, the letters *J* and *K* were in the same square.

The first series of taps was for the horizontal rows. One tap meant the top row, two taps the second row, three taps the third row, and so forth. The second series of taps was for the vertical rows. One tap was for the vertical row on the left, two taps for the next one, until five taps for the vertical row on the right.

From the Shadow of Death

The block looked like this:

A	B	C	D	E
F	G	H	I	J-K
L	M	N	O	P
Q	R	S	T	U
V	W	X	Y	Z

To tap out a letter, for instance, the letter *O*, the men used three taps in the first series for the horizontal row and four taps in the second series for the fourth vertical row.

To spell a word required the tapping out of one letter at a time. "However, we developed this code to the point where we had a shorthand we could communicate pretty rapidly," explained Bob Jeffrey.

As each man was incarcerated, he was taught the code by the prisoner in the next room. Most prisoners were very slow with the code at first, but as they practiced, their speed increased, and before long they were able to communicate with a high degree of speed. They even developed a type of shorthand.

If the prisoners were caught, it meant punishment. To prevent being caught, the men would clear for each other by peering out the vent over the doorway or through a crack in the boarded-up windows to see if there were any guards around.

Shortly after arriving at the Hanoi Hilton, the Americans were given their standard prison issue: a straw mat, two sets of long clothes, two sets of short underclothes, sandals made of rubber tires, a toothbrush, toothpaste, a bar of soap, a tin cup, a mosquito net, and two blankets. "I didn't realize how great an instrument a toothbrush was," commented Jay. The prisoners were given a new tube of toothpaste every two months and a new bar of soap every month. They were given a razor blade about twice a week with which to shave, and they received a haircut from one of their fellow prisoners about once a month.

The prisoners were to arise daily about five A.M. at the sound of a gong. If they were permitted to bathe that day, that was taken care of about six A.M. They would eat breakfast usually around ten A.M. and an afternoon meal about three P.M. Most of the day they were confined to their rooms. "There were years that we went without outside time, except to bathe and wash dishes," explained Jay.

"The worst thing about the food," said Larry, "was that it was so repetitious. We had pumpkin soup day after day, month after month, and then it would change and we would be given kohlrabi soup every day. Then we'd get cabbage soup. Intermittently, we'd have some kind of greens. We called them sewer weeds."

Jay also talked about the food. "We always had soup. This was for the two meals we had each day. As a second part of each meal, there was either rice or bread. This was before the treatment changed. When the treatment improved, they would bring a roll around early in the morning, or some bread. Later, we also received milk sometimes."

The prisoners called each other by their first names. Although rank was not used in addressing each other, there still existed a military organization on all levels of the camp and in the rooms. There was a senior man (the man with the highest rank) for the entire camp, and one for each room, whether there were just a few men or as many as forty or fifty.

From the Shadow of Death

Beds differed in different rooms. Some were concrete beds with built-in stocks; others were just boards. Many times the prisoners slept on the floor on a straw mat that could be unrolled. Lights were usually left on in the rooms during the night and turned off during the day. However, men in solitary confinement or those being punished were usually in rooms completely darkened for twenty-four hours a day.

The Hoa Loa was certainly a "hell-hole"—where torture, punishment, hunger, humiliation, and depravations were daily occurences.

The Power of Involvement

Chapter 27

Yvonne Williams—A Prayer of Thanks

Mrs. Yvonne Williams of Clinton, North Carolina, was concerned. She wanted to get involved. And buying a POW/MIA bracelet was one way that she could do a small part. At least, it would be a constant reminder to her of the sacrifice made by so many American servicemen.

In October 1972, Mrs. Williams, publications manager at Pope Air Base in North Carolina, went to the base director of personnel to purchase a bracelet. The director had been selling them for only two months, and he had more than two dozen to choose from.

"Previously," said Mrs. Williams, a convert to the LDS Church, "I had not been very interested in what seemed to be an unpopular war, but I decided it was time that I did show some interest and concern about the American men who were fighting, dying, and being captured in that far-off country of Viet Nam.

"Voice in Vital America (VIVA), an organization which played an important part in publicizing news and important happenings for the families of the prisoners of war and men missing in action distributed pamphlets and quarterly newspapers to our base. Until I read some of these pamphlets, I did not realize that some of the POWs were cooped up in cages, treated like animals, and put on public display. The pamphlets told of the torture and terrible treatment our men were being forced to endure. My heart went out to the men who were sacrificing their lives for my country, and I wanted to help them."

At the base personnel office she carefully looked through every one of the names and birthdates on the bracelets. She did not know any of the men but she came back again and again to one bracelet, and she finally decided it was the one she was going to wear.

It carried the name of Captain Larry Chesley.

"I had no idea that Captain Chesley was a member of the Church, nor did I know that he was from Idaho," she related. "I chose Captain Chesley's because I liked his name, and because he was captured April 16, 1966. Less than a month later, on May 9, 1966, my son was born.

"I thought these dates being so close together would give more meaning to the bracelet. I could be thankful that I had had my son for six and one-half years, and I prayed for the mother of this prisoner because through the tragedy of this terrible war, she had been without her son for six and one-half years."

Once Mrs. Williams had purchased the bracelet, she became active in telling others about America's prisoners of war and those missing in action. "I helped sell some bracelets and obtained several hundred POW/MIA pins from base personnel to distribute in the high schools around our area. I wanted other people to know more about our fighting men, and wearing my POW bracelet made me more aware of my aim to be concerned about them."

Mrs. Williams had joined the Church in 1949 when she was thirteen years old. After World War

II, the missionaries had started contacting people in the area for the first time since before the war. In early 1949 the elders held meetings for five nights in an old abandoned garage in the small community of Piney Green. The subject of their meetings was "Come and Learn the Truth About the Mormons."

"My family and I attended every night." My first impression of the missionaries was that they knew the Bible and could prove all their statements with Bible scriptures. They were very humble and friendly.

"The elders started coming to our house in March 1949 to give discussions. The one thing that thrilled and impressed me most about this new-found religion was that it taught that God and Christ have bodies. Previously, I had been taught that they are only spirit, and I just couldn't believe it.

"The elders worked faithfully with my family, and I finally decided to be baptized on May 29, 1949, in Goldsboro, North Carolina. Five months later in the middle of October 1949, my mother, father, and brother were also baptized into the Church."

After attending Brigham Young University in the mid-1950s, she returned to her home in North Carolina, where she met her husband-to-be, helped teach him the gospel, and married him.

After becoming involved in the POW/MIA affair and purchasing Captain Chesley's bracelet, she said she felt a real closeness to him. "I felt that he was still alive and that the Lord was hearing my prayers in his behalf.

"I often thought of him and the other POWs and wondered how they were being treated, if they were well, and if they had enough food. As the mother of one son, I could only imagine how awfully hard it would be for me if my son were one of the

POWs, and I knew that the mothers of these men must have suffered terribly."

In January 1973, Mrs. Williams suspected that Captain Chesley might be a member of the Church when she read his address with the list of prisoners in the newspaper. Later, she talked on the telephone with a friend at Hill Air Force Base in Utah, and she was informed that Captain Chesley was indeed a Mormon, and that there were stories about him in the *Church News* and in the *Ensign.*

"It still seemed impossible that I could have chosen out of all those names a POW who was a Mormon.

"My first thought was that my choice must have been made through inspiration. I feel I was inspired to choose a member of the Church to make me more humble and help me to know that I am my brother's keeper."

Although Mrs. Williams knew when the release of prisoners would take place, she didn't know which prisoners would be released first. "We live out in the country, and there was a big snowstorm. We didn't receive a newspaper for three days, so I hadn't read any names of the released prisoners.

"As I watched TV waiting for the release, I had a prayer in my heart that Captain Chesley would be on one of those planes. Then when the information officer got mixed up on the names, I thought maybe he was one of the first to get off and I didn't know it was he.

"But then he came. 'Captain Larry J. Chesley, Burley, Idaho,' the announcer said. When I heard his name, tears came to my eyes and a prayer of thankfulness and peace entered my heart. I was so glad that he was now home and safe."

Dr. Roger E. Shields

Chairman of the Prisoner of War and Missing in Action Task Group
for the Department of Defense

Chapter 28

Dr. Roger Shields—An Exciting Time

It was an exciting moment for Dr. Roger E. Shields as he stood in front of the terminal at Hanoi's commercial Gai Lam Airport. Dr. Shields, a member of the Potomac (Virginia) Stake high council of the LDS Church, is a tall man, standing six feet three inches. With his short crew cut and dressed in a civilian suit, he stood out in the crowd.

As chairman of the Prisoner of War and Missing in Action Task Group for the Department of Defense, Dr. Shields was in Hanoi to assist in the repatriation of the American prisoners of war. It was the culmination of many months of hard work. The prisoners—longest held prisoners of any war in U.S. history—were coming home.

Dr. Shields had arrived in Hanoi on a C130 aircraft, the first American plane to land in the capital city since the cease-fire. There were a lot of reporters and photographers to greet him and his party as they walked from the plane. "We were met by the North Vietnamese and taken inside the terminal," Dr. Shields reported. "We sat down and chatted for a few minutes, and then we went upstairs where we worked out the details of the release.

"The men had been taken earlier to a building just around the corner in front of the apron of the terminal. After we worked out the procedures and our C141 had landed to take the prisoners out, the men were brought out from the building and placed in camouflaged buses. There were about fifteen to twenty men in each bus.

"We went outside in front of the terminal to meet them. As I saw the first bus come around the corner, it was a very exciting moment for me." The buses pulled up in front of the terminal. The prisoners looking out of the window immediately recognized Dr. Shields as an American.

"I gave them the 'thumbs up' signal, and they returned it. They were all grinning, and it was a very, very exciting time. The men got out of the buses with great dignity. They were dressed in clothing that the North Vietnamese had given them, which I think looked very presentable. They came out holding their heads high; that is the thing I remember more than anything—how straight they stood, how proud they looked, and how dignified they were.

"I think they had planned it that way. They seemed almost oblivious to the things that were going on around them, and they maintained that air until they came through and were in our hands. It was just great."

A green awning had been set up in front of the terminal. A table had been placed beneath it, and around the table were seated officials of the United States and of North Viet Nam. The POWs walked in one side of the tent-like awning for processing, made a right turn, and walked out of the adjacent side and to the waiting medical evacuation C141 airplane.

Dr. Shields rode back on the first plane. The men boarded the huge aircraft through big clam-shell doors in the rear. Three men were carried in on litters. "When those clam-shell doors were closed,

From the Shadow of Death

they all gave a great big cheer, and as soon as the aircraft lifted off the ground, there was another big shout. But once they got over the coast and away from North Viet Nam completely, it was bedlam. The feeling I got from this was something that will last for a lifetime. It was fantastic."

At the controls of the first C141 was Major James E. Marrott, thirty-eight, a member of the Church from Provo, Utah, who called that flight the most important of his career.

Dr. Shields continued: "The men were concerned about whether they had really come out with honor. They had talked about that being something they wanted to do very badly. They wanted to know if they had achieved it."

Enroute to the Philippines, the men talked about many things, and they joked with each other. "It was interesting to know their concerns were for each other," Dr. Shields said. They had also maintained a good sense of proportion and perspective, and a sense of humor.

"One man noticed my wide tie and asked, 'When did men start wearing bibs?' "

For maximum comfort and relaxation, each aircraft was equipped with a bed and a seat for each returnee. Aboard also was a complete medical staff to care for any medical needs, and each man had a service escort.

The release of the prisoners climaxed months of preparation and planning. As early as 1969, a review of the status of all actions and efforts relating to the problems of servicemen missing or captured and their families was directed by Melvin Laird, then Secretary of Defense.

"This symposium provided us with some of the insight and knowledge of the captivity situation and its effects on our men that are necessary for repatriation planning that will meet the needs of returned prisoners and their families," Dr. Shields told the House Armed Services Committee in October 1972.

Also, in 1969 the Defense Department assembled all former United States POWs who had up to that time been released from North Viet Nam, together with expert military and civilian behavorial scientists. "Information gained from this effort provided the basis for additional evaluation and refinement of our plans."

"In 1971 and 1972 we conducted, over an eight-month period, an exhaustive survey and analysis of the problems of our returned men, the families of the prisoners and the missing, and our then-current policies and plans. Some fifty recommendations for changes in existing policies and procedures and for the development of new programs were made." In January and August of 1972 worldwide conferences were held to again review the repatriation plans. Participants included sixty officials from the office of the Secretary of Defense, the military services, the unified commands, and subordinate echelons.

At the House Armed Services hearing Dr. Shields told committee members, "I believe our plans and those charged with their implementation are in a high state of readiness."

The repatriation plans had come a long way since the first hints of prison releases. "Back in those early days, we really didn't know how many men we had. We didn't know who they were; we didn't know where they were located; we didn't know where their repatriation would occur. We were talking in those days about obtaining good treatment for them, so they would be alive when the time came for them to be released. We were very concerned about the kind of treatment they had been getting.

From the Shadow of Death

"Some men had been released, and we knew from the things they had said that conditions were very difficult. We knew particularly with regard to South Viet Nam, Laos, and Cambodia that the conditions there were more difficult and arduous than conditions in North Viet Nam, as far as natural factors were concerned.

"Aside from mistreatment and that kind of thing, we knew that in South Viet Nam the Viet Cong didn't have any capitals, any cities or prisons where they could take care of these men, as they did in Hanoi. Because of this we knew the conditions were very, very difficult. As it turned out, when the men were finally released, we did learn that relatively large numbers of our men captured in the south had died in captivity.

"We were more concerned in those days with obtaining the kind of treatment for those men that could sustain their lives, and also in getting some communication for their families, to give the families the comfort and assurances that come with knowing their loved ones are all right.

"So we were engaged in the Paris peace talks. [Dr. Shields made several trips to Paris to participate in talks concerning the POWs.] We were basing all our action on the Geneva Convention Relative to the Treatment of the Prisoners of War. All of the parties of the conflict were parties to the convention and were legally bound by international law to provide certain minimum standards of living to our men, but our men were not receiving the advantage of any of these things."

At first, the repatriation plans were called Operation Egress Recap. The name had no special meaning, but was merely a short term used for ease of reference to the operation. Later the name was changed to Operation Homecoming. Every detail for a smooth release was worked out, with alternate plans to insure maximum efficiency. When a peace settlement seemed at hand in October 1972, Dr. Shields and his team were ready with a number of processing sites in both Asia and Europe.

Dr. Shields continued: "We did not have any certainty that our men were going to be released in Hanoi, or in the south, or even in Asia. We had seen some men released on the battlefield and others through Europe. We had no way of knowing whether our men would be released through Europe, flown to someplace in Europe by a Soviet airline, or released some other way. We had to plan on meeting these men and processing them wherever they would be released. That meant we had to cover Europe as well as Asia."

In addition to the site selection, there were many other contingencies to cover. "We didn't know how many prisoners we would get at a time. We didn't even know how many were prisoners. We really didn't know who we were going to get back until the list came out. We didn't know if they would be released at one time or in increments, whether we would have advance warning, or whether they would be released on a moment's notice.

"We were not sure where they would come, but had our preferences. We felt we ought to go to Hanoi to pick the men up. We knew some men were in the Hanoi area anyway. Those not in Hanoi we felt should be picked up at their detention sites. We didn't want them to have to take a long journey. A year or so ago when an Army sergeant in South Viet Nam was released he had to walk a number of miles, and he came out with a herniated disk in his back, two or three different types of malaria, an elbow that was immobilized, and shell fragments in an eye, which rendered him partially blind in that eye. He should not have been walking out in that condition.

"So in the negotiations, we said we would like to pick up our men from their detention sites. As it turned out, most of the men were in the Hanoi area, and it was most convenient to send those C141s to Gia Lam. Many of those captured in the south had been taken to Hanoi for release, but there was one large release in the south."

Because the prisoners were released in increments, it was necessary to use only one processing site, and that was at Clark Air Force Base in the Philippines. "If they all had come out at one time, we would have activated one or both of our alternate sites in the Pacific."

"The story of the POWs is a great story, and I think it is one that people everywhere ought to know about," said Dr. Shields, who is a professor of finance and was on leave from the University of Texas in Austin. "These remarkable Americans have done great things and have served their country very well under extremely difficult conditions.

"Many of these fellows were prisoners of war three times longer than any American had ever been held as a prisoner before. We were dealing with so many new problems just because the time element was so much greater. Another factor was that the men were used as political hostages in a way our men had never been used before. I think that without any question, in general, and by and large, the conduct of the prisoners was examplary. On the whole, the Vietnamese did not get any valuable information from our men.

"We have found that a lot of the things the Vietnamese did were aimed at harassment and acquiescence, getting a man to say, 'All right, I am your prisoner and you can do anything you want to me, and I've got to do what you tell me to do— you own me in effect; I must give you total obedience and acknowledgment that here I am and I am power-less.'

"The Yankee ingenuity is great," he went on. "Some of our men did answer innocuous questions. This was part of their way of evading the real questions. Our men did all kinds of things, some ludicrous in the extreme. They would talk about Major Flash Gordon. These were things that would be immediately obvious to an American, but not to the Vietnamese."

Dr. Shields talked about the Code of Conduct. "The Code of Conduct is exactly what it says it is it is a code. It does not have the force of law. The Uniform Code of Military Justice is the legal code. "The Code of Conduct is exactly what it says it is: a code. It does not have the force of law. The Uniform Code of Military Justice is the legal code. The Code of Conduct gives a man the guidelines he needs to survive.

"When they talk about giving name, rank, serial number, and date of birth, they are talking about the things that a prisoner is obligated to give. When you become a prisoner, there are certain things you have to do. We accede to the Geneva Convention. One of the provisions of the convention is that a prisoner gives that kind of information to the capturing force. That means you are bound to give them the information needed to identify you, so they can fill out the capture card. Beyond that, you have no obligation.

"That does not mean that this is all a person is permitted to say. That would be an incorrect in-terpretation of the code. It is not a legal code, and you do not prosecute under it. Prosecution comes under the Uniform Code of Military Justice, which spells out many things, including fraterni-zation with the enemy.

"The code gives a man something to live by and

something he can hang on to. A man being captured finds himself in a totally new situation. The prisoners will tell you that there is nothing like it. You are no longer your own man, and you can't do anything without permission. The captors have absolute power over you."

The Code of Conduct in its written form grew out of the Korean War in which the conduct of a few American fighting men cast a shadow over the great majority of their comrades in arms who acquitted themselves honorably and with distinction. The code was not intended to provide detailed and exhaustive guidance on every aspect of military life. For that purpose, there are such things as the Uniform Code of Military Justice, military regulations, rules of military courtesy, and the well-established traditions and customs of each of the military services.

Written in the form of a creed, the code contains 247 words, and was prescribed by the President of the United States in 1955. It contains six articles dealing with devotion to American principles, behavior on the battlefield, and what is expected of the American fighting man who has been captured by the enemy.

Dr. Shields said that the prisoners were called war criminals by the North Vietnamese early in the war. "At one time, they threatened to try our prisoners as war criminals, but they never did. Our prisoners were never convicted by their captors for any war crimes. In fact, they were not criminals, and the North Vietnamese and Viet Cong finally dropped that assertion and never mentioned it anymore. In Paris, they talked about the prisoners of war."

When the giant C141s arrived at Clark AFB enroute to the United States, Navy Captain (now Rear Admiral) Jeremiah A. Denton, the senior officer, was selected to give the waiting crowd a word of greeting. "The men were not sure there would be a reception, or even that anyone would be there. But they were told the arrival would be televised.

"Captain Denton asked what he might say," Dr. Shields continued. "I told him to say what he felt was appropriate. He sat down and wrote his few lines and then got on the public address system of the aircraft and said, 'This is what I would like to say on behalf of all of you,' and as he continued, the men all gave him a thumbs up signal."

Captain Denton was the first POW off the C141 Starlifter evacuation plane. He told the waiting crowd, "We are happy to have the opportunity to serve our country under difficult circumstances. We are profoundly grateful to our commander-in-chief and to our nation for this day. God bless America."

Dr. Shields continued, "The men had long used the saying, 'God bless America' and they really meant it. Many of those men knew the power of prayer. Several of them told me that they really learned what it was like to get down on their knees and really communicate with our Heavenly Father.

"They said it meant so much to them when they were held in solitary confinement for so long, without even being able to tell anyone that they were there.

"Their captors would tell them, 'No one knows you are here and when something happens to you, nobody will ever know.' Many of the returnees maintained their spirits through the ordeal through their real feeling of communication with the Lord. They knew the power of prayer and came out with a real feeling for their relationship with their Creator."

He talked about the processing of prisoners at Clark AFB. "A great many changes had taken place during the many years the POWs had been away

From the Shadow of Death

from their families. There was good news, bad news, family relationship changes, births, and deaths. We had up-to-date photographs of families, letters, and other background information so when the men got on the telephone to make that call home, they would have a bit of a background. We wanted to do all we could to reassure the men and to make them as well prepared and presentable as possible when they met their families.

"We had very extensive medical tests arranged and good procedures in follow-up. It was all recorded. We had debriefers who were ready to listen to all the men had to say. They needed to tell their stories to someone who understood and would listen. At the same time, we gathered information about casualties. A more intensive debriefing was conducted in the United States, but we wanted to get the men home to their families as quickly as possible."

Each POW was given an escort to help him through his debriefing and see that he was fitted into a new uniform. The men were provided with information concerning their promotions, back pay, and future benefits. Every effort was made to gain information about men missing in action. "We still have many questions about men in Laos and Cambodia," he said.

In a memorandum to members of the United States Senate and House of Representatives, dated February 2, 1973, Dr. Shields outlined some of the procedures in attempting to identify missing servicemen:

"The United States Joint Casualty Resolution Center (JCRC) has been established at Nakhon Phanom, Thailand, and is assigned the mission of resolving the status of U.S. missing personnel. Personnel from the JCRC will locate and investigate crash sites throughout Southeast Asia as arranged through the Four-Part (U.S., South Viet Nam, North Viet Nam, and the Viet Cong) Joint Military Commission.

"The organization of the JCRC will provide the expertise for these investigations, utilizing air search and ground search teams and a central identification laboratory with a pool of specialists to inspect located crash and grave sites and recover remains.

"It is expected that endeavors in remote areas will normally include air and ground searches for crash sites. In the more inhabited areas, personal contact with the local people following extensive information programs and coordination will be a primary technique."

On May 31, 1973, Dr. Shields testified before the House Foreign Affairs Subcommittee on National Security Policy. He told them, "We do not consider the lists received so far to be a complete and accurate accounting for our men. The most agonizing and frustrating problem that remains concerns those who are thought to have been captured alive but who have not been returned."

He said there were "cases of men who were seen on the ground or whose pictures were released subsequent to capture but who, for one reason or another, have not returned and for whom the other side has yet to provide a satisfactory explanation."

Dr. Shields told the committee members that the Defense Department was seeking to recover the remains of the missing who have died and those who are listed as killed in action.

He said that on May 11, 1973, a U.S. inspection team inspected burial sites in North Viet Nam, allegedly of American servicemen, but Hanoi would not allow identification or recovery of the remains.

"We are currently trying to arrange for the exhumation and repatriation of these remains and of any other American dead known to the other side.

Another unresolved issue between the United States and the Communists is the acquisition of entry rights for our search teams to areas throughout Southeast Asia where our men are missing."

While at Clark AFB, Dr. Shields attended Sunday School and sacrament meeting at the Clark Branch. "I met Colonel George Kiser, who is the branch president. It was interesting and instructive to find out that he was involved in meeting the LDS men because there was no LDS chaplain to meet them. Many members of the branch turned out to welcome the POWs and a packet of information was prepared for each Latter-day Saint POW It meant a lot to them."

Dr. Shields said that his experiences connected with the release of the POWs "could not help but increase my faith. When I saw the faith of those men, it was certainly something to build my own."

Dr. Shields made a report directly to President Richard M. Nixon on the release of the prisoners. "I reported to the President the whole operation of the release," he said. "The President was very proud of the men. He feels that they are great Americans. At the same time, he was very concerned about the missing, and wanted me to pass on to the families of the missing his personal pledge to press on with the problem of accounting for the missing."

POW, using crutches, is assisted by Dr. Roger Shields as his release is effected at Hanoi; press photographer prepares to take picture as Vietnamese look on

Dr. Roger Shields, responsible for Operation Homecoming, is a member of Arlington LDS Ward in Virginia

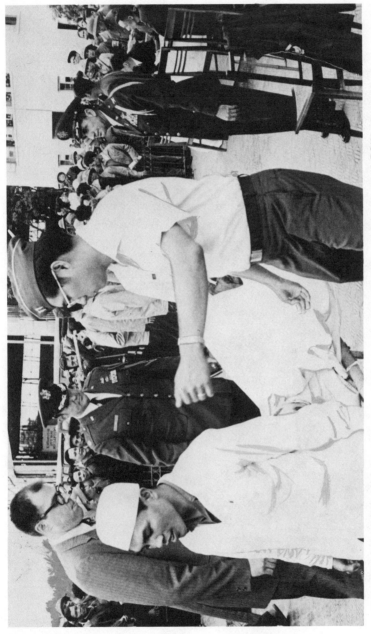

Dr. Roger Shields supervises activities of Operation Homecoming, which removed POWs from Hanoi

283

Colonel George C. Kiser

Branch President at Clark Air Force Base, Philippines

Chapter 29

Colonel George C. Kiser—Putting Their Lives Together

A hero's welcome greeted the first group of American prisoners of war from Viet Nam when the first big C141 Starlifter evacuation plane landed at Clark Air Force Base in the Philippines on February 12, 1973.

Crowds cheered and waved banners. The whole world gave its attention to the dramatic moment. America watched the historic event on television, many weeping for joy. The first fleeting glimpse of POW husbands stirred the emotions of waiting wives.

In fairly quick succession, a second and third plane carried a total of 116 freed POWs from Hanoi to Clark, a distance of 900 miles.

At Clark, the POWs started to put their lives together. They had received sketchy letters on a hit-and-miss basis while in prison. Their minds were filled with uncertainties. They harbored unanswered questions, questions about what happens to a man's home and family when he isn't heard of for four or five years.

The word *repatriation* was being spoken often, and it carried with it an uncertainty. The POWs found the first step of repatriation was a complete medical examination, including a thorough dental check.

Debriefing was a welcome opportunity to talk to a friendly ear, to unload the concerns of imprisonment. Some POWs knew of casualties. They had watched a buddy grow ill and disappear, taken from his cell and not seen again. They knew it mattered; they wanted to tell someone who would understand, who could put it all together and tell a widow.

Chaplains were provided to assist the men in their spiritual needs and to help ease the rough moments. Colonel George Kiser, president of the Clark Branch, was the acting chaplain for returning Latter-day Saint men. He also was the chairman of the department of prosthodontics at the base hospital, where the released prisoners were taken.

"I had the responsibility of screening the POW patients in terms of dental emergencies. I also got an idea of what the problems were, missing teeth, fractured teeth, and so on. The returning men came in on Sunday, and we took care of the emergencies at that time. On Monday we saw them all again and gave a complete examination besides taking care of their other dental problems.

"It was very important to me, with regards to my particular responsibility, to make sure that every man was not only functionally capable, but also cosmetically acceptable to meet his family and friends.

"Some of them would have reflected some serious cosmetic dental problems if we had not been able to accomplish what we did. We saw them Monday, Tuesday, Wednesday, and they were gone. Then we got ready for the next group," Colonel Kiser said.

Kiser, who had been president of the serviceman's branch of more than three hundred members since January 14, 1973—less than five weeks before the first POWs arrived—was seriously dedicated to his responsibilities.

From the Shadow of Death

"When I knew I would be meeting the POWs, I was very concerned. I talked a great deal with my Heavenly Father about what to do to help those fellows. I just told him that I needed strength and help."

"The senior chaplain briefed me on the LDS men who were expected to come through. I became aware of their problems, and I prayed about the best way I could prepare myself to help them.

"I had been told there could possibly be nineteen LDS men returning. These were individuals who for some good reason—some positive reason, such as sighting of a parachute opening, or a sound from a beeper, or a photo taken in Hanoi—were thought to be held captive. The Department of Defense felt there were eighteen LDS POWs and one MIA. This was before we had contact with any of the men coming out. As it turned out, another one was added, Captain Lynn Beens, making a total of twenty.

"Only nine of the twenty were released. As each man came through, I would question him about the other LDS men, trying to establish how many there were and get word about the others. There was information on only two members. One individual had been captured in a cave with two other Americans, but he never reached Hanoi. He was delirious at the time of capture. The other POW was a pilot of an F-4 Phantom jet. While close to the ground, the back-seater ejected. The plane crashed. The informant did not see the pilot get out," Kiser explained. "I do not know what happened to the other men on the list.

"I had one patient who was not LDS who that came through with a broken denture. It had been broken when the villagers who had captured him tied him to a tree and took a stick with a rag on the end of it and shoved it in his throat.

"But his life was literally saved by a North

Vietnamese soldier who came up and stopped the villagers. The military men had orders to save as many of the U.S. airmen as possible because the Vietnamese government wanted to utilize them for political propaganda and bargaining reasons. If the villagers captured a downed flier, they would oftentimes kill him," he said.

The branch of the Church at Clark and the mission headquarters in Manila were involved in helping the returning POWs. With the help of his counselors and others, Kiser prepared information packets to present to the returning members of the Church. Each packet included a copy of the Book of Mormon, pamphlets, and publications, such as the *Ensign* and the *Church News*.

"I wanted them to see what was happening in regard to the Church. I think the packet was very helpful to the men. They had a lot of things given to them all at once, but this was something for them to read as they traveled.

"It was very interesting that they were not aware of the things that had transpired in the Church, the changes in General Authorities and the programs of the Church. They were not aware that President Joseph Fielding Smith had died and that President Harold B. Lee was the new president of the Church. I was able to bring them up to date on what had happened."

In addition to the information packet, arrangements were made to provide temple garments for the men who wore them. Oil was available for adminstration, if they desired it.

This was a period of adjustment. From long years in prison to freedom with unlimited resources at their disposal, the POWs did not seem to grasp the full meaning of time. They did know, however, that they wanted to get home to their families, and they did thrive on freedom.

"When the released men came off the airplane, they got on a bus. Once the bus was full, they were escorted by the military to the hospital, where they were briefed by the director of Operation Homecoming and by the hospital commander, Colonel Jack Ord, who is also a Mormon. An escort was assigned to each man to assist him and walk through the entire process of debriefing with him.

"I knew the names of the LDS men and made an effort to contact and speak with them. In every instance, they were glad to see me, for which I was grateful. Their feelings varied. Some had stronger feelings about the Church than others, but nothing negative. They were very attentive and interested in what I had to say.

"With Captain Larry Chesley, it was a situation where everything developed so beautifully. I can really see the hand of the Lord in it. Larry had a rather severe challenge in his adjustment," Kiser said. He had received word by mail while in Hanoi that his wife had divorced him. When he arrived at Clark, he received further details. He described that time as his "darkest hour."

"I was in the clinic, and Larry came down the hall with his escort. There were a lot of people around and it was a busy time. My intention was that after I had finished working with my patients that day, I would go up and see Larry—sit down and have a talk with him. I came out of my treatment room and looked down the hall of the hospital. Someone said, 'That's Larry Chesley.'

"I knew I wanted to see him, so I just went down the hall and introduced myself. 'I'm George Kiser; I'm the branch president at Clark,' I said. It was just like an electrical shock. It went right through us and we sat down and started talking right there."

The two men sat, heads close together, Chesley in hospital clothing, Kiser in his white dental smock.

Their voice tones were low, a reassuring clasp of hands was frequent during their conversation. They were oblivious to the activity around them.

"It wasn't long until we were both choked up. Both of us were crying. It was a time when I arly needed some spiritual ministering. The Lord understood that, and some of the things that were said were said through the Holy Ghost. That conversation set the stage for a brighter outlook.

"I turned to him and said, 'Larry, you have no right to judge. You cannot understand unless you have walked in other people's shoes.'

"I think he began to understand that perhaps there was an answer to his problems. Larry had been very close to the Lord while in prison. He felt that his prayers were going to be answered as he had anticipated they would be. But he had some tragic disappointments. I think he felt that perhaps he had been abandoned."

"He was concerned about his family, his two children. Tears were running down his face, and I was choked up with emotion. But there was a strong feeling that came over me at that time. I felt that it was the Lord speaking to Larry through me—that is how strong the feeling was.

" 'Larry,' I said, 'if you will live in accordance with the gospel of Jesus Christ—and everything depends on your performance—and if you keep his commandments, I promise you that the Lord will bless you, and in his eternal plan, your children will be yours.' I said it so strongly and so emphatically that I knew it was inspiration."

As the two men stood to go, their moist eyes met, they shook hands, then embraced. The branch president returned to his dental work and the POW to more debriefing.

"What were you guys doing down the hall? It

looked like you were crying," a dental assistant asked Kiser. He only smiled.

That night arrangements were made for a small group of Church members to meet with Larry. They met in the Red Cross lounge of the hospital. At that time Larry addressed them and told them of his feelings.

He was experiencing some frustration. He was a bit confused, but the way was opening up for him.

"When he left, a very touching event occurred. I didn't realize the full impact of my message to Larry until after he had gone.

"He had taken his hospital slippers and on one side of them he had written the statement, 'Don't judge a man until you have walked in his shoes.' He gave those slippers to me," Kiser said.

The colonel's eyes were moist as he stood in his dental office, the slippers in his hands. He knew that Larry was on his own feet. He would treasure the slippers; they had special meaning to him.

"It was obvious that the Lord had touched Larry's spirit and changed it. This was verified later when I talked with his mother and she mentioned the change in Larry's attitude between their first conversation by phone and the second one."

This was the first of many experiences Kiser had as he met most of the returning LDS POWs.

"We called them returnees, but someone was quick to remind us, with pride, that they were POWs. They had been treated as prisoners, even criminals, and they had done it for their country, with dignity and pride."

"Commander Dale Osborne of San Diego, California, was the POWs POW," Kiser said. "He was a hero to the POWs. I say that because of what the other POWs have said about him. Everybody had a great deal of respect for him, for his courage and endurance. I was impressed as I talked with him in the dental clinic."

When Commander Jack Rollins met Kiser there was a special attraction. "I wear Navy wings on my Air Force uniform," Kiser said. "During World War II, I was a Navy pilot on an aircraft carrier. The Navy men that came through wondered how I got my wings.

"Well, Jack and I had an opportunity to become acquainted in terms of common experience as Navy pilots, even before we knew each other in terms of church experiences. We talked about tying ourselves to gospel principles and not people. We talked in some depth.

"We talked of the restoration of the gospel of Jesus Christ and the importance of it in our lives and the blessings that can come from it. I talked about some of my experiences as a young man when I first became converted.

"I think my real conversion came when a good friend of mine was killed. We were flying together, and I was in a period of questioning. I asked, 'Why was he killed? Why did it happen to him and not me?' " Kiser related.

"I was born and reared a Mormon and received good training, but when I went in the service in World War II, I left that environment, and questions began bothering me. It was at that time that my good friend went out night flying and never came back. The next day as I landed my plane, I could see the black spot where he had crashed.

"I began to question, 'Who is God and what is my relationship to him?' In the process, I took a look at many religious philosophies, even non-Christain philosophies, because I wanted to know.

"I found some truths in the various religions, and then I would find a flaw, which eventually brought me back to the Joseph Smith story. I wanted to know if Joseph Smith was really a prophet. I reread the Book of Mormon. I read it in one night. I just couldn't sleep.

"It was just like the people, the characters in the book, were leaping out at me from the pages. They literally came to life and bore record to me, to my spirit, that the Book of Mormon was true," Kiser related.

Rollins and Kiser talked long into the night.

Some firm friendships developed between Kiser and the men he met and counseled. "However, I missed seeing Major Robert D. Jeffrey," Kiser said apologetically.

"It was a great experience to meet Major Jay Hess of Bountiful, Utah. He was quiet and introspective, and I wondered if what I was saying was of any value to him. Yet, in reflection, I can see that the Lord really touched him. I went to see him in the evening and took some literature. We just started talking. Jay was a bit hesitant at first. I wondered if I was saying the right things or not, but he began to understand some of my feelings, some of the things I wanted to discuss with him concerning the gospel.

"He was interested in the things that had been happening in the Church. He wanted to know about the Church leaders who had died and who had replaced them. He had a good understanding of doctrine. We kept talking about events, and I would explain the things that had happened."

A bond of brotherhood developed in a few short minutes. Jay's eyes would sparkle and his eyebrows would lift as he would discover new information.

A light tap on his door, made in a polite way, interrupted the conversation for a moment. It was a corpsman.

"They are having dinner, Major Hess," the

corpsman said, with a smile that reflected admiration

"Thank you," the major returned, with appreciation.

The conversation retuned to the Church.

"Yes, President Joseph Fielding Smith died unexpectedly early in July 1972. But, of course, he was 95 years old," Kiser said, and he went on to explain the succession of President Harold B. Lee.

There was another tap on the door and the corpsman entered, almost without being asked.

"Don't forget your dinner. It's steak and eggs, if you like," he said.

Hess acknowleged the invitation with gratitude.

"It is hard to believe that Elder Richard L. Evans isn't giving the Spoken Word with the Tabernacle Choir," Hess said. "You know, my wife sings with the choir. I found out while I was in Hanoi. That made me very happy." They talked about the choir and the strength of the music.

The tap on the door was a little sharper. "Major, you don't want to miss dinner," the corpsman said with determination.

"No, I'll be there," Hess replied. "Tell me," he went on, "more about the conference in England. It is great to know that the Church is growing that much."

They talked on, about the new skyscraper church office building in Salt Lake City, "and they are going to build one in New York City too," Kiser said.

When the next knock came on the door, Colonel Kiser was getting uneasy. "Here was a guy who had been living on pumpkin soup eighty percent of his diet and now, for one of his first meals with good food, he wasn't interested. I was getting a little concerned because the corpsman kept coming in, and I knew that Hess would have to eat."

From the Shadow of Death

Hess was motioning that he would be there when Kiser said, "Jay, you've got to eat,"

"Never mind the food. Let's talk," Hess replied.

"Have some food sent up," Kiser told the corpsman, who gave a nod of approval and left.

"I realized that the need and desire for spiritual food was far greater than the need for physical food. We talked on into the night. None of the guys slept that first night. It was a great spiritual experience with Jay," Kiser said. "We had the privilege of providing temple garments for him."

They would have talked all night if Kiser had not had a five A.M. call and a twelve-hour shift ahead of him.

"Jay is a very outstanding person. He smiled as he told me he had the shortest tenure in the Church as a group leader. He was set apart one Sunday, attended MIA the following Tuesday, had a mission the following Sunday. Before the next Sunday he was shot down.

"As he was going down in flames, he said to himself, 'This can't be happening to a group leader. I'm a group leader; it can't happen to me.' He felt it was a miracle that he was not burned by the fire in the cockpit. The Lord preserved him," Kiser said.

"His big concern was how he would adjust to his family, and that came off beautifully, I understand. I'm sure he will be a great strength to the Church and to society," he added.

Kiser tried to meet every man on his list, which was not completely accurate. One returning POW in the hospital was approached by Kiser. He had the same last name as a man on the LDS list. "Hi, I'm George Kiser, Clark Branch president. Are you a member of The Church of Jesus Christ of Latter-day Saints?" Kiser asked.

"He just stood there acting rather surprised and

then said, 'No, I'm not a Mormon, but I know of the LDS Church.' He smiled and was very friendly. We talked about many things. It was a warm conversation, and I offered to help in any way I could. The man I was looking for did not return. He didn't come out," Kiser said.

During the time the men were at Clark, Kiser asked many men if they were LDS. Many times the answer was, 'No, I'm not a member, but I have a friend who is."

"I took a man in for examination; that was all I had to do—he needed no further treatment from me. His name was Lieutenant Gary L. Thornton [captured February 20, 1967]. He was a Navy man from Porterville, California.

"Following the examination, on several occasions he showed up at my door. It just seemed as if there was a strong feeling between us. We talked about patriotic things and gospel fundamentals. We got to be good friends. I didn't know he was a Mormon until after he had left. This brother needed something and he was guided to me by the Holy Ghost," Kiser said.

"I feel very strongly about my experience with the returning POWs. At first, I was disappointed with my assignment to come to Clark. I hadn't expected to be transferred from the School of Aerospace Medicine at Brooks Air Force Base in San Antonio, Texas. I liked the assignment as well as my Church work. I was Sunday School president at the time, and things were going very well.

"I rather teasingly mentioned to the ward in San Antonio that I was probably going over there to play the piano in priesthood meeting. The first Sunday at Clark Branch they asked me if I could play the piano, so my joke turned out to be a little prophetic.

"I didn't realize at that time that the opportunity of being branch president and the assignment of

From the Shadow of Death

working with the POWs would be mine. I am grateful to my Heavenly Father," Kiser said.

"As I look back, I can see many events in my life that prepared me for this special opportunity.

"I flew torpedo bombers in World War II. I had wanted to go on a mission, but had been interrupted in my plans by the war. When I got out, I was twenty-five years old and was counseled to get married and raise some missionaries. I proceeded to speak with a very attractive and talented young girl, Patricia Anne Robinson, to convince her I should follow the counsel, and she agreed. Pat and I have five sons and one daughter." The two eldest sons have completed missions, and one is now serving as a missionary. The other two are planning missions in the future. "I haven't seriously talked to Kimberly Anne, who is three years old, about a mission, but I understand she wants to go," he said with a twinkle in his eye.

Kiser flew in the Navy Reserve while he finished his degree at the University of Utah, and then went back into the Navy as a flier for a couple of years.

"When we were expecting our first baby, I elected to leave the military service and return to school for my doctorate in dentistry. Four years of private practice followed, all of which time I had remained in the reserve program. I went back to active duty in 1960, accepting an Air Force commission since the Air Force had specialty training not then available in the Navy. I had almost thirty-one years of active and reserve service when I went to Clark," he said.

"I have had some marvelous experiences in the service. I have had church assignments as stake high councilor, district councilor, district mission president, and many other assignments. I have worked with some great men in several different countries. My testimony has been strengthened. I know without a question that the gospel is true," he testified.

The military service has been a great church experience for Kiser. "I didn't have a chance to go on a full-time mission, but when I got my patriarchal blessing, one part stood out—that I would serve as a missionary throughout the world. This has literally come to pass. I've had the opportunity to speak of the gospel in many different lands.

"I received a call as a district missionary in Germany. This was a very meaningful experience and approached the feeling I have experienced dealing with the prisoners of war," he said.

"I know that the Air Force thinks they sent me over to the Philippines to be a department chairman in the hospital, and, of course, they did in reality. But by the same token, I'm confident that the Lord's influence was there in terms of performance and service in the kingdom. I know he blessed me with health and strengthened me to do what I had to do.

"I approached the assignment from the senior chaplain the same way I approached any assignment, in the Church or in the military service. I attempted to do the best job I possibly could.

"I'll be eternally grateful that the Lord allowed me the privilege of being there at Clark at that particular time to help in any way that I could as servant. I realize that we all have a great mission in helping to build the kingdom. Meeting the POWs was one of the most choice experiences of my life.

"I give credit to my Heavenly Father, because there is no possible way I could have helped the returning prisoners without the help of the Lord. If their spirits were touched it was through Holy Ghost helping them to understand."

"There were plenty of people helping; my counselors and the branch members worked hard. Roger

Shields, who was appointed by the President to organize and oversee the entire repatriation of the POWs, is a member of the Church. He did a very effective job.

"I asked Roger to speak to the members of the branch. He accepted very graciously. While at Clark, he met with us in our meetings as well as socially. One evening, we had a barbecue at my quarters. Afterwards, the members of the branch sat on the lawn surrounding Brother Shields. It was a tropical setting: papaya, avocado, and banana trees. A comfortably warm night in February. Roger wove a fascinating picture of the POW story in terms of gospel principles. His convictions greatly strengthened the testimonies of all present. I feel knowledgeable and dignified approach in resolving the POW assignment brings honor to himself and reflects great credit to the Church."

Colonel George C. Kiser explains homecoming procedures for POWs released from Vietnamese prisons

To: all of your fine people God Bless you all—

Colonel John P. Flynn, left, Commander and senior ranking POW, poses with Colonel George C. Kiser at Clark Air Force Base in the Philippines

A Proud America

Chapter 30

Homecoming—"Our Hearts Have Been Touched"

"Step forward when your name is called and go home," the North Vietnamese officer called out to each group of American prisoners of war arriving at Hanoi's bomb-shattered commercial Gia Lam Airport.

One by one the Americans—587 of them—stepped forward to freedom. For many, however, it hardly seemed possible.

"When I heard I was going home," said Larry Chesley, who had been promoted to captain while he was in prison, "I went to bed that night and went to sleep. I wasn't very excited then.

"But the next day, I was a little more excited. I was on the number five bus from the prison to the airport. After the first two buses unloaded at the airport, they said, 'There's no more room on the airplane.' And we thought, 'Oh, brother, you've got to be kidding.' But then the Vietnamese said, 'Here comes another one now.' We looked out of the bus and saw another 141. And boy, it was beautiful, just beautiful.

"And then the men on the next two buses loaded on the plane, and it was filled. 'There's another one that is supposed to come,' someone said. The next two or three minutes were pretty long, just waiting for that other airplane to come in," said Chesley, who was among the first group released.

Navy Commander Dale Osborne, who also was released with the first group, described his feelings:

"We had heard of the peace tries in October 1972 and that the United States and South Viet Nam would sign. We felt that with the B52 raids—we hoped strongly—we were optimistic—that the war would be coming to an end.

"It was hard to believe it when they told us. I had had so many ups and downs expecting peace that I was afraid to let myself go for fear something would happen and I would get another let-down."

"This thing had been going on for so long that it was hard to get excited," commented Jay Hess, who had been promoted to major while in prison. "But we never lost hope. We had slogans, like 'Golden Gate in '68,' for every year.

"In the fall of '72, it looked like we might be released, but we were all skeptical. It was really hard to believe. However, things began to happen in the prison camps, signs that indicated that perhaps a release might be possible.

"There were little steps along the way," Jay went on. "First we were moved together, by shootdown date and rank. That was a sign. And the food began to improve. The rumors began to circulate. 'What did you hear today?' we would ask each other.

"We knew when the releases started," Jay, who was released with the third group, said. "Everybody's optimism was really high. It was great to know it was finally happening.

"When I got up that morning and these buses were in the camp, I thought, 'I never thought I would see those buses here in the camp to take us out.'

"Later that day, an international inspection team came through the camp. A Canadian came up to the

From the Shadow of Death

window and popped a salute to us. It was the first salute we had seen in a long time. The bow was the customary greeting in Hanoi. Well, that was a real thrill to see that salute."

As Jay and the others were taken from the camp in small camouflaged buses, the streets were lined with people. "There were a lot of school children," he described. "They were as happy as we were that we were leaving. Someone got a chant going in Vietnamese, which I can only imagine was derogatory. But the guard stopped it immediately, and they all went back to smiles.

"As we approached the airport, we saw the tail of that 141 above the trees, and that was quite a sight."

However, the real impact of going home didn't hit Jay then. "I didn't really feel the joy of being released until I stepped over the threshold into my house in Bountiful." It was a new house that his wife and family had moved into while he was in prison. "When I walked in the door, that's when I yelled, 'Yippee!' "

Captain Lynn Beens, who had been a prisoner about three months, commented, "I never really got the feeling that I would be there very long. All of us (the B52 people) were shot down in the period when the talks were going on, and we already thought that the war was almost at an end.

"We received the word before the actual announcement. Some of the Vietnamese workers who were cleaning up the camp had pointed out to us a date on the calendar and indicated that that was when the cease-fire was coming, and, of course, we were all very happy.

"We found out we were being released the night before. We were really excited. We got up at five o' clock in the morning and cleaned up the camp and packed our stuff. There was a wall outside my room in the courtyard. I climbed up on it, and I could see the buses arriving to take us to the airport. It was a real thrill to know we were going home," Lynn related.

From Gia Lam Airport the giant steel birds carrying the repatriated POWs flew to Clark Air Force Base in the Philippines. "At Clark," Larry related, "there were many children, chanting, 'Welcome home.' I cried. We all cried, because we were coming back to freedom."

And then from Clark, it was the long flight across the Pacific Ocean to home—home in the United States.

The prisoners were given heroes' welcomes as they arrived in their home towns.

Thirty thousand persons lined the streets of Burley, Idaho, on March 10, 1973, to pay tribute to Larry Chesley during a homecoming parade. That's more than four times the population of the city of 7,508, located on the banks of the Snake River, some seventy-five miles west of Pocatello.

That evening he addressed some 3,500 people assembled in the Burley High School, from where he was graduated in 1956.

For him, it was the Fourth of July, Christmas, and apple pie all wrapped up together. Santa Claus was at the homecoming assembly in the high school, and at the Chesley home stood a six-foot Christmas tree, with several gifts underneath. "I had lots to do around the world," Santa told Larry. "I just couldn't get in to see you for seven years."

Perhaps the most dramatic moment of the Burley parade was one of total silence. As the vehicles carrying the parents and relatives of area men killed in Viet Nam passed by, the crowd stood in complete silence in reverence to those servicemen who had paid the supreme price.

Letters poured into the Chesley home by the

From the Shadow of Death

hundreds from people throughout the United States. School children wrote letters thanking Larry for what he had done in helping to preserve the cause of freedom.

One letter he received was from the eighth and ninth grade English classes at the Robert Stuart Junior High School in Burley. It was thirty feet long and contained a letter from each of the students and various pictures cut from magazines.

One girl brought Larry up to date on the latest treat in Burley. "I've heard you like ice cream," she wrote. "There is an ice cream parlor in the Blue Lakes Shopping Center that has thirty-one different flavors that are real tasty and very, very fattening."

On March 12, 1973, Larry spoke at the elementary school in Ogden, Utah, where his children, Debbie, eleven, and Donnie, nine, are attending.

"I thought about it many times in prison," he told the youngsters, "that the very most important thing you can learn in school is English—the ability to communicate in speaking and writing. After English, take a foreign language as soon as you have an opportunity.

"When we were in prison, we didn't have pencils, papers, books, crayons—all we had was our minds. We taught each other all we could.

"To me, this land of America is so important," he stressed to the school children, "because you are allowed to learn at any rate you desire. This country deserves good children like you.

"This country is worth dying for—don't you ever forget that," he emphasized as he ended his talk to the youngsters, who someday will take their places as leaders of communities, states, and perhaps even of nations.

Jay Hess was met by thousands at the Salt Lake Airport on March 31, 1973. Several thousand others lined the streets into his home town of Farmington,

Utah, where he was honored on the courthouse steps.

"I suppose," he was told by the master of ceremonies, Nephi W. Taylor, "as you were thinking in your prison cell lots of times, you remembered some of the good things of life, particularly the nice things you like to eat. One of your friends has baked a nice chocolate cake, and we'd like to present it to you at this time."

In a more serious homecoming setting, Jay was honored at a banquet at Woods Cross High School in Bountiful. The banquet was attended by Utah Governor Calvin L. Rampton and Elder Marion D. Hanks, an Assistant to the Twelve Apostles of the LDS Church.

One touching scene was when Bountiful Mayor Morris Swapp, who was master of ceremonies, asked the parents of the twenty-seven Bountiful servicemen killed in Viet Nam to stand. As the parents arose, Jay was overcome by emotion and took from his pocket a handkerchief and wiped his eyes.

The governor paid tribute to him: "The thing that impresses me most about this man—of whom so much has been demanded and who has given so much for all of us here—is that he shows no trace of bitterness or resentment for what he has sacrificed.

"These people," Governor Rampton said as he spoke of those who came to the banquet to pay tribute, "are not here in a sense of gratitude, but more—although we haven't known you before—in a sense of love, and to say to you, 'We are glad the family is together again.' "

And there were spiritual homecomings too.

On March 11, 1973, Larry Chesley spoke in sacrament meeting in the Star Ward on the outskirts of Burley. The congregation filled the chapel, the cultural hall, and the stage.

It was a very emotional meeting. In introducing Larry, Bishop Lee Lamont Frodsham said, "This boy has had an impact on the life of nearly every one of us. Our family has remembered him by name in our prayers. In some strange and wonderful way, we had a bond with him. I realize that Larry is someone else's son, but in no way could I love my own son better."

As Larry talked, he removed his eye glasses several times and wiped his eyes with his handkerchief. His voice was filled with emotion during the entire talk, and he broke into grateful tears as he described the story of his father visiting the patriarch.

He told the congregation of some of the songs the POWs had sung while in prison. One was from the inscription on the Statue of Liberty:
"Give me your tired, your poor.
Your huddled masses yearning to breathe free,
The wretched refuse of your teeming shore.
Send these, the homeless, tempest-tossed to me,
I lift my lamp beside the golden door!"

"That song meant a lot to us," Larry said. "We also often sang 'This Is My Country,' 'The Battle Hymn of the Republic,' and 'What Is America to Me?' Songs were important to us in prison."

He continued, "I would like to talk to you about my homecoming a little bit. The thing that has impressed me the most about homecoming is the little children. I have received a letter from President Nixon thanking me for my courage and for doing my duty to our country, but I received another letter that means more to me than that, from a nine-year-old boy. I cannot quote it to you, but I will tell you what it said. It said, 'I have prayed for you for many years, and finally God has answered my prayers. I would give my life for you, but I don't think my mommy and daddy would let me.'

"Then when I met my mother and father at Travis,

they hugged me and kissed me and we cried. They told me that they were proud of me. I have thought many times since that day, 'How great—how great it will be if I should live righteously enough to meet my Father in heaven at homecoming.'

"And he will throw his arms around me, and say, 'I love you, Larry, and I'm proud of you.' I am working toward that end."

Larry then talked about the importance of families. "One of the bishops in one of the wards I was in was bearing his testimony and he said the most priceless possession that a man can have is his family. And I said, 'No, bishop, the most priceless possession a man can have is a testimony of the gospel, because without that he probably won't save his family. And without saving his family, everything is for naught.'

"During my captivity, I thought constantly of my wife and my lovely children. And I celebrated every birthday they had, and I went to school with them the first time they went to school. And being alone—you know, God said to Adam or to the people when they were creating the earth, it is not good for man to be alone. I can attest to you that it is not good to be alone.

"I want you to do me a favor," he told the congregation. "And that is, the next time that you become angry with one of your loved ones, just stop and think how lucky you are to be there with them so you can be angry at them—and then, don't be!

"Love in our family is the only thing that will ever hold this country together, and it seems to be the thing that is most lacking in these trying days."

Larry then told what had happened to the five hundred dollars, two hundred of which was for tithing, that he had placed in his Book of Mormon shortly before he left on his ill-fated flight nearly seven years ago.

From the Shadow of Death

When he was shot down, all of his personal belongings were returned to his parents in Burley. Included in the belongings were his Book of Mormon and the five hundred dollars. When he returned home, he inquired about the money in the book. His parents got the book from its storage place and found the five hundred dollars untouched.

"I guess the Lord took care of his own money," Larry said.

Jay Hess spoke in sacrament meeting at the Bountiful Thirtieth Ward on April 29, 1973. He gave thanks to all who had played roles in the lives of his family.

"I am grateful," he said, "that my children have been taught by teachers who have had a little special inspiration and were touched by understanding.

"I've kinda triggered on the words of a Primary hymn that you all know well. We used to sing it and apply it to ourselves, but I felt like I was past the point of needing it for myself, so I turned it around from 'Lead me, guide me, walk beside me,' to 'Lead them, guide them, walk beside them,' and I feel you people in this ward have done this for my family. You have taken them by the hand, and I am grateful indeed to you.

"One of the things that this experience has done for me—it has helped me see things a little clearer, things I couldn't see before, like words of songs, like words of poems.

"I was released from Hanoi on March 14 [1973]. That was Wednesday or Thursday. The Sunday preceding that, a group of us who were in a particular camp—about 120 of us—were assembled outside our brick building having a church service. It was a misty morning, with the rain falling gently.

"Most of us were dressed in our usual attire, a pair of shorts, and many of us wore our shirts.

Captain Gillespie, who was acting as chaplain, stood before us and led us in the church service.

"The words of the choir, a double quartet, singing 'You'll Never Walk Alone' really touched me at that time. Those words were, 'At the end of a storm is a golden sky and the sweet silver song of a lark.' That really struck me. And I was impressed that things might be looking up.

"I was at Hill Air Force Base the other day. They thought it would help bring me up to date if I flew over the valley. So I flew from Ogden down to Farmington and along by my home and saw how things had changed. We came down here and circled around and saw how the chapel was situated in relationship to my house and the school. Then we went to Salt Lake. I couldn't believe the changes on the campus of the University of Utah since I was last there.

"Then we flew on to Provo, and lo and behold, there was a temple down there. You know how far behind I am. A month ago I thought David O. McKay was president of the Church. And I just wasn't brought up to date. I needed some news.

"I got to chatting with the pilot. He seemed especially understanding and sympathetic, and I enjoyed talking with him. He finally confided in me that we all have difficulties in our lives, and he mentioned that his wife had been in a coma for the past six years.

"Well, we live in a world of sorrow. Sometime it will. probably come to each of us, somewhere along the way. The object is not to figure out a way to avoid sorrow, but to become a better person for having gone through the experience, and to look about us and help those people who are in need of help and who have sorrow in their hearts."

Jay summed up his feelings by bearing witness to the truthfulness of the gospel. "In the test I put

From the Shadow of Death

the gospel through, I found more than ever that it is true. Would a man curse God and die, or would he turn to see more clearly that it was true? Every principle I have been taught became clearer to me. I became more convinced of its truthfulness, and it became more valuable. Indeed, I could see that the most important thing is eternal life."

Jay and Larry and Navy Lieutenant Commander David J. Rollins from San Diego attended the priesthood session of the 143rd Annual General Conference of the LDS Church on April 7, 1973, and were honored by President Harold B. Lee.

President Lee rose to the pulpit. He stood, paused for a moment. Nearly 8,000 priesthood holders were assembled in the Tabernacle on Temple Square. Another 180,000 were listening to the session by closed circuit, gathered in some eight hundred locations in the United States and Canada.

President Lee spoke slowly. He paid tribute to the three LDS servicemen who had recently been released as prisoners of war from North Viet Nam: "Captain Larry Chesley, United States Air Force, was a prisoner of war for seven years. He comes from Burley Stake, Star Ward. Major Jay Hess, United States Air Force, was a prisoner for six years. He is from Bountiful East Stake. Lieutenant Commander David J. Rollins, United States Navy, was a prisoner for six years. He is from San Diego North Stake."

As each man's name was called, he stood and faced the congregation. There was silence. Captain Chesley and Commander Rollins were both in uniform, bedecked with medals. Major Hess was dressed in a suit.

President Lee continued, "These three young men represent many of those boys who have gone through the fire. We just want you men to know that our hearts have been touched by the announcement of your faith, the confidence in your country and in the commander-in-chief.

"We want to say to you, we have been praying, we have been hoping, with every means at our command, and we now say to the priesthood generally, will you put your arms around these boys and help them now to make their adjustments as may be necessary?

"The Lord bless you brethren. We love you and the many others who have been under these circumstances, and have come through the fire and are now being prepared to carry forward. You be the kind of men," President Lee told the servicemen, "that we look to for the standards for our youth in the years that lie ahead. Thank you, brethren. We welcome you home."

The POWs had returned to a cheering America. After they had had a chance to become reacquainted with their families, three major welcome-home parties were held for them, providing opportunities to renew friendships that had been made in Vietnamese prisons.

The first of these big parties was held in San Francisco April 27-29, 1973, for the prisoners housed at Camp Hope in Son Tay and the Green Berets who made a rescue attempt. Because the prisoners had been moved four months earlier, the rescue attempt fell short of its goal.

This party was sponsored by H. Ross Perot, wealthy Texas businessman. Most of the former POWs attended, and some of the Green Berets came from as far away as Laos. Highlights included a ticker-tape parade for the men in downtown San Francisco and a banquet.

At the banquet, movie star Ernest Borgnine was master of ceremonies, Red Skelton entertained, and John Wayne was the guest speaker. California Governor Ronald Reagan sent a message to the

From the Shadow of Death

POWs, which was read by his wife. The former prisoners mingled with the stars and special guests, chatting and being photographed.

A scale model of the Son Tay camp was displayed, and for the first time, the rescuers and the prisoners had an opportunity to tell their separate stories. "They didn't know that we had been moved four months earlier," said Captain Larry Chesley, "because, as Secretary of Defense Melvin Laird put it, 'there isn't a camera that looks through buildings.' We were not allowed outside at the prison camp, and it would have been a miracle to have been photographed outside by our reconnaissance planes.

"Even after we were moved, the camp continued to have guards and there were people in the camp. The guard towers were manned the night the Green Berets came in, and there was a battle. No Americans were seriously hurt, however," Captain Chesley explained.

As the banquet ended, Mr. Perot explained that San Francisco was a town for fun, with plenty of food and entertainment. "But, you need a little oil to get around," he said, and he handed each POW and Green Beret an envelope containing a $100 bill.

There had been some concern that demonstrators and picketers would mar the downtown parade, but it went forward in the tradition of a hero's welcome.

"The parade through San Francisco," said Captain Chesley, "was very impressive. There must have been three hundred thousand people lining the streets and looking from windows. They were cheering and waving. On my side of the street there were only six demonstrators and three signs, but you know, they got half the TV coverage."

The next big party was given by the President of the United States, Richard M. Nixon. He scored a special triumph on May 24, 1973, when he hosted a welcome-home dinner on the White House lawn for more than a thousand jubilant and grateful former Viet Nam prisoners of war and their guests.

The POWs had gone hungry in Viet Nam, but that was not the case during the parties that followed their return. In Washington, they "brunched" and dined and had late snacks, and the food was just great.

The servicemen met senators and representatives from their home states, and they heard President Nixon thank them in person for their sacrifice. They had a chance to shake hands with the Chief Executive, and some even had their pictures taken with him.

President Nixon took the opportunity to address the ex-POWs at a meeting at the State Department. He was stopped several times by wild ovations during the speech. "He got a standing ovation when he said, 'I wanted to bring you home on your feet and not on your knees,' "said Captain Chesley.

While the men listened to President Nixon, the women were entertained by Mrs. Nixon and her two daughters, Julie and Tricia.

But the dinner, held that night under a giant red and yellow striped tent, was the highlight of the day. Surrounded by stars and celebrities, the men and their partners were hosted in a gracious way.

"The man who waited on us at our table was a New York City lawyer who had flown down to serve us. He was outstanding and really enjoyed doing it," Captain Chesley said.

Henry A. Kissinger, national security affairs adviser and the architect of the Vietnamese cease-fire, was at one of the tables, and he was a popular man indeed.

There were many toasts during the evening. One was to the men of the B52s, which many feel brought an end to the war. "We stood and toasted with our water glasses," said Captain Lynn Beens.

"We all become members of the 'Red River Rats' with this as our first reunion," Captain Beens went on. "It all started," he said, "with the fighter pilots who had been shot down north of the Red River in North Viet Nam."

Captain Beens and his wife, Kristine, have a special souvenir of the event. "President Nixon came right down among the guests," Captain Beens related. "He stopped at our table, and we had our picture taken with him. We just asked, and he was willing. One of our friends at the table took the picture with our own camera. We have the negative."

The most moving moment of the evening was when Irving Berlin, along with President Nixon, sang "God Bless America." "We all joined in singing with them, and there were plenty of tears before the song was finished," Captain Beens said.

The ex-POWs displayed an American flag that had been made in the prison camp, and a plaque was presented to President Nixon with the inscription, "To Richard the Lionhearted."

All stops were pulled for the POWs. The third floor of the White House, the Nixons' residence, was opened for the servicemen to visit—a very unusual occurrence.

Following the banquet there was a dance in the White House. Like the Cinderella story, it is traditional for all events at the White House to stop at midnight, but the President announced that he would assert his authority and the dance would go on until two A.M. There was a big cheer, but soon the party-weary guests started to make their way from the ballroom back to their hotels.

It was the biggest party they could remember. More than thirteen hundred ex-POWs and their guests attended the celebration.

The celebrations were not over, however. The

next big event was June 1-3, 1973, in Dallas, Texas, sponsored by the people of Dallas, and again, H. Ross Perot was at his home town to help with the occasion.

Dallas was the site of another ticker-tape parade. The crowds were large, and the welcome was great.

Banquets and entertainment, brunch at the Marriott Hotel, open house at the Perots' home, and food was offered everywhere. A Texas barbeque of beef, chicken, and Polish sausage was served—a far cry from the pumpkin soup the prisoners had received so often in North Viet Nam.

At the Cotton Bowl on the final evening, about seventy thousand people filled the stadium to cheer and honor the repatriated POWs. Bob Hope and a score of others provided entertainment, dubbed by the former prisoners as "fantastic."

Each former POW was introduced individually, and the crowd cheered with warm response. When Major Robert Jeffrey, the home town hero, was introduced, the crowd showed great appreciation. Major Jeffrey had a special seat of honor.

The crowd "went wild," recalls Captain Chesley, when the entertainers sang the song about a returning prisoner, "Tie a Yellow Ribbon Around the Old Oak Tree." One of the lines in the song says, "The whole bus cheered," but at the Cotton Bowl that night, they changed the words to "The whole Cotton Bowl cheered." "It sounded like the Dallas Cowboys had just scored three touchdowns in a row," described Captain Chesley.

Nothing is more American than baseball, and no one was prouder than Major Jay C. Hess as he displayed a treasured lifetime pass to both the American and National League baseball games. "I would like to take a few of those games in," he said with a smile as he tucked the red metal pass card back in its leather sheath.

In addition to the parties, there were speeches by the returning prisoners at schools, churches, and civic events.

Captain Chesley, for instance, kept up a steady pace of speaking engagements—sometimes as many as ten a week—until he left for his honeymoon in Jamaica following his marriage on June 19, 1973, to Annette Huntsman in the Salt Lake LDS Temple.

The former POWs enjoyed the parties and speaking engagements because they could share the excitement of returning home with their wives and partners, and with the people of this country. They have been able to meet each other on a basis of freedom and friendship, and it is apparent that they appreciate the welcome given to them by America.

Welcome home. What a long-sought greeting, a greeting many POWs wondered if they would ever hear again. It wasn't very long ago—although to them, it might have seemed like another world, another time—that they had been prisoners of war in a hostile country nine thousand miles away.

Members of the United States reception team meet with representatives of the Democratic Republic of Viet Nam at Hanoi's Gia Lam Airport before release of POWs

American POWs line up for short march to freedom as they leave their bus at Gia Lam Airport at Hanoi

POWs were transported to the airport from the prison in a camouflaged bus to await flight from Hanoi; North Vietnamese guard was called "Mark" by POWs because of birthmark on his head

Master Sergeant William A. Robinson, obviously glad to be free, was model used to make prison clothing for POWs. He was a large man, weighing about 260 pounds. So most of the prison suits were a bit large

Thumbs up, cheers, and smiles broke out as a C-141 Starlifter took to air from Hanoi, flying the POWs to freedom after years of imprisonment

Admiral Demon W. Cooper, commander, Task Force 77, hugs returning prisoner of war at Clark AFB

*Air Force
Lieutenant
Colonel John
A Dramesi
displays
prison-made
flag as bus
leaves flight
line at Clark
Air Base in
the Philippines*

*Flight crew and auxiliary support teams that assisted in
Operation Homecoming line up following flight in C-141
Starlifter plane, used to remove POWs from Hanoi*

Elder David B. Haight, Assistant to the Council of the Twelve of the LDS Church, greets former POWs in Mormon Tabernacle prior to general conference session: left to right, Major Jay C. Hess, Commander Jack Rollins, Elder Haight, Captain Larry Chesley

It was a reunion for former POWs as they meet Colonel George Kiser, center, who had greeted them at Clark Air Force Base upon their releases: left to right, Warren Hess, standing next to his father, Major Jay C. Hess; Colonel Kiser; Commander David J. Rollins; Captain Larry Chesley; Gene Rollins, son of Commander Rollins

Watching and Waiting

Chapter 31

Cathleen Caras—"I'll Never Give Up Hope"

"I'll never give up hope," said Mrs. Cathlene Caras as she sat in the overstuffed chair in the front room of her small home in rural Benjamin, Utah. "If I give up hope, then I have nothing. They'll have to prove to me that he is dead before I give up the hope that he'll be back home again."

Mrs. Caras is one of thirteen hundred American women whose husbands are missing in Southeast Asia. They are referred to as "missing in action" or MIA. Air Force Captain Franklin A. Caras (who has since been promoted to major) has been on that list since April 28, 1967, when he was shot down in an F-105 over North Viet Nam.

For Mrs. Caras, the mother of four children, the years have been long—always waiting, always wondering, always hoping. The years that have passed since her husband was shot down have failed to erase the constant ache she carries in her heart.

She aches for her children. They are growing up without a father—but they are also faced with never-ending comments of other children, which may be said innocently, but which cut deeply, "Children hear their parents say something, and they immediately pass it on to my children. 'You don't have a daddy,' I've heard them say, or 'Well, he's dead and he won't be coming home.'"

And then there are the questions. "I have often heard my children say, 'If people just didn't ask us questions that we can't answer.' Children have a habit of asking questions that even adults can't answer, and my children are faced with it nearly everyday. Oftentimes, it is really hard for them."

Mrs. Caras and her four children, Anna Marie, twelve, Tony, eleven, Cathy Lynn, ten, and Christopher, seven, have found strength in prayer, but even with that, there are many times when it is difficult for them.

"Sometimes, you know, with all of us, the answer to prayer is, 'You will have to wait.' I have never asked is he alive or is he dead, because I feel that when the Lord wants me to know, I will. I still pray for the things I always have—'If it is thy will, please let him come home.' My children still pray the same as they always have, 'Watch over my daddy and please bring him home.'

"It has been more difficult the last little while with the release of the POWs because there is a greater chance that he won't be home, but I don't think my children have given up hope. However, the last time when the men came home (the fourth and last general release of POWs) one of my children said, 'Mama, now I don't know how to pray.'

"They have been really good children. They have adapted to the situation, and they still pray that he'll come home. I hope I have done right by them, by giving them this faith, this hope that he will be home, and I think that through the years it has helped, because I have been able to talk about him and hopefully help their love for him grow. I think it would have been a great deal more difficult had he just been declared dead. Christopher was just a few months old when Frank left and has

From the Shadow of Death

never known his daddy. But by praying for him and talking about him, all my children have grown close to him.

"My children seem to have a greater urgency to pray than lots of children do. I mean by this a greater need. Prayer has sustained us. It has been the best tool that God ever gave us, I am sure. I hope the children never look back and think, 'I prayed all that time and it didn't happen the way I wanted it to.'

"I have tried hard to express to them that even though we want something desperately, we have to accept the Lord's will no matter what it is. I haven't seen that they feel any bitterness, or that they feel that their prayers aren't being answered,"

The last time Cathlene Caras saw her husband was during the Christmas season in 1966. He had been in the Air Force for eleven years. They were stationed in Texas when he received orders for Southeast Asia. His orders stated that he was to undergo F-105 pilot training in Las Vegas, Nevada, and then survival training in Washington before being sent to the Orient. He came home for Christmas, and then left.

Captain and Mrs. Caras both had heavy hearts when he left. They knew that he might never return.

"While in Texas, Frank had a dream," Mrs. Caras related. "He dreamed he had been shot down, and he saw the things that were happening after he was shot down. It was just a short time after he had received the orders for Viet Nam.

"He told me about the dream, but I guess I was slightly like an ostrich; I didn't want him to tell me. I felt that as long as I didn't thing about it, it wouldn't happen, so I wouldn't let him talk about it a great deal. I know he knew it might happen.

I'm sure he thought it could happen because of the things he did tell me."

Captain Caras stayed close to his wife during those four months in Viet Nam before he was shot down. There was much concern for her. "I received letters almost daily; occasionally he would miss a day but almost every day I would receive a letter. He didn't say a great deal about what they were doing. Most of it was classified, and there wasn't a great deal that he could say. I could always tell when one of his buddies had been shot down. I could tell by his letters that he was nervous about it. It wasn't an enjoyable thing to go through. However, he always said he felt that it was good that he was over there rather than the war being over here.

"He told me about some of the targets, what they were after when he hit them. Sometimes he sent maps home. I don't know what the target was when he was shot down. Our communique just said it was in North Viet Nam, and that was all."

Perhaps because of the dream he had had and the possibility that he would not return, Captain Caras prepared for the worst. "He took care of all the details very specifically in case anything should happen to him. He had left specific instructions with the government, that they should go first to his parents, and then his parents in turn would call one of my brothers so I would have some of my family with me if I had to hear bad news.

"I think this was a very considerate thing, because it is not a very pleasant experience, and it would be harder, I am sure, if you didn't have someone with you that you love."

The day her brother and a representative from the Air Force came to tell her the sad news that her husband had been shot down and was missing, Mrs. Caras was preparing for the Primary program in sacrament meeting. She had all her Primary materials sitting out on the table.

A knock came at the door. When she saw the Air Force man, she knew something had happened, but she didn't want to believe it—or accept it. "I kept thinking that maybe they had rescued him right after he was shot down. I could not believe it; it was not true. I would find out soon that it was not true."

Her sister-in-law came to the house and picked up the Primary materials. She was going to take them to the Primary counselor so that a substitute could be arranged for. She unintentionally left one picture face down on the table.

"It had been mass confusion in the house while everybody was here," Mrs. Caras reflected. "After they had all gone, I started to straighten up a bit. I really wasn't aware of what I was doing, but I went about my normal chores, and I happened to notice that picture face down on the table." She picked it up and turned it over. It was a picture of the resurrected Savior.

"I remember well looking at that picture and then praying with all my heart, 'Where do I go from here and what am I going to do?' At that time, I felt a very warm, wonderful feeling, which I truly feel was the Holy Spirit, and I heard, 'All is well; all is well.' That was all I heard, but it is what has sustained my for all these years—all is well.'

"For the longest time I felt that 'all is well' meant that he would come home, and I just had complete faith in the Lord that if he hadn't called him home, he would send him back to me. Now, as I look back at it, I think maybe the Lord was saying, 'all is well, he's home with me.' What better place could anybody be? That is where we are all going, and I am sure it is the best place because this life isn't always so much fun."

One of the hardest days for Mrs. Caras was

when the Air Force returned her husband's personal belongings to her. "It was really hard to go through his personal things—things that were with him after I was. All the things that he had taken with him came back. They were shipped in a long box, like the type of box the moving companies use. It was about the size of a coffin. In fact, one of Frank's friends in the military who had seen the box thought Frank's body was being shipped home."

Sorting through the box, Mrs. Caras found some poetry that her husband had written before being shot down. "These are things that I will cherish forever. My husband loved to write poems. Whenever he had a particular thought, he liked to write it down as a poem. He wrote one song—a special verse to the Ballad of the Green Berets," but the majority of the poems were about the love of his family and his home and the importance of it and about the good times we enjoyed together."

One poem Mrs. Caras especially enjoys, and which is most meaningful to her, portrays how he felt about his family:

My fortunes are great. I don't have to be told.
I have all the treasures a lifetime could hold.
Not diamonds, not rubies, not emeralds or gold.
My treasure's more precious than all kingdoms
    of old.
I've the smiles of my children, the love of my wife,
And a blue sky above me the rest of my life.

I've the warmth of their nearness, the joy of
    their touch,
The comfort in knowing and sharing their love.
These are the treasures that give life its cost.
These are my riches; without them I'm lost.
True, I'm a miser, but worth it, I say.
With wealth such as mine, there's just no other
    way.

From the Shadow of Death

After she received word that her husband had been shot down, Mrs. Caras wrote letters and sent packages to him as often as she was permitted. "We were allowed to send three letters per month and one package every three months to Hanoi. For the first three years or so none of the letters or packages came back, but after that I started to get them back. In fact, I am still receiving packages. I got one in May [1973] that I sent last October.

"I think the reason they started coming back was that pressure was put on Hanoi, and they felt that they either had to send them back or account for not delivering them."

The Saturday night before the list of POWs who were to be repatriated was released, Mrs. Caras received a telephone call about eleven P.M. from her bishop, Clair O. Anderson of the Benjamin Ward, Palymra Stake, in central Utah. "He told me that a major from Brigham Young University was coming to let me know one way or the other whether or not Frank's name was on the list.

"I called Jim, Frank's brother, because I wanted him to be with me when we went to tell Dad Caras whatever it was. The children were asleep, but I didn't wake them."

It was late when the man from BYU drove into the lane next to the Caras home. Mrs. Caras and her brother-in-law were waiting. "They just told us that Frank's name was not on the list, and that was all they could tell us. They didn't know whether there would be any further lists, or if that was it, or what."

The next morning she told the sad news to her children. "I thought this would be really hard for them, but they handled it very well. I told them if they didn't want to go to church they didn't have to. But I told them that putting off until tomorrow doesn't make things any easier, and so we got ready and went to church. I was really proud of them. They could have sat home and worried about it."

When the POWs started coming home, it was particularly hard on the Caras family. "We had mixed emotions. We had extreme excitement for those who were coming home, thinking how good it would feel, and then thinking that we were not feeling the same thrill. It has been hard, but I am so glad that some of them have come home."

The Caras family tries to remember the good times they had with Frank, and to do some of the things they did when they were all together. Camping, fishing, or just hiking in the canyons were among their favorite activities. "Frank loved nature, and I have tried to instill his love in the children because it is something that too many people completely overlook. But to him, God's works of nature were wonderful. He could sit back and look at a tree and just marvel. Now we don't camp like we used to, but we still spend a lot of time in the canyons."

Mrs. Caras tries to keep busy and keep her mind occupied. She is president of the Primary in her ward. "When they asked me to be president, I was so stunned because I couldn't believe that I would be called. I felt that there were a million people who could do it better, but I am so grateful for the opportunity to serve because I have found that it has given me a more well-rounded life and many spiritual blessings."

Mrs. Caras and her children all wear MIA bracelets with her husband's name inscribed on them. "I don't think I will take it off unless Frank comes home. It has become a part of me. It is like a wedding ring, symbolic of Frank, just one more thing to help keep me closer to him."

Mrs. Cathlene Caras and four children, Christopher, 7, Tony, 11, Cathy Lynn, 10, and Anna Marie, 12, work in garden near family home in Benjamin, Utah

Mrs. Cathlene Caras walks with daughter Cathy Lynn, 10, along tree-lined lane adjacent to their home

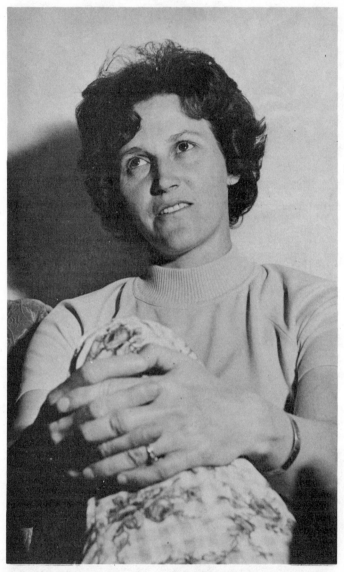

Mrs. Cathlene Caras, in a reflective mood, ponders
question asked about her husband who has been
missing in action since April 28, 1967

From the Shadow of Death

INDEX

birthday party in, 181; Osborne taken to, 206; chapter on, 245; Hoa Loa known as, 251; built by French, 251; three sections of, 251; description of, 252

Harassment, submission through, 275

Hartness, Mrs. Paula, went to Paris, 20

Hate, for POWs, 22; in eyes of people, 79; told not to, 112

Hathaway, Don, a friend of Chesley's, 63

Heartbreak Hotel, Jeffrey incarcerate in, 14; Beens moved to, 239

Hell-hole, Hoa Loa a, 258

Henley, William Earnest, Chesley quoted, 46

Hepatitis, Chesley treated for, 42

Herman, Willis' lizard, 172

Hero, Osborne was hero's, 218

Hess, Cameron, Hess' son, 142

Hess, Heather, Hess' daugher, 146

Hess, Heidi, Hess' daughter, 142; writes to father, 142

Hess, Holly, Hess' daughter, 146

Hess, (Major) Jay C., section on, 133; never got angry, 218; Osborne wanted to meet, 219; Kiser talks to, 295; dinner missed by, 296; group leader, 297; peace exciting for, 306; homecoming for, 309; sacrament meeting, 313; at conference, 315; baseball pass for, 320

Hess, Marjorie, Hess' wife, 146; chapter on, 148

Hess, Warren, Hess' son, 146

Highway One, Willis crosses, 165

Hill AFB, Utah, news from, 150; Yvonne Williams calls, 265; Hess visits, 314

History, most popular subject, 52

Ho Chi Minh, referred to, 145

Hoa Loa, Hanoi Hilton, 10, 251; main prison, 246; built by French, 251; a hell hole, 258

Holidays, not overlooked, 57

Holy Ghost, speaks through, 292

Home, a source of strength, 63

Homecoming, repatriation of POWs, 273; welcome, 291; freedom for 587 POWs 305; hero's welcome, 308; hero's welcome in Bountiful, Utah, 310; at general conference, 315; Son Tay, 316; President Nixon's party, 317; Dallas party, 320

Honor, home with, 87; of POWs, 271

Hope, came to Chesley's mother, 69; POWs learned to go easy on, 219

Hope, Bob, at POW party, 320

Hospital, Chesley taken to, 42; Alfred N. Knight confined to, 66; Osborne taken to, 211

House, mentally constructed, 45, 173

Hue, South Viet Nam, shelled by mortar fire, 161; 50 miles south of DMZ, 164

Humor, chapter on, 55; POWs', at release, 271

Huntsman, Annette, Chesley married to, 321

Hut, Osborne woke up in, 196

Hymn, Jensen's favorite, 81; appropriate in Hanoi, 111

Hymnbook, songs remembered from, 81

I

Ingenuity, American, 276

International Commission of Control and Supervision, members of, visit, 85

Interrogation, Jeffrey subjected to, 6, 11; Chesley subjected to, 36; a diversion, 115; often ended in beating, 117; Hess faced, 136; Willis faced with, 169; once each month, 178

Interrogator, talked to Osborne, 207; tried to get Osborne to sign papers, 207; Beens faced, 232, 235

Interrogators, Jensen stood before, 79

"Invictus," Chesley learned in prison, 46

J

James, (Major) Goble, Osborne's cellmate, 213

Japan, Chesley served in, 63; conference held in, 64

Jayroe, Julius, talk by, impressed Chesley, 50

Jeffrey, Joy, chapter on, 20

Jeffrey, (Major) Robert D., section on, 1

Jensen, Larry, Jensen's brother, 86

Jensen, (Major) Jay R., chapter on, 77

Jensen, Jay Roger Jr., Jensen's son, 82

Jensen, Mr. and Mrs. Milton L., Jensen's parents, 86

Jensen, Sherrie, Jensen's daughter, 82

Johnson, (Major) Sam, pilot of Chesley's plane, 34

Johnson, Sandra, teacher from Rhode Island, 167; selected to be shot, 167

Judge, don't, others, 292

64; Mrs. Rollins offers, 96; role of, 111; comfort to Rollins, 111; brought assurance, 138; POWs remembered in, 264; spirits maintained by, 278; Chesley tells of, 292; President Lee asked for, 316; sustained Caras family, 333

Prayers, were answered, 111; for forgiveness, 112

Praying, a lot of, 82

Pride, POWs released with, 270; served with, 293

Primary, Rollins thought about, 101; Mrs. Rollins worked in, 104; Mrs. Caras taught, 334; Mrs. Caras president of, 338

Prison, shortage of everything except, 251

Prison life, a lighter side, 55; test of endurance, faith, 124

Propaganda, Vietnamese study books, 215

Prophet, at head of church, 66

Puddles, Osborne drank from, 204

Pumpkin, boiled, good for headaches, 121; served by captors, 121

Pumpkin soup, Hess lived on, 296

Punishment, for hitting guard, 120

Q

Questions, not of military value, 12

Quiz room, Osborne taken to, 205

-R-

Radio, Beens makes statement on, 236; broadcast simple, 237

Ragsdale, Tom, killed in bombing, 168

Raids, warplanes in, 226; bombs dropped in, 227; helped end war, 306, 318; Beens shotdown, 307

Railroad complex, was target, 229

Rampton, (Governor) Calvin L., Hess honored by, 310

Randolph AFB, Texas, word from, 151

Rat, eating on Osborne's wound, 202

Ravine, Jeffrey kneeled at, 9

Reagan, (Governor) Ronald, message from, 316

Red Cross, letters went to, 69

Red River, Willis crosses, 184

Red River Rats, members of, 319

Regulations, POWs forced to read, 253

Religion, popular subject, 52; Jensen asked about, 82; explained through

wall, 83; actions became, 110; talked about, 211; was comfort to Beens, 241

Repatriation, at Hanoi, 270; early plans for, 272; Operation Homecoming, 273; preparations for, 274; debriefing necessary for, 278; first POWs at Clark, 287; feeling about peace and, 306

Reunion, spiritual, joyous, 126

Reynolds, (Major) Jon A., Jeffrey's cellmate, 15

Ride, wildest ever, 93

Risner, (Colonel) Robison, highest-ranking POW, 15

Rocks, Chesley's target in, 33; thrown at Rollins, 97

Rollins, Connie, Rollins' wife, 91

Rollins, Gene, Rollins' son, 92

Rollins, (Lieutenant Commander) Jack, section on, 91; at conference, 315

Rollins, Patricia, Rollins' daughter, 92; watched homecoming, 125

Rollins, Richard, Rollins' son, 92; at Naval Academy, 125

Rope, put around Rollins' neck, 94; Willis tied with, 165

Rope treatment, Jeffrey subjected to, 12; Chesley subjected to, 37; Beens given, 235

Rules, violation of, meant punishment, 17

S

Sacrament, blessed by Baptists, 53; Hess partakes of, 141

Sacrament meeting, Chesley at Star Ward, 310; Hess at Bountiful 13th, 313

Salem, Mass., Rollins thinks of, 101

Salt Lake City, Utah, Osborne from, 193; Osborne reared in, 210; Osborne and Wood talked about, 212

San Diego, Calif., Rollins from, 91

San Diego Naval Hospital, Osborne at, 220

San Diego Union, newspaper reporter from, 98

San Francisco, Calif., homecoming party, 316

Sandbags, ordered from Japan, 162

Sandstrom, Carla, Jensen's sister, 86

Sandy, Utah, Jensen from, 86

Savior, source of strength, 144; picture of, 335

Scavengers, looted Osborne, 196

Toilet paper, used for writing
    paper, 84, for papier-maché, 119;
    used for bandage, 214
Toothpicks, made from bones, 119
Torture, Jeffrey subjected to, 12;
    Chesley, 36; Jensen, 79; Rollins
    went through, 100; emotional,
    psychological, 117; Osborne, 208;
    Osborne not tortured with rope,
    215
Towel, used for cross, 49
Travis Air Force Base, Calif., Chesley
    landed at, 70, 311
Treatment, started to improve, 83;
    progressively worse for Osborne,
    199, medical treatment for Osborne,
    209, 214
Tree, Jensen landed in, 79; Hess looked
    at, 250
Troutman, Konrad, Hess' cellmate, 141
Truce, declared for Tet Holiday, 161;
    hoax and fraud, 163
Truck, Osborne on, 198, Osborn
    thrown from, 205; Beens taken on,
    233
Twenty-Third Psalm, quoted by
    prisoners, 47
Typhoon, flood prison camp, 179

U
USS Kitty Hawk, Rollins aboard, 91
Uniform Code of Military Justice, legal
    code, 276
United States Joint Casualty Resolution
    Centur (JCRC), established, 279
Unity Section, Part of Hanoi Hilton,
    251

V
Values, Hess reflected on, 140
Viet Cong, attacks Hue, 161; ready to
    shoot Willis, 165; had no capital,
    273

Vinh, Osborne shot down near, 193
Voice, an American's, 14; absolutely
    indescribable, 149
Voice in Vital America, publicizes POW
    needs, 262
Voice of Viet Nam, a broadcast into
    rooms; 56
Voice of America, Willis was manager
    of, 161; listened to, in Alaska, 174;
    Willis makes broadcast for, 186

W
Waiting Wives, Mrs. Hess belonged
    to, 150
Wall tapping, forbidden, 115
Wallow, Hoa Loa pronounced as, 206,
    251
War criminals, POWs called, 277,
    treated as 293
Wayne, John, party guest, 316
Weber State College, attended by
    Chesley, 45, 65
Webster, Carrie, daughter of Jensen, 82,
    86
Webster, Heidi, Jensen's grandchild, 86
Westover, Jan, Jensen's wife, 87
Widow, "don't make me a," 218
Williams, Yvonne, chapter on, 257
Willis, Charles, section on, 161
Willis, Charles Riedel, Willis' son, 173;
    student at BYU, 186
Willis, Howard James, Willis' son, 173;
    seminary graduate, 185
Wire, acquired by Rollins, 118; made
    into needle, 118
Woods, (Commander) Brian, in room
    with Osborne, 208

Z
Zoo, the, Jeffrey incarcerate in, 15;
    Rollins sent to, 98; Osborne
    at, 215; Beens moved to, 239; had
    been French movie studio, 239; a
    prison, 251

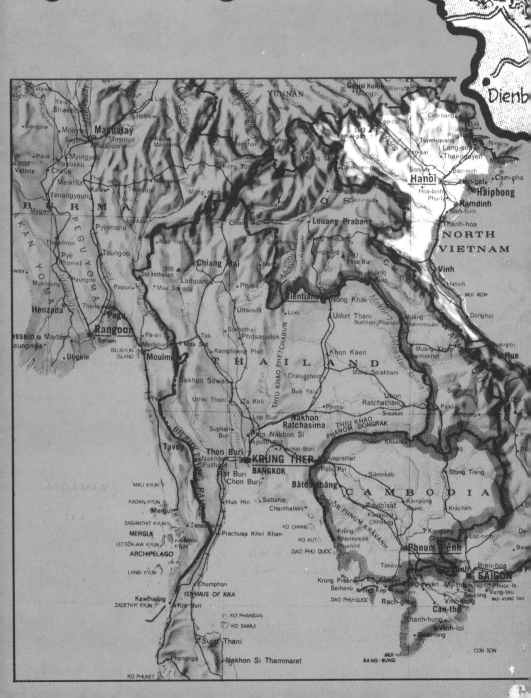

1 Robert Jeffrey
2 Larry Chesley
3 Jay Jensen
4 Jack Rollins
5 Jay Hess
6 Charles Willis
7 Dale Osborne
8 Lynn Beens